Phyllida

# LET LOVE HEAL

Phyllida Anam-Áire

# LET LOVE HEAL
## A NEW CONSCIOUSNESS FOR A NEW AGE

*Ennsthaler*

PUBLISHER ENNSHALER
STEYR (AUSTRIA)

## LIABILITY EXCLUSION

The exercises and meditations in this book are not intended as a substitute for professional, medical or therapeutic treatment. Each application of listed suggestions herein is done at the discretion of the reader.

Neither the author, publisher, consultant, distributer, dealer or any other person associated with the contents of this book is liable or responsible for any consequences directly, or indirectly arising from said contents.

Cover design by Christoph Ennsthaler
Interior layout by Damian Keenan, Heidelberg

*www.ennsthaler.at*
ISBN 978-3-85068-881-9
Phyllida Anam-Áire · Let Love Heal
All rights reserved
Copyright © 2012 by Ennsthaler Verlag, Steyr
Ennsthaler Gesellschaft m.b.H. & Co KG, 4400 Steyr, Austria
Published by Ennsthaler Verlag, Steyr

# Contents

| | |
|---|---|
| What Is This Book About? | 11 |
| And How Did The Book Come To Birth? | 11 |
| Acknowledgements | 15 |
| **1. Hallelu-JA** | **17** |
| A "New HalleluJA" For A New Consciousness | 17 |
| Time To Awaken ... Now | 21 |
| A New Language For A New Consciousness | 24 |
| **2. Becoming Conscious** | **31** |
| What Is My Soul's Purpose? | 31 |
| So Why Have You Come To Earth? | 32 |
| Incarnational Healing | 33 |
| My Mother's Story, My Own Story | 36 |
| Healing Visualization | 39 |
| From Tribal Consciousness To Unity Consciousness | 46 |
| Survival Consciousness | 49 |
| Struggle | 52 |
| Inviting The Problem | 53 |
| States Of Consciousness | 54 |
| From Unconscious To Conscious | 57 |
| Consciousness, The Stuff Of Miracles | 65 |

3. Beliefs And Love ............................................................ 73
   According To Your Belief .............................................. 73
   Healing Is About Loving ............................................... 76
   Focusing On Love... Meditation For The Heart ........... 82
   Love And Relationships ................................................ 85
   Love Illusion ................................................................. 89
   Evolution And Love ..................................................... 95
   True Reality Is Love ..................................................... 97
   Mary Magdalena And Her Dedication To Love ........ 100

4. Forgiveness Revisited ................................................. 105
   Forgiveness And Illusion ............................................ 105
   Perpetrator And Victims ............................................ 107

5. The Hidden God ........................................................ 111
   Disguises Of The Divine ............................................ 111
   I Am That ................................................................... 116
   Identification ............................................................. 122

6. Experiencing Soul ...................................................... 125
   Experience .................................................................. 125
   Soulful Living, Living Love ....................................... 128
   A God Without Soul .................................................. 133
   Living The Symbolic Life ........................................... 134
   Spiralling Lives .......................................................... 136
   Walk Lightly On The Earth ....................................... 139
   A Sound Mind... A Sound Body ............................... 141

7. Universal Heart .................................................................... 145
　Emotional Versus Universal Heart ........................... 145
　From Head To Heart ................................................ 148
　How Do We Break The Code? ................................. 150
　New Bottles For New Wine ...................................... 152
　Intuitive Awareness And Spiritual Growth ............. 156
　Intuition And Decision-Making ............................... 159
　Intuition And Conscious Imagination .................... 161
　The Pineal Gland And Intuition .............................. 161
　Intuition And Instinct .............................................. 163
　Intuition And Discernment ..................................... 164
　Examples Of Intuitive Guidance ............................. 167
　Intuitive Responses In The Christian Scriptures ... 167
　The Chakra Energy System And Intuition ............. 168
　A Summary ............................................................... 170
　Count The Ways ....................................................... 171

8. Beyond Freud ................................................................ 175
　A Little Bit Of Freud And Beyond .......................... 175
　Freud And Women ................................................... 177
　The Absorbing Psyche Of The Child ...................... 177
　The Old Time Religion ............................................ 178
　The First Force In Psychology ................................. 179
　Freud's Triplets: The Id, The Ego And The Super-Ego ... 180
　The Third Force: Humanistic Psychology .............. 190
　Me And My Shadows ............................................... 191
　The New Consciousness Or Fourth Force .............. 193
　An Open Letter To My Dear Earth Mind Or Ego .... 194

## 9. Beyond The Fear of The Feminine .......... 199
  Patriarchal Religion And Its Fear Of The Feminine ......... 199
  Jesus And Women .......... 202
  The Age Of Awakening .......... 203
  Religion, Enlightenment And The Feminine .......... 205
  Integral Spirituality Or Fragmented
  Patriarchal Beliefs? .......... 212
  Women's Work And Worth .......... 218
  From History To Our Story .......... 221
  Woman Soul And Sexuality .......... 222
  The Cauldron, The Grail And The Soul -
  The Trinity Revisited .......... 225
  The Grail .......... 228
  The Soul .......... 230

## 10. Letting Go In My Time .......... 233
  A Child Learns About Grief .......... 233
  Letting Go In Their Time .......... 235
  Consider The State Of The Soul .......... 236
  We Are Not Alone .......... 240
  A Blessing To All .......... 244
  No Other Saviour .......... 247

  Books I have referred to .......... 249

# What is This Book About?

I am an Irish woman who has for the most part of the last six years lived in Germany. For the last three years I have lived, loved, written and worked in beautiful Bavaria. What has drawn a full-blooded Gaelic speaking-singing woman to this part of the world near Hitler's birthplace? Of course there is only one answer and it is, to heal.

Next question, heal what? And therein lies the mystery of my soul. I only know that in this place of green pastures, beautiful lakes, high alpine mountains, strange speaking inhabitants, beer drinking lederhosen men and dirndl dancing women I have found inner peace, joy, affiliation, beauty and friendships that forever sing in my soul. I have also found great and wonderful healing for myself and for my ancestors. I believe in the collective unconscious-consciousness. I believe we are all interwoven together like a beautiful multi-patterned quilt and that each of us plays our own part in the beautifying or darkening of the threads for this quilt. I hope to beautify the overall pattern with my contribution because I know I have come to earth to heal into unconditional love. Seemingly, here in Bavaria is where I am challenged to do just that. And so far the challenge is full of insights, love and joy!

**AND HOW DID THE BOOK COME TO BIRTH?**

**Author's note:**
This book is not written in sequence as such; therefore you, the reader, can decide which topic speaks to your heart at a certain time, then open that page and just experience.

Truth is, whilst I physically typed the words and arranged them into sentences that read more fluently, most of the contents of this book are straight from an inner tutor in residence whose wisdom has taught me these past years. The lessons that I learned were written in the downloading of spiritual truths, wrapped in everyday challenges that I had forgotten. This book is the container that holds some of the contents of these truths. As a Psychotherapist I have woven some psychology, as I interpret it, into the threads of the Chapters, hopefully giving some "grist for the mill" of understanding. I realized a long time ago that therapy alone cannot heal. Neither can ungrounded spirituality as such heal. One needs the combination of both together with awareness of the importance of our physicality, in order to reach a deeper appreciation of the beauty of a congruent personality. At one time I thought that by being a so-called pious nun I would reach sainthood. But I began at the wrong end! Instead of working from the base chakra upwards I began at the top and worked down but only as far as the waist! I was very "holy" but not a "whole" woman. The fragmented parts showed themselves in the life choices I made.

To be honest, this book was written in a short time every day for about two months in all. Sometimes the words would come to me whilst travelling on a train, waiting at an airport or in the middle of a concert. I also received some of the contents during workshops. Naturally I added my own understanding to most of the "downloaded" information, since I wanted a more coherent expression for my readers.

My gratitude to dear friends and students such as Janet Caranas Cobb, who has proof read the English manuscript and has been true to the original text, Cailianna Silvia Lange, Bettina Heidsiek and Alannu Hogger were always near to translate into German. Patricia Ploss also gave her precious time to helping with the translations. The texts were then distributed to the students for their own reading. Alannu said one day, "Why don't you make a book from all this?" So, dear reader, here you are: the result of what I learnt for my own healing. I was challenged to either "Walk your talk or stop talking!" Not easy for an Irish woman! My inner scribe or inner tutor was strict with me, as I had to really understand that I was the one who had to learn the lessons first and then pass them on to others.

When you find that many themes here are repeated, perhaps cloaked in a different language, this is how I learn. Through repetition I gain a deeper understanding of the subject. Please forgive the recycling of certain topics. Friend, I am still learning the lessons, so maybe now that you have the book in your hand we can learn together … you in your way and me in mine, creating a New HalleluJA together.

With joy in connecting with your soul, I send you all love and great healing for your very precious life and for your ancestors. Remember that we are the *"Spiritual Compost"* for the next generations.

We had a conference in Bayern in November 2011 titled "Creating A New HalleluJA", where we collectively visioned a consciousness of gratitude and love.

My references to a "New HalleluJA" in this book refers to this vision.

PHYLLIDA ANAM-ÁIRE
*(Anam-Áire is the Gaelic for soul carer.)*

# Acknowledgements

My deep and everlasting love and gratitude to Alannu Hogger for all she has endured, as she untiringly helped me in the writing down of the contents of this book. You are a computer guru who patiently waited as I tried to understand the German for "save" and "delete" - sometimes with disastrous results as you tried to retrieve lost material! You are such an amazing woman, full of grace and, I believe, a true Bodhisattva. May you know the wisdom of your own soul.

I give gratitude also to Geraldine Ennsthaler for your eternal beauty and listening with love; and thank you so much dear Dorothea at Ennsthaler publishing for your patience with my terrible Deutsch and your kind understanding.

Bettina thank you for saying yes to translating this into German. I am so honoured that you said "Ja".

This book is dedicated to some great people in my life: my adult children Anthea and Richard Templeton and their partners Martin and Mel for encouraging me. Not forgetting my grandson, Riley Templeton, who has shown me in a short time the sheer abundance of life force.

I also say thank you to all my students wherever you are. You have all been my spiritual teachers.

May you know, dear friends in Germany, the great joy I experience living amongst you all. May we have many more glorious years zusammen. Ich bin mit Euch, damit ich heile … my soul's song.

CHAPTER 1

# Hallelu-JA

## A "NEW HALLELUJA" FOR A NEW CONSCIOUSNESS
### *What do I mean by a "New HalleluJA"?*

The question should be: what was meant by the old HalleluJA? It means praise God. Many Christian hymns and prayers end with the acclamation HalleluJA… praise to God. It suggests jubilation and celebration. I translate it as enthusiastic gratitude!

Why give it a new meaning when it has been around for a long time and used in ceremonies that give praise and jubilation? There is nothing wrong with that surely?

> *For the past ca 5.000 years we have lived under the guidance and teachings of the patriarchy. That means all our conditioning since then has come from the male collective or male dominance. This is just the way it was. We have, however, internalized male philosophies, male religious instructions, male social conditioning etc. Now we are looking at another possibility not that of returning to the matriarchy, but rather the possibility of building together a New Consciousness from the ashes of the old that includes female and male wisdom.*

It is time to rename the sacred, the divine in our daily lives, as a way of becoming more consciously involved with the mystery in each precious aspect of life. Can we celebrate the sacredness of children's voices, of dance, of our feeling hearts, our emotions, of making love? This is all part of the "New HalleluJA" of living and loving.

The "New HalleluJA" is saying: give thanks not to an ethereal being in the sky but to the sacred, the beauty in each other, in nature, in life with its triumphs and grief. It says: do not wait until Easter to sing HalleluJA; sing it now, today and rename what is sacred in your life. It may even be a healed hurt or an old hatred that has become a blessing. It is saying: you do not have to believe in God to sing. Believe in your own ability to co-create something beautiful and uplifting and be a co-creator with all. Our collective consciousness is the mystical body of the divine. The new HalleluJA is saying, wrap your own arms around your own heart and bring out the parts as yet unlived, unloved.

When we said HalleluJA in the past we offered praise to the God of our fathers. I have asked many people the question: "Do you believe in God and if so, tell me about your belief." Some of the answers came from the Christian catechism, such as "I believe in God because He sent his son to save me" or "I believe in God because He helps me" or "I believe in God because He is my father in heaven" etc. Each time I was amazed at the way the old religion with its emphasis on gender and relationship through fear still permeated people's lives in the 21$^{st}$. century. I was saddened that the old patriarchal God still held power over people. Other people, who had left tribal religion answered, that God is a being of love, a source of healing etc. I was surprised when a seven-year-old boy answered me, "God sends us love from heaven and sometimes when it gets to us it is all gone." His mother had died and he was trying to make sense of the belief that God is love. What I heard him say was: God is love but when that love filters through the many interpretations and conditionings it gets diluted.

I do not believe in the God of the patriarchy because this belief no longer serves humanity or me. We were taught that He, God, punishes the evildoer and loves the righteous person. This sounds very similar to human love with all its conditions. What I believe in does not have a name, as it is pure consciousness so I refer to it as "IT". I have to let go of all concepts to find what supports and serves my life and my spiritual evolution.

As I look at social and religious history I see that we are still evolving and that this New Age is bringing in radical changes that require total transparency and accountability in all walks of life, from industry to finances, from corporate concerns to the way we love our neighbour.

The scientist, Louise B. Young in her book: "The Unfinished Universe" (Oxford University Press, 1993) says, "We are not finished yet." Meaning, we as evolving humans must cooperate with an evolving Universe to allow past experiences to be integrated into a new awareness, a more intense and fuller appreciation of the Universe as it unfolds and we along with it. The Over-Soul of creation is vibrating at a higher frequency and we are affected by this because we are part of the whole. There is no need for panic as this is natural and is all about harmony and balance. It has to do with staying centred when everything seems to be in chaos.

What does a "New HalleluJA" have to do with all this? I believe it is time to look at old beliefs and values and at that which does not serve us any more. When we live only by old rules and traditions we cannot enter the more vital aspects of our souls. When we stay in the old regimes of religion and psychology we cannot enter fully into the abundance of life, because guilt and dysfunctional patterns of behaviour act as barriers to our own and others' actualization. If we believe we are part of a whole Universe then we have our part to play in its evolution. We are not cogs in the wheels of institutions; we are the activators of the wheels. Religion and state have told us that all life is precious and only God has the right to take a life, but we are still sending boys to kill, with the blessing of both religion and state. The ancient wisdom suggests that our internal world of discrimination creates our outer world of reality. Religion does not allow for autonomy, so we remain God's victims instead of taking responsibility for how we live.

If we believe that we are powerful beyond belief, things will change in our personal and collective worlds and social and religious reform will be imminent. We can remain as children and be led and manipulated by old values and norms, both social and religious, or we can stand up and be counted amongst the ones who declare that:

> *Something new is here.*
> *Something vital is asking to be birthed.*
> *Something vibrant is longing to emerge.*
> *If we decide it can be so, then it will be.*
> *We must all play our part in this new birth.*
> *This new child belongs to us all; we all have to parent it.*

We have not named it yet. We know we are powerful and that scares us even more than being overwhelmed by our weakness. This new awakening, or new creation, belongs to those who are tired of bending a knee to the internalized politics of the patriarchy, tired of having no power and who are now willing to take responsibility. The old feminist battles for freedom and equality were important to achieve a new breakthrough for women, but they were based on patriarchal standards of re-action that keep us all, women and men, stuck in institutionalized abusive values. In this book I take a look at some of the ways in which we are all changing, whether we know it or not. It is better when you have a say in what gets changed and how this is accomplished so you can become aware of the shifts in your own being, your own transformations and your own belief system. One thing is for sure, we all need each other now since "The Times They Are A-Changin'" (Bob Dylan, 1964) - not in the future, but here and now.

The idea of a "New HalleluJA" is about personal transformation, co-operation and global consciousness rather than creating barriers to expansion. It is about the power of collective consciousness, believing in abundance rather than deficit, and feeling great gratitude for all we experience in our magnificent Universe. When we see through the inner eye of innocence and love, instead of through the eyes of judgement and fear, we see with the eye of Creation.

To live the "New HalleluJA" is not to bow low to a God of overpowering might, but to see the wonders of this magnificent creation and stand up with our arms outstretched with gratitude and joy, awed by the miracles of molecules and particles of light that constitute all beings, including all the worlds of created phenomena. When we can allow tears of joy to wet our faces at the splendour of a sunset while singing loudly "Hallelu-JA", we will understand the meaning of true humility and true religion.

This book is about praise and gratitude – not to a projected God with personality or gender - but to a magnificent healing energy, a boundless, limitless intelligence, a vast sea of endless consciousness. It is that love in which everything lives, moves and has its being.

*We are that love.*
*We are that healing energy.*
*We are co-creators with this magnificent intelligence.*
*We are self-actualizing every moment.*
*And we are awakening together.*

And that is why we sing a New Hallelu-JA (composed for the conference with the same title, November 2011, Laufen, Germany).

*We'll sing a New Hallelu-JA*
*We'll gather together hand in hand*
*We'll sing a New Hallelu-JA*
*Consciousness singing throughout the land*

*We'll sing a New Hallelu-JA*
*The old stories we leave behind*
*We'll sing a New Hallelu-JA*
*Soulful healing we now find*

*Hallelu-*
*Hallelu-*
*Hallelu-JA*

## TIME TO AWAKEN ... NOW
*What does it mean to awaken? Do we need to awaken?*

To awaken means to be awake - it is as simple as that. But are we not all awake? "We are all doing the best we can to help others and to help the earth", I hear you say. This is true for many people. Awakening is not a once-and-for-all-time phenomenon. I have to awaken a little bit more every day because I easily fall back into old well-worn habits. Many dear ones are experiencing radical change, total break up of relationships, finance failure, children on drugs, excessive drinking, etc. In society the old walls of power are crumbling and no one feels secure anymore. One would think that is horrific. From the outer appearance of things that may be true, but one can also believe that only the Great Oversoul of creation itself could create such radical transformation all around. A song of mine reminds us of the so-called chaos around us at this time.

> *Everything's transforming, earth must break her bones.*
> *Forests burn out blazing, raging waters overflow.*
> *Energies are quickening as the prophets have foretold.*
> *Chaos and confusion shatter what we owned.*
> *But we belong to the light, we have befriended the dark*
> *Time to let our sparks come alive, cause we belong to the light*
>
> *Old beliefs are crumbling as the hierarchies fall.*
> *The old HalleluJA is up against the wall.*
> *The wall itself can't hold out, all our barriers must go.*
> *As consciousness bursts from us, now at last we know.*
>
> *We belong to the light...*
>
> *We feel our second coming a new and glorious birth.*
> *We are all preparing for heaven here on earth.*
> *It is a time for healing; we have come out of the past.*
> *Raise your voice and sing it, our time has come at last.*
> *For we belong to the light ...*
>
> (FROM CD "SOUNDS OF THE HEART" 2010)

It is true that the Mayan calendar suggests that as we are all entering another age, confusion and transformation are now natural phenomena. In the Hindu religion it is known as the Kali Yuga, the time of darkness between times. This new era is bringing back the spiritual fusion of yin and yang, of Anima and Animus as they co- create in us as female and male.

We have spent enough time honouring the intellect as the main controller of the psyche. Now it is time for the creative juices of our souls to sing a New HalleluJA in each and every socio- religious- psychological structure that affects human beings. We will be guided into a new awakening, a new golden era known as the New Jerusalem, one that can serve us all with compassionate energy. We are now witnessing our fall from the old Garden of Eden. Together, we men and women have to be allowed to eat from the tree of knowledge. We must be able to say no to the father, the patriarchy, and not feel guilty or fear that we will be punished. We have to recognize that the social elite and the hierarchical control-structures did not work for the ordinary people, but served to maintain a social structure of have and have-nots. The standards of law and order were also derisive, as they produced one law for the poor and another for the rich. At times throughout history it is easy to identify many situations when social laws were in actual fact abusive, for example, permitting slavery or the abusive interrogation of prisoners of war etc. Peaceful demonstrations ended up as blood baths in Northern Ireland due to the over-enthusiastic control of police and army. We have had laws that were at times not at all legal and order that was unruly and inconsistent. One can say the same for the other social systems that seemed to be serving the populace but in actual fact were serving only what Lucia Rene calls the global elite.

Patriarchal Religion has not honoured the feminine at all, but subscribed to a male populace to the detriment of females. Neither has education really afforded young people the full range of information and experiential practices that could have enriched their curriculum. Wisdom-keepers are not usually hired as professors at high schools or universities, but those with an accumulation of intellectual information are readily employed. When education once more lives what it means, i.e. to draw out from the student knowledge that is already there, then we will have teachers of wisdom and wise professors. Perhaps then the joy of knowledge will once more return to our schools.

Everyone has their own story regarding the inconsistencies of the world order that exist at this present time. As long as we support governments that enslave the people, as long as we consent to children's' minds being abused by advertisements, as long as we stay silent in the midst of pornography, we are helping to maintain the status quo of ignorance. But we cannot go to war as our ancestors did since that was the way of fear. We have more knowledge now and with this great advantage we can invalidate the value systems that defined the past centuries. If we each take total responsibility for our part in the manifestation of peace and goodwill on earth, we can and will bring this to pass. But in order to achieve this, our thinking has to change.

Each person can delve into the archives of their own experience and draw out stories that can support the theory that the time for radical change has come. It is time for us to awaken each day to a new consciousness so that the next generation can really benefit from our present challenges. It is also time to let go of blaming the old age where conflict, control, confrontation, condemnation reigned and make way for connecting, for congruence and for a radical raising of consciousness.

May we all earnestly look at the ways in which we have to awaken, so that our children's children to the seventh generation can be proud of us their ancestors.

## A NEW LANGUAGE FOR A NEW CONSCIOUSNESS

Language is an amazing tool of communication. Let us take a simple look at how it affects us and our world. Confucius said, "If language is incorrect, then what is said is not what is meant. If what is said is not what is meant, then what should be done remains undone." Although communicating verbally is only one way of connecting with another, it is a strong and vital skill. Its function is to help us understand what we say to each other when we share our views, our beliefs, our feelings etc. Clear words help us follow instructions better so there are fewer misunderstandings. In this way, as Confucius would agree, things get done that need to be done. People with speech dysfunction know only too well the difficulties they experience when trying to express their thoughts and feelings to someone who has no such difficulty. Sign language for the hearing impaired has been a great innovation, as has Braille for people with sight problems.

It is interesting to look back at the ways human language has developed through the centuries, from grunting animal sounds to the symbolic drawings and gestures of cave man, and realize just how language has advanced with evolving consciousness. It is said that if we change the language of a nation we also change the culture. So language has to do with culture and belonging. The Irish saying: "You can't make yourself known in a language that is not from your own tongue!" bears some truth. It means you cannot be truly known for who you are in a language that is not the native language "from your own ones".

Language describes various states of being; for instance, there is the language of love, the language of grieving, the language of war, the language of reconciliation, the language of healing etc. It is as if the different states of consciousness have their own language of expression. In the forties the language of war "raged" throughout Europe, and that included the language of want and poverty, death and destruction. The every-day vocabulary included words such as war, dead, terror, bombs, ammunition, brutality, hate, disastrous, hopeless, victims, dying, starvation, helplessness, overpowering, suffering, etc. If we believe that words are energetic beings and hold various impulses that contribute to the atmosphere, then one can understand how depressed people felt in regions where war ravaged. People who listened to the news of wars in other parts of the world would have become depressed as well. We know that words of compassion and love have a different affect on our psyches than words of condemnation and shame. Try this exercise yourself.

**EXERCISE**

- *Write down all the negative words you can think of. Read them aloud slowly to yourself and feel the impact of these words on your feelings.*
- *Then write down all the positive, loving words you can imagine.*
- *Read them aloud to yourself and notice the difference in the way you feel.*
- *For the rest of the day it might be interesting to notice the times you or others use any or many of these words, whether they are negative or positive - no judgement, just an exercise.*

In the fifties, the language we used was mostly of release and rebellion. The younger generation introduced a new vocabulary to include expressions like real cool, square, teenagers rule ok, freedom for all, no to war, jukebox, pop fans, fantastic, rip it up etc. Seemingly, young people had something to say to the older generation and were daring to say it. I remember the words of my father in 1959: "It will all end in pain yet; these young ones are going too far." (He was referring to pop singers rebelling against the politics of war.) The sentence held doom and gloom because he, like most adults at that time, was still recovering from the effects of war. There was no room for expansive thinking in Europe since people were trying to live beyond mere survival and the language naturally echoed these thoughts. Their philosophy was: "Young people should do as they are told. They do not have a right to their own opinions. We got it hard and so should they." So the psychological mindset was carried over from the forties and it was difficult for the older generation to admit that they had anything to learn from Cliff Richards' "Young Ones".

Politics also began to change its language in the form of J.F. Kennedy in the early sixties. His election and subsequent speeches had radical effects on the world in general. Like Martin Luther King, J.F. Kennedy made visionary statements that began to rock the boat of the patriarchy that wanted to maintain the status quo of the hierarchical political dualistic language of "us and them". Kennedy's language was about inclusion not exclusion. It was so unlike the raging language of Hitler twenty years earlier, when roars of hatred and terrorism filled the street corners and political platforms in Germany and Austria! I lived in Northern Ireland during the so-called "troubles" in the seventies when the language of hatred incited people to kill and destroy. One day my daughter, then six years old, said: "Mummy, are you *the other side*?" I was a Catholic who had married a Protestant and in his tribe the Catholics were the enemies, just as in the Catholic tribe the Protestants were to blame. I felt the pain of having to tell my daughter that we did not take sides. She had heard someone, a Protestant, say that "the other side should be shot dead."

Women have been denied their own language in the workplace and in the churches for centuries. Our language is naturally not one of war and terror (although many women who have internalized the patriarchy use violent language). If we are to cultivate a society that is soulful and that honours human life, we have to use a language and speech that supports this. When we listen to good poetry we realize how it touches the places in us that have been stonewalled for a long time. Poetry brings mystery and the grace of symbolism back to life in us and satisfies our thirst for a spiritual language. My own Gaelic language is an earth language and touches a very creative chord in our cellular memory. It opens the heart into a warm place that many thought they had forgotten.

In the past years science has begun to take a closer look at the way in which it expresses its theories in words. In the early nineties the scientists John Wheeler expressed the belief that we as humans are not only observers of the world but full participants in it and, as such, are co-creators. In 2007 the American scientist Gregg Braden reiterated this belief at his conference in Italy ("The Divine Matrix"). He even went as far as to postulate that consciousness transcends form and that thought manifests as matter. His studies show that the ancient religions knew about such things as thought projections affecting the material world, and the heart being the true vehicle of transformation. So perhaps we can also say that the words we use, language our reality. As we believe, we speak; as we speak, we create. Words like compassion, healing, spirituality, co-creators, formlessness, consciousness beyond death, are examples of the language Gregg Braden includes in his wonderful lectures. From such soulful language we can build a different concept of science and therefore live from a different perspective. One might say this is the language of spirituality. So maybe the language from one state of consciousness is compatible with that of another, as long as we let go of our former stringent cognitive use of language.

In his book, *The Science of Oneness*, (O books, 2006") my friend Malcolm Hollick says: "It is not the atoms of which our bodies are made that makes life real for us, but our consciousness, our awareness of the world around us and of our own inner selves" (page 126). We have moved from the scientific language of materialism to a language that considers the possibility of consciousness and in doing so we have brought about a more friendly coexistence between religion and science.

This closer communication helps us to understand our world from a deep universal perspective, one of awe and wonder. When we reach the stage where the poet and the mathematician, the scientist and mystic, the healer and the professor of medicine, the scholar and the story-teller can sit together and share what they know, we may find a soul language that all can truly hear.

Religions also have to look at the ways in which the language of scriptures no longer serves the soul of humanity. In the sixties the Catholic Church decided that the language of liturgy should be in the vernacular and so the prayers and gospels were changed to fit a new consciousness. It was a movement towards the people and one that addressed the needs of the congregation, rather than complying with old encyclicals that fed only the analytic mind and left the soul hungry. The old story of condemnation that includes the language of damnation and hell fire does not set the soul free but binds it further. It is interesting that the language of Jesus was one of encouragement, love, compassion, forgiveness and toleration - the language of the heart.

In the late sixties we also had the language of encounter groups - the beginning, as it were, of the "workshops and self development" culture. Psychologists like A. Maslow, F. Perls, Timothy Leary, Ram Dass and others were declaring that we are all capable of self-actualizing and self-healing. From then on the language of healing seemed to flow into the universe like a tidal wave, bringing a sense of creative newness and hope, of autonomy and power. We could heal our past traumas and enter a space of more congruency within ourselves and with each other. It seemed as though humanistic psychology was the new religion that was offering healing forgiveness, the healing from the sin of self-guilt and shame. We could experience this heavenly release here and now through the medium of soulful gatherings which included words like transformation, self-actualisation, sharing, self-love, the higher self, healing the past, karmic release, soul retrieval etc. Since then we have all adapted to terms such as self-compassion, inner child work, transcending the past, working on your ego patterns, creative drawing, dancing into healing, dying to the old, etc.

Now we seem to be entering into a whole new field of language consciousness and as a result our language is again becoming more and more refined. Whilst my parents would not agree with how I language my world today, the fact that I have changed my beliefs means I have also had to change my mode of expression. As I become more aware of myself and others, so also will my mind and heart open to a more expressive language that reflects this internal transformation. Together we can begin a new way of communicating with each other, a way of sharing from the heart, from our feelings, with joy and exuberance for life. As we appreciate more and more the wonder of life and are really grateful for this chance to participate in the transformation of our planet, let our language be the outward sign of inward change and healing. With the knowing that our words materialize into beings, we can create a more loving and tolerant society, thus reaching out into the whole universe with supportive love.

May we all bring out the language of a New HalleluJA for ourselves, the world and for the planet.

As we all sing the New HalleluJA we remember the people who had to live the language of war and terror, and who have gloriously risen up again to sing a new song, to speak in a different tongue.

CHAPTER 2

# Becoming Conscious

**WHAT IS MY SOUL'S PURPOSE?**

This is a very important question that many people ask. Why am I here on the earth? And what is my soul's work? Actually, there is only one question: "Why am I on earth this time?" The answer seems very simple, yet very few really understand it and even fewer live it.

Can you imagine that you are on earth to become more and more conscious and so to live divine love? That is all and this takes lifetimes to actually achieve. Why is this?

The Christian religion teaches that we are on earth to serve God and later we will be happy with him in heaven if we have done well and have not died in mortal sin. This is not truth since this is human manipulation. It suggests that God is a god of condemnation who has preferences and loves conditionally, as mortals love. Can you imagine a gospel that says you have come to earth to live your precious life fully, to experience and honour every situation and to eventually reach a place where you become more and more aware of your thoughts and actions and so live from a more soulful place of divine love? You decide when you come to earth and you also decide when you return to formlessness, never to take form again. You have the power to live fully in each moment without judgement of yourself and others. You have the power to live divine love here and now. When you become more conscious, all your actions come from divine love because all you are is love.

Imagine if the first time you went to church the priest or parson had said that you were a wonderful being of pure love and all you do is from love itself! Imagine if you had been told the truth: that you are totally innocent and you are deeply loved and cherished. How different your life might have been!

Imagine if you had always believed that the reason you came to earth was to do everything with full awareness! Then you would have had no need for any great ambitions nor would you struggle to be anyone magnificent because you would know you already were so. Then you would stop setting unattainable goals for yourself. How different might your self-image be if you truly believed thus? You are asked by universal law itself to live in mindfulness of who you are – a divine being that has taken on the amazing contract that the angels found too difficult and that is: to embody, to be on the earth plane with all its pains, confinement and contractions. Your work is mighty; you have contracted to live divine love on earth in your body-mind.

Now, most of us do not live thus. In actual fact we live the opposite because we have lost sight of why we came. The earth mind took over and we often got lost in power struggles and manipulation. This can be said of religious people as well as of those who for selfish reasons use others. There is no condemnation, no judgement. As we leave the physical body, we will realize our errors and recognize the pain we have caused others. I have now consciously contracted to live a more congruent life every day. The raising of consciousness in thousands of people at this time is creating waves and waves of divine outpouring on the earth and we yes we, are responsible for such transformation.

Because you are a work in progress of transforming your earth mind into the mind of the Christ, or universal love, you are a helpmate in the transformation of your world, here and now. That is the work of warriors of the divine order.

### SO WHY HAVE YOU COME TO EARTH?

You have come for this moment. Every breath, each thought, each movement, becomes an act of grace and love. Whether you laugh or cry, it matters not because the intention to raise your own consciousness is what counts. You see, it matters not what you do, it only matters in what state of consciousness you do it. Your intention is everything. The more conscious you become, the more you will be aware of the beings your thoughts are creating in you. If you have conscious loving thoughts, all that flows from you is love and so you add to the collective love and light-consciousness of creation. So if you are enjoying a beautiful meal at the moment, just know that… for this moment you have come. All our actions become spiritual practices when done with consciousness.

Our precious lives are worthy of joy and laughter. Of course, the more you look with love into your own so-called dark shadow, the more lightsome it becomes. The more you work on your earth grounding energies and free them into the place of love, the more you are helping in the raising of consciousness. Just imagine, the more you are willing to embrace your fear and anger and see their origins, the more you help the entire universe in the healing, cleansing process that is taking place at the moment.

So let us rejoice together and know that we are healing every moment. Be very loving with yourself and know that you are doing the work of your soul when you ground love on earth. For this you have all come into birth this and every other time.

*"We are together that we might love"*
*(FROM CD "TOUCHED", PHYLLIDA 2007).*

## INCARNATIONAL HEALING

It seems that when we left the womb we experienced a deep energetic wave of grief. This so-called grief energy was the result of the loneliness experienced by the psyche having, first of all, left the formless place of unconditional love in order to experience and heal human emotions. This required leaving the warmth and comfort of the womb where all the earth-needs had been met. Of course this deep energetic longing of the newborn baby went unnoticed by those around her since so-called spiritual realities were not taken into account. With more enlightened awareness as to the mighty trauma of birth and the subsequent emotional stress, we began to look more deeply at this very important and highly influential journey of the child, where she learns once more the various components of physicality and its attendant states of loss. I personally believe that we all experience what I call primary grief, the descent from pure consciousness to the adaptation to form - form in which we learn to judge ourselves and others.

Before birth great miracles were set in motion forming all the complex attributes that make up our human biology, emotionality and mentality. We were spiritual beings voluntarily taking on the winter coat of form in order to ground Spirit on earth, and this required much adjustment and adaptation. Making this journey to the earth plane is not an easy choice for a soul, even though the decision is not based on emotional intelligence, but rather on wisdom from the completion of the previous incarnation, the outcome of which determines how the soul prepares itself for this limited form in which it has to live, move and have its being. As the soul, or life force, of the individual is a component of the Great Oversoul of creation, it is in essence sacred, holding both masculine and feminine energy. Matter has a very dense frequency and vibration, so the magnificent unlimited shapelessness and spacelessness of the Great Oversoul allows itself to be confined by the template of the form in which it shapes itself. Thus the human body is created in a way whereby the individual soul, a particle of the Great Oversoul, may find a home and begin its journey of literally widening itself into the cellular system of the physical, thus giving vitality and movement to form. The individual human soul takes on the journey of earthing divine love and this constitutes the ultimate self-sacrifice. Since the Great Oversoul loves all form unconditionally, whether it is a tree or flower, sun or mountain, animal or plant, it always breathes it with life. The soul in us is the mediator between pure love and human expression and helps us to find balance and harmony through the medium of spiralling earth lives. It assists in our being made sacred, being sanctified. Eventually, the individual expression of the Great Oversoul will fully unite with formlessness and will not be earthed again in physicality. This is called the holy marriage, unity consciousness, returning back to the one. Soul is also not confined to time - it lives in the eternal now.

When the individual soul enters human form at the moment of conception, the divine becomes grounded. Actually, great miracles of grace had been happening all along the way from the moment the sperm went on his love quest to unite with the egg. But the fusion between sperm and egg is an all-important phenomenon without which the soul cannot be grounded. The moment the soul unites with form, trauma begins for the emotional body. Although the soul is without emotionality, it does not feel pain; it directs all emotion to the centre of the body and from there the sacred heart of the child may express the feeling. So, the stage is set for the continuation of form to build itself on form and produce a beautiful well-formed human being at the end of nine months. This is the work of a genius and a highly intellectual and orderly mind, in conjunction with the soul wishes of the human being.

From the moment a soul takes on form it begins to feel its own presence and its own state of individuation on earth. The form is produced by the millions of neurons and photons, molecules and particles that are transmitted through electromagnetic pattering throughout the potential form, thus giving shape and materialism to these electric impulses. Later on, as the soul widens into the form, the feelings of the mother are transmitted to the child. The mother's state of being affects the baby's emotional growth and, in turn, the child's physical growth is affected by her own emotional re-actions. At this stage, the baby's emotionality is that of stimulus-response, basically instinctual, since it is not yet equipped with the internal mechanisms of discrimination and individuation. The child uses its psychic abilities to begin to soulfully sense its internal states of consciousness, since there was no way of differentiating between its own emotional impulses and those of the mother.

Many people when undergoing regression therapy attest to the fact that whilst in the womb they became aware of the presence of energy around them. One man told me he experienced a sadness and helplessness that "was not mine". When he later asked his mother how she had felt about being pregnant she said: "I was very sad and helpless as I felt I could not imagine being able to birth you." Strangely, she had used the same words as her son to express her feelings. My own story of embodying is very interesting regarding this non-discriminating emotional bonding with my mother.

## MY MOTHER'S STORY, MY OWN STORY

Three months after the deaths of her two children who died within one week of each other, my dear Mother became pregnant with me. Her little son of eight months died in my mother's arms. At her child's graveside my mother cried her tears of grief until the parish priest said, "No more tears or God will send you another cross!" My parents went to visit my father's sister for six days and when they got back home they were told that their two and half year old little daughter had died two days before. No one had told them, since no one could take the responsibility of being the messenger of this further grief. My Mother told me she did not cry one tear as she had remembered the words the priest had prophesied. They still had a four-year-old daughter and their fear, no doubt, was that God would also take her if they cried. What a deep wound for these two dear people, broken-hearted and helpless in their pain! God was not a comforter but a tyrant who denied them their humanness. I cannot imagine that my mother welcomed another pregnancy. But the Catholic Church demanded that mothers become pregnant every year, so she was a "good mother" and obeyed. She told me that she had a lot of pain in her pregnancy with me. Dear woman, full of suppressed grief and deep sadness that later became depression and scruples, inappropriate guilt and self-punishment. When I was born mother could not bond with me as it was too painful for her to express love, fearing that God might just take me too. The lesson she learnt about love was that it not safe emotionally. The message she received about God was that HE was not happy with feelings and certainly not with a mother's tears. The church declared all was God's will and we have to suffer in silence and prayer. God became the love/fear object of her unlived life, with the result that she became addicted to religion. Father was not able to support her emotionally, so he became melancholic and drank at times in order to numb the pain. Poor people with locked in feelings, too hurtful to imagine, too painful to express. When I was one year old Mother took me to the chapel and presented me to God, disowning me emotionally. I belonged to God and she would not cry if he took me from her.

Clearly, my own story began with the emotional transference from my mother when I was in the womb. I knew about grief and sadness from then on. Seemingly, I did not want to come into the world, as I was a long time struggling with life and death. In the end, I made it and I appreciate my own courage for having done so. Evidently, my particular contract in this lifetime was to come to earth and live grief fully, so that I could help others to deal with it, instead of trying to cope like my dear parents did in the only way they knew how. It was also the only way the priest knew how to help - by saying it was God's will. I truly marvel at the perfection of the choice I made prior to conception. I chose exactly the parents who would throughout their sad unlived lives teach me to risk living fully and risk feeling all that my heart needed to feel and express. For all the gifts I received from them I am forever grateful.

---

A near death experience in 1973 confirmed my beliefs years later that death is not dependent on form and that consciousness, or soul, transcends the material. When I met with Dr. Elisabeth Kübler-Ross M.D. in 1983 I realized that she was going to be my most important teacher in this lifetime, and so she was. I worked with her in the U.S. and in Europe and I was the one who worked mostly with mothers and fathers whose children had died. Thanks to my own dear mother and father for their teaching, beginning in the womb, I could bring the message that grief is a very fundamental feeling that needs to be expressed, along with the attending stages of anger, depression, bargaining, fear, jealousy, denial and acceptance. No doubt, through the years I attracted other very wise teachers who taught me about loss and rejection through my relationships with them. I hope I have learnt these lessons well!

For the rest of her life, my dear mother suffered with ill health and isolation. I could never get close to her because she denied any human closeness. My father tried to carry the wounding silently but his bouts of drinking revealed suppressed grief when he cried his songs rather than sang them. Although my father was happy to have his five children around him when he breathed his last breath, when my mother was dying she asked to be allowed to die alone, without her family, as she said it was too painful for us all to see her dying. The nurse in charge when she died told us that just before my mother died, she sat up in the bed and said she had seen the mother of God and that she welcomed her. My mother then lay down and smiled and left the earth, that place of suffering and loneliness for 71 years. Maybe she has come back to experience self-love and to trust the wisdom of her feelings. Above all else, that is what I wish her. May all beings be blessed as they come and leave.

Sometimes it is not easy to see that the earth journey is all about stages of love, yet when we draw back the veil of understanding and begin to see through the eyes of perception rather than the eyes of judgement and ignorance, we begin to see the beauty and the amazing web of consciousness surrounding all our experiences. We move in and out of this web, from incarnation to incarnation, as we grow deeper in love with love itself, continuing on each time until, in the end, there is only the love that was in the beginning, is now and ever shall be, love without end.

In the last century the spiritual journey of coming into birth was not emphasized. Physicality was of the utmost importance. "Both are doing well", meant that both mother and child had survived the trauma of physical birthing. That was a blessing - all one could possibly hope for. In many cases, babies who had just left the womb were immediately held upside down and slapped on the back to initiate breathing and help express the phlegm that may have gathered at the back of the throat. Imagine the torture for a small insecure being trying to learn to trust this new world. But in the ears of the midwife a crying baby meant a happy one! Then the child was wrapped in a towel on a cold stainless steel scale to be weighed. There was a strict procedure for feeding the baby. "Feed them every four hours", we were told as young, ignorant mothers. "Do not feed them more often or they will want more!" It was as if giving them what they wanted was wrong, as it could become a habit! The little child had to struggle, cry loud, make a fuss and then, possibly, the adult, out of exasperation and annoyance, would listen and do something. How could we develop any trust or security when our first experiences were so painful, due to the insensitivity of our caregivers? Many babies simply gave up in the end since no one had heard their cries. I have worked in psychotherapy with adults who had cried and cried as babies and then became helpless and invisible for the rest of their lives. They found it difficult to share their lives, as their habit had been to remain quiet, because no one cared enough to hear them.

How could we possibly grow into self-affirming beings when our first sense of self was one of inadequacy and worthlessness? We have physically survived, most of us in good enough health, but some of us did not survive emotionally.

Some are still suffering from the emotional trauma of primary grief, of psychic loneliness. We are still split off from our souls, still grieving silently to ourselves. The deep longing for home and for unconditional love creates such a void in ones life! Forgiving ourselves for having incarnated is, I believe, an important stage of healing this deep sense of isolation. Grieving the need for acceptance and approval is not easy for many since the soul's memory of pure consciousness is still present. Some of us never healed these early instinctual egoistic experiences and today we are still looking for that spiritual home, that place where we are loved into healing and joy. Thus we are not fully present here and now, as we are mostly out of our bodies. If we have come from pure love and love is the ultimate journey of soul, then how can we apply this belief to heal our body-minds instead of always flying off to blue perfection? I believe that as loneliness is the first emotion we need to heal, we need to begin at the beginning.

## HEALING VISUALIZATION

I suggest the following visualization, which may be experienced with the help of another caring person. The caring helper makes sure that the friend is lying down in a comfortable position and that there will be no interruptions. She then reads the following, slowly, using consistent pauses and soft expression in the voice.

**VISUALIZATION**

*"Breathe deeply into your solar plexus.*
*Keep breathing in this way for three breaths.*
*Imagine as you begin the fourth, fifth and sixth breaths that you are building up a reservoir of breath.*
*These deep breaths help you to travel deeper into your own heart.*
*Keep breathing this way for the next four breaths and then relax the breath into slow quiet breathing, still deep in your solar plexus.*

*Now slowly accept a place of deep quiet and stillness.*
*A quiet secure soft darkness fills the place with peace.*
*You feel safe and are surrounded by safety.*
*The safety of love surrounds you here.*
*You are so safe (helper pauses here).*
*Imagine you can lie down here in total safety.*
*You are warm and cared for.*
*Breathe into this space gently with slow breaths.*
*Watch what images come to you from here (again pause here).*

*Breathe into those images with soft deep breaths.*
*All is well. All is well.*
*Breathe deeper into the images.*
*See them clearly and become one with them.*
*Enter into them.*
*Now.*
*Do not judge them or yourself. Just stay in this space of acceptance of them and yourself (pause here).*

*Now imagine that you are being lifted up high -*
*High out of the place where you are lying.*
*Keep breathing deeply and quietly,*
*Letting go with each out breath...letting go.*
*That's it, letting go.*

*Slow breaths of security and peace.*
*Lifted up, up, gently, securely lifted up (pause here).*

*Now you see a place clearly.*
*It is full of light and softness.*
*Softness, such soft, soft light and security.*
*Feel the softness of this light.*
*Breathe into soft security as you drift away on the softness.*
*It carries you deeper and deeper into a place where you are laid down -*
*Very gently you are laid down on a soft cloud that feels like silk.*
*Breathe into the silk feeling.*
*All is well. You are safe here (pause here).*

*Now hear a voice from this place ...*
*Listen, it is calling your name.*
*Softly it calls your name.*
*It says:*
*Now it is time, dear one.*
*Now your time has come to be in the world of form.*
*Now, dear one, we support you in leaving -*
*In leaving this place of love and security,*
*This place of lightness and joy.*
*Now you have chosen to go to the earth plane.*
*And once more take on the cover of darkness.*
*Well done, dear one (pause here).*

*As you go, as you leave this consciousness of love*
*You will forget more and more the joy and pure love*
*That now surrounds you.*
*You will forget more and more the purpose of your going.*
*You will soon forget all about this space of pure love.*
*This is the way of incarnating.*
*This is natural (pause here).*
*Feel that you are surrounded by light beings.*

*Beautiful healing music fills the space*
*And you are so safe and loved.*
*Breathe now as gently as possible.*
*Now, dear one, take the step,*
*The step into your new life; for all is life.*
*And know that you are not alone.*
*Beings from here are going to assist you,*
*And by so doing, they will work out their own contracts*
*(pause here).*

*Your mother is waiting. The one you have chosen to womb you,*
*The one who will teach you your first lesson in earth life:*
*The lesson in grief and the pain of separation.*
*For you cannot live earth life without first being part of her.*
*And then separating from her.*
*Just like this moment that now beckons you,*
*The moment of leaving (pause here).*
*Your father is also waiting for you -*
*The one who will teach you the second lesson in earth life -*
*The lesson in support or none, whichever is your particular theme.*
*For you cannot live with just his support. You must stand alone.*
*Just like this moment that beckons you – the moment of aloneness (pause here).*

*Other loving beings are also at the threshold waiting to serve you.*
*You know that they travel to serve your earth journey.*
*But when you meet again you will not always be able to see through their disguises.*
*Some you will call friend, some enemy.*
*But in this space of true love, you know that there is no enemy.*
*All beings present themselves in order to serve you fully and also to work out their own stories through you (pause here).*
*Now, dear one, you will have to take on what is called breath in order to live in the density of earth existence.*
*As you learn to breathe, you will one day learn that this is the*

*connecting force between your earth mind/body and your soul, and is the direct communication with me, Holy Spirit.*
*The day you know this you will begin to remember and heal from the pain of your longing.*
*When you breathe into this primary grief, you will be able to heal the other sorrow held captive in your heart beat (pause here).*

*Your longing for home will be your sickness.*
*Your living in a space which you call non-love will be your sickness.*
*Your insistence on caring only for temporal things will be your sickness.*
*Your inability to trust that you are not alone will create sickness.*
*Your fears of life will create your sickness.*
*All sickness carries a fear.*
*Open your heart now to the love that surrounds you.*
*In nature.*
*In friendship.*
*In the breath your breath.*
*And in the life you have chosen (pause here).*

*Remember you are free to choose at every moment.*
*This gift was yours throughout each incarnation.*
*You are creating your life by your choices.*
*You can change your mind (pause here).*

*Now, dear one, take another deep breath.*
*Keep this breath in your body and count to 4.*
*Release it slowly into the ether.*
*Follow this by another deep breath and hold it for 4 counts.*
*Release it into your lower body/mind.*
*Accept all of yourself as you do this (pause here).*
*I accept all of who I am, and am becoming right now.*
*I accept the fact that the same love that created me is still breathing me alive.*
*I accept the love that surrounds me now.*

*I accept the fact that I am a being of light and joy, unbounded joy.*
*I breathe all these gifts now.*
*I free myself now from all contracts of suffering.*
*Suffering is a choice I make.*
*I free myself from suffering.*
*I will myself to live more within the pure abundance of my life here on earth (pause here).*

*Slowly bring your awareness to your breath.*
*Allow it to flow out of your mouth into the whole of the room.*
*You are bringing yourself into light here and now.*
*Breathe gently into your whole body with joy.*
*Remember the words:*
*I am not alone.*
*All are here to help me.*
*I just need to open my heart and receive all.*
*All beings in all the worlds of life creation now bless me.*
*Ahh!*
*Stay here in this place of blessing (pause here).*

*Hear the whole of creation singing a New HalleluJA to you and for you.*
*Earth welcomes you.*
*Breath welcomes you.*
*All your friends welcome you.*
*See how the souls of so-called enemies welcome you.*
*And you have been initiated into earth life.*
*Welcome beautiful form of love.*
*Breath of love.*
*Expression of love on earth.*
*Welcome to you (pause here).*
*Now gently come down.*
*Down, down into the density of the body.*
*Feel your feet, legs, torso, hands, and head.*
*Without opening your eyes, roll them in your head,*

*from right to left, up and down, to centre and back.*
*Breathe very gently, rhythmically, with compassion for yourself.*
*Feel the love of your soul totally surround you.*
*Feel the compassion of the entire Universe serving you now.*
*Feel the warmth of your own blood circulating with loving-kindness throughout your entire body/mind system.*
*How wonderfully you are made!*
*You are a being of such light!*
*How soulfully aware you are!*
*Well done! (Pause here).*

*Now imprint this image in your mind, like you are copying this download on to your computer.*
*See yourself marking this page and going to save.*
*Then save it in your mind computer.*
*You know you can retrieve it any time your want (pause here).*

*When you feel totally in your body/mind, SLOWLY move your body.*
*Breathe into the whole of your body/mind and sit up VERY slowly.*
*Take time to get up and walk very slowly as if you are learning to walk the earth for the first time."*

Drink water and stay quiet for a while. For the rest of this day be aware of your feelings and sense any changes in your body/mind.

May you be blessed and be a blessing. May your incarnation serve your soul journey this time and for all times.

## FROM TRIBAL CONSCIOUSNESS TO UNITY CONSCIOUSNESS

Having healed our ego-self to a certain stage, it is natural progression of our soul-selves to then have an intuitive need or calling to join the collective, to co-create a higher consciousness for us all. We have reached a higher degree of individuation, are more individually responsible for our own creative forces, so we want to share what we have experienced and what we have healed with others. You are now surrendering more and more to your inner guidance and inner authority. This authentic self now wants to reach out and become part of the process of healing of the Universe and making it whole. In order to do the work of letting go of old messages etc. we had to individuate and become self conscious. We had to discover the difference between ourselves and "the other". This was an integral part of the healing process. Now we refer to "we" and "us", the theme of togetherness, unity. Whatever unites us is important now since we cannot achieve this global healing alone. We must not, however, lose ourselves in the one-making; we remain forever and always individuals whilst, at the same time, becoming more and more united to the bigger story of our incarnations. We become more of who we are in the process of becoming, and that is the mystery of our individual soul-selves. The creator is forever delighting in its differentiated self as seen in the varieties of all created phenomena.

We are now more self-regulated and self-responsible within this internal shift of the collective. We become helpmates in the evolution of consciousness. Your place is now in the shaping of a new being, a New HalleluJA of evolved spirituality that will include a more spiritually imbued psychology and philosophy. Once, the scientists were in an empirical world of their own with their own language that separated them from the artistic and religious. Now they are being invited to sit at the table of metaphysics and soul so that language, as such, need no longer create the gap that has separated us all for too long. Now all disciplines including physics, astrology, geology, etc. can participate in this story of human evolution, each contributing its own jewel to the crown of a deeper understanding. To create a higher consciousness we have to be part of creating a culture in which language and customs have to change in order to accommodate this new being that is emerging. We need each other if we are to approach the changes with integrity and love. We will see a new world being created from the ashes of the old.

Whether we know it or not, we are all coming together, our egos and souls at last able to co-exist and create something beautiful, something totally new and innovative, something that separatism cannot create. This is magnificent, and only fear can keep us back from being totally wonderful and powerful. We are co-creating with a mighty force that is too awful to imagine. And yet it has chosen us as its co-workers, harvesting the field called "awakening".

Our tribal values are also being questioned at this time and we will not have it easy, as tribal customs will revolt against anything that is new and transformative. We will be viewed as breaking with past ideologies. That is very threatening to the tribe which, in turn, will try to deny any innovations to their fundamentalist beliefs. The more aware we become, the more we will experience the fear that exists in the clan or tribe. The old fundamentalists will fear the changes in family affairs. The tribe is scared that we will be lost or will travel too far from home and leave them all behind. This is a great grief, often unspoken by a family member or a friend, and is often expressed as anger toward the one who leaves the tribe. If they could be encouraged to bring their pain to the openness of loving sharing, this would be beneficial for all.

We are representing the Anti-Christ for those still referring to a one true God, one true religion, one true way of life, one ideology for the masses etc. We are living more symbolically and spontaneously and this is difficult for the tribe as they still live literally, according to the word and the law. It takes time for such cultural attitudes to change. We need to have patience with the ones who for "our own good" try to keep us safe in the old beliefs. It is not necessary to try and change these dear ones, as this is seemingly not their journey this time. And all is well - there is no judgement.

Our business is to re-create ourselves, here and now, at every moment. If we pay careful attention to language, that helps the tribe to be calm. If we use language that is foreign and unacceptable to them, then fear again sets in and we create war, rather than peace. We need to be respectful at all times with all beings who do not believe as we do. Spiritual arrogance is a great scourge. We need to be respectful of the culture that reared us and helped us to survive. We are not better than they; we are just on a different pathway. There are no hierarchies in Spirituality.

> *To integrate the past is to honour it.*
> *To honour the past is to heal it.*
> *To heal the past is to respect the struggle of our ancestors.*

We need inclusiveness, not elitism. Everything is looking to be honoured, since everything is longing to be made sacred again. It is up to us to rename the sacred in everyday living. This is a powerful grace, to rename what is holy and bless it in our lives. We no longer have to depend on a religion to make our decisions.

Tribes need to feel that they are powerful and autonomous and this is threatened by our growing power. Our power comes from our inner authority that needs no bravado or outer show of strength. It is good to be open to discussions regarding tribal values and we must make sure that the language of war does not prevail. When debate turns into an argument then the ego takes over for sure. Defensiveness sets in when we are threatened, so we use defence strategies in order to be safe. Tribes act like this as well, so when an institution feels that its values are being questioned it will re-act and in doing so may overpower someone in the process. Remember, the patriarchy has not used power well in the last 5,000 years. Before that there was matriarchal rule, which was more about honest networking and inclusiveness rather than the club mentality. But we now see that the cornerstone on which the patriarchy was built was that of fear. Institutional hierarchies are all built on fear because of their internal tribal value systems. One needs to be aware of the outcomes of such fear. Hierarchies, both political and religious, are falling; they have to, in order to become part of the transformation that is happening all around.

You are part of a new emerging consciousness. Now is the time to begin to come out of the closet and start to activate the soul within you. It was good and necessary to spend time incognito so that you could build up a strong spiritual self. Now it is time to bring the amazingly powerful spiritual beings that we have become into the world so that we can be the difference, wherever we go. As Gandhi said, "Be the change you want to see." We have to become what we aspire to and not just dream it. We will do that with joy and great love for all beings, because we do not work alone.

*We're coming out of the past*
*We're healing at last*
*With blessings from the tribe*
*We're washed in the tide*
*Of love.*

(FROM SONG "COMING OUT OF THE PAST"
BY PHYLLIDA ANAM-AIRE)

## SURVIVAL CONSCIOUSNESS

What is meant by survival consciousness, and how will I know if I am still living from that place of powerlessness and victim hood?

As children we all learnt to survive - otherwise we would not be here today. This is good, this is amazing, and especially for the many people who suffered great abuse and serious illness. Our dear ego mind helped us survive by gifting us with defences so that we would not feel the pain. Some people left the body when life was too awful for them to be fully present here and now. Many people drifted into daydreams so as not to be present. This is fine since we needed these skills and they served us well until now. Now we want more, the more of life. Now we want to transcend survival and enter into the dance of life and live fully. It is not wrong to want this and it is great that we are looking at the possibility of achieving it.

Before we can go beyond the survival pattern, before we can take the armour off, we need to see what the armour has been. We have to look at the mechanisms we used, and maybe still use, in order not to feel.

Here are just some survival skills we use:

1. I stay with what is safe and known, rather than take a risk for transformation.
2. Fear dominates my choices. I do/don't do something out of fear.
3. I keep referring to the past when I need to make a choice for the future.
4. I blame others, both for my mistakes and for my feelings.
5. I cannot face certain truths about myself or a relationship.
6. I am addicted to certain substances or attitudes of mind.
7. I am "small- self" focused most of the time.
8. I give in to primitive impulses like rage.
9. I do not listen to others when they disagree with me.
10. I choose to remain a victim, rather than move to the place of a victor.
11. I become defensive when I perceive that someone is against me.
12. I have irrational feelings, for example, thinking people are always against me.
13. I have a fear-controlled relationship with money. It always controls my choices.
14. I keep myself hidden so I am invisible. I do not trust anyone.
15. I do not make a choice for love unless it carries a guarantee that I will be happy.
16. I cannot change my job even though it makes me sick, as I am afraid I will not find another one.
17. I believe others are always better or worse than me.
18. I need to have my family near by, since I want to be loved.
19. I believe life is good for some but not for others, and it is not really fair.
20. God controls all. I have given him my power. I will find happiness when I die ...I hope.

These are some of the states of unconsciousness many of us have learnt in order to function in the world, but they do not bring us joy and aliveness. It is a good idea to check the above list and ask yourself if you can find any other ways that you personally have learnt to help you survive. If so, add them to the list. Then notice with ease and non-judgement in how many ways you hide from life in spite of the fact that life is always there awaiting your arrival. A song I wrote in 1989 shows how one can remain a victim all ones life.

> *I've been victim all my life,*
> *Used to darkness, never light.*
> *Survival was the name of the game I played.*
> *And now I know there's more*
> *To life than a half-closed door.*
> *Somehow I'm sure that there is a better way.*
>
> *As long as I just survive*
> *I won't taste the joys of life.*
> *I won't dare to open out to my own sound.*
> *And as long as I don't fly*
> *Like an eagle to the sky,*
> *I'll stay here cold and lonely on the ground.*
>
> *Though my prison door is free*
> *I stay here upon my knees,*
> *Not daring to go forth and face the sun.*
> *And I know what keeps me back*
> *Is the energy I lack*
> *To challenge life and know that change can come.*

This was my own story for a long time until I realized that it was not serving me to stay on my knees. Life is a journey to be lived moment by moment. I hope you will reach out and allow life to touch you.

May you be blessed as you go for life and leave survival where it belongs, in the past.

## STRUGGLE

To struggle means to resist what is here and now. But you say, "What is here and now is painful, and I am trying to change it so I don't have to struggle". I believe that we cannot heal what we do not feel. The inner child struggled to change things but did not have the wherewithal to do so. Her outer world was dictated by the adults around her. So we have to go back to this feeling child-self again in order to really heal, because as adults, we can have access to our reason, and from there make sense of the past. You do not have to change the outer environment in order to stop the struggle. The only thing that has to change is your own attitude to the pain. You will read this again and again in this book. Whatever we resist causes pain in the emotional being and then gets transferred to the physical. What are you now resisting? Resisting is a re-action. Re-acting is about hooking into a past wound.

Go to the place of the re-action. What about that situation causes you to contract, to shorten your breath, to feel a charge going through your body? It will be some hurt from childhood needing attention. You will probably find that whatever you have been resisting is just looking for integration, for inclusion, for your love.

Just sit and feel the child's unmet need. Once you contact the unmet need, feel this pain that you have been resisting. Now you do not have to struggle against it. It is the resistance to investigating it that causes the contraction in you, so you struggle against it with all kinds of distractions. But it still persists like the stone dear old Sisyphus tried to push up the hill! When he reached the top of course it tumbled down after him every time. So you keep pushing the problem away from you and yet it comes after you again and again. When you take time and get in touch with the inner hurting child you will realize that she was unable to express her feelings and therefore they became repressed. Over the years, you yourself suppressed them so the feelings got stuffed down even deeper. Now at least you say you need to finally stop the struggle.

You may be struggling at the moment with a lack of money, a lack of power or a broken relationship. These are the situations that call us to look at our lives and see where the real problems lie. Your problem with money may be a problem with accepting the fact that you deserve money or power. It may be a message from the past that "money is the root of all evil", so it is wrong for you to attract it. You may even have the unconscious thought that spiritual people should not need money and so, subconsciously, you don't have anything to do with it. Feelings of powerlessness in the here and now have their origin in the past and are looking for healing. The same goes for relationship issues, self-control issues, issues of addiction etc. They are now asking for you to get to the root of your struggle, to look deeper than the obvious problem because the real wound lies underneath it.

Your amazing soul-self uses a crisis brought on by your unconscious self, the ego, in order to let you see that wounds from the past still operate quite strongly in your life. The soul utilizes all painful situations in order to show you where the wound is so you can heal and be free.

### INVITING THE PROBLEM

To struggle with something means to go to war with it. It does not give energy, it steals it. So there is a war between "me" and "it". I do not want "it" in "my" life, because "it" hurts "me". So "it" becomes the enemy.

Now breathe. See the object of your struggle. It threatens you, you hide from it, it pursues you and is unrelenting. It makes you feel small and helpless. The more you run, the harder it pursues, until in the end you fall down. You cannot run any further. This is the moment of recognition, the moment of healing, though it does not feel like it at the time. This is the moment you can breathe and look at the hurt behind this struggle.

You have to recognize "it" at last and see why "it" is here. You have to include what is not easy to integrate. If "it" is not integrated, "it" will take over. So where does "it" come from, this powerless feeling, this feeling of not being in control of your life? You have the feeling that others are giving you the scripts and you are just reading them and calling them your life. This place of pain comes from the past when you were overpowered and became helpless. This situation now asks for healing into personal soul authority, here and now. "It" is here to show you that you have learnt to give your power away to others, and that you cannot have any authority in your life as long as the initial wound is not healed.

Who first overpowered you as a child? Why do you have a struggle with authority, with relationships? Why is your mind always telling you that you are not good enough? You will soon see that your struggle is not about any of these situations but, rather, a particular hurt from the past that is calling for help, for your attention and love. All situations, all experiences in your life, are midwives to new realizations and freedom. If you can see life situations as such, you do not have to struggle any more. You only have to look at the gifts hidden in all the situations that you struggle with and heal them into the presence of this moment. Then you can love all of your precious life and live from joy instead of from struggle. Leave the heavy stone to Sisyphus to keep pushing up the hill - you can just roll down the hill for fun!

## STATES OF CONSCIOUSNESS

It is not always easy to truly define states of consciousness because energy is forever in movement, forever in a state of flux. It must be so, as it is life itself manifesting itself in various ways through unfathomable channels of created phenomena, from invertebrate to vertebrate, from one-cell being to the multiplicity of intricate cellular systems. For example, the consciousness of a jellyfish is different from that of a blade of grass, and that of a tree is different from that of an animal. When it comes to human consciousness, we are delving into an even more complex manifestation that calls for a more complex understanding.

One might say, for example, that a tree cannot be more than a tree. It is not able to choose nor can it feel as humans do. Although through the process of natural transformation it changes its outer form, it is controlled by nature herself. However, biofeedback has shown, according to biologists such as Rupert Sheldrake in his book, "Rebirth of Nature", that trees, in actual fact, have responded favourably to loving human touch and human vibrations, such as sound. Dorothy Maclean from Findhorn claims that trees and vegetables respond favourably to human love (see "An Ordinary Human Mystic", by Dorothy MacLean, 2010 and also "Trees for Life", by Alan Featherstone B.S., Findhorn Press).

May one assume, then, that created beings, such as trees or flowers or animals, are not only affected by human interactions but, in fact, have an inner response to them, either favourably or unfavourably? There is an old Irish belief: "Tá croí mör na gcloiche ag canadh dom" that translates as: "The big heart of the stones sings to me." That suggests that even so-called inanimate phenomena have a certain energetic pulsation, a certain consciousness. We have learnt, of course, that stones or crystals do pulsate and therefore can be said to have life. So now we have the question, if non-humans such as animals or trees actually respond to the frequencies or electromagnetic fields of humans, is it likely that they can also heighten their own consciousness by association with loving human beings? Let us go further and ask: "If human beings are affected by the electromagnetic fields of each other, is it also likely that they can respond positively to the energies of higher evolved beings?"

It would seem that never before in the story of creation has humanity been so infused with such high spiritual energy. We are preparing for an even stronger and deeper infusion. As the earth herself shifts and transforms to bring in more light energy we are facilitated to in-body more and more light. This divine outpouring of high voltage energy, of course, disturbs our so-called personal equilibrium. We are stirred in the great cauldron of Bronwyn and in this stirring we are awakened to our own inner unrest, our own inner chaos. This is natural. But we do not like it! As we become less earth-mind driven, our fears and confusion will be welcomed into the heart of love and our emotional energy will be strengthened by the grace of our spiritual immune system.

During the day one can enter into many states of consciousness. In the morning one can awaken the physical body with the help of its biology. This brings the psyche to ordinary awareness. One may or may not remember the time spent between falling into the altered state i.e.

sleep and the other state of wakefulness. Then, as the day precedes, one may sit in the garden and admire nature in all her beauty. We may find beauty in trees and rivers. This helps us to connect with our creative souls. These states of natural connectedness with all nature are really important for human beings as they raise our vibrational impulses. They also help us to conserve our energy, instead of losing it through too much talk and activity. These uplifting states of consciousness can also help us to be more aware of our responsibility to nature and to our own inner landscapes. If I am not conscious of my own inner landscape, i.e. my actions and responses, all the altered states of consciousness, all the visualizations on the beauty of nature will not help me to maintain a stable spirituality. Altered states of consciousness could be used as escapes from my everyday life. Raising our vibrations is not about losing touch with earthiness; rather, it helps to bring us into a more intimate awareness of our moment by moment interconnectedness with ourselves and all beings. We meditate not to go further from earth awareness, but to help bring more intimate consciousness to it.

According to many yogi masters, we have the ability to transcend ordinary consciousness. This happens to many people when they meditate, when they go beyond the ordinary mind and enter into a place of no thought. Scientists, such as Dennis Dale Purcell (California) in his paper "Detecting the Astral Body", Pim van Lommel (Netherlands) on "Consciousness beyond Life", J. Kenneth Arnett, PhD, on "The Mind Body Problem", are looking into the phenomenon of the "Near Death Experience" and tests are being done at the moment regarding the whole issue of consciousness transcending death, transcending the body. Now scientists are realizing that consciousness is not dependant on brain function (see Goswami, A. 1995 *"Self Aware Universe")*. Whilst we are still in-bodied we have much to learn from our earth connections.

Although knowledge of various states of consciousness equips us with inner awareness of how we can evolve, it is also wonderful to know that the more we clear our energy centres from the past unconscious, the clearer we become to transcend earth-mind control and so, with great joy, naturally, and without any formal teaching aid we evolve spiritually. We do not have to learn ways to get in touch with our higher energies- it is a natural result of having cleared our lower channels, so that grace and joy may filter through without blockages. Love consciousness infiltrates our D.N.A. and the nuclei in the cells in the body become more lightsome. Only love consciousness can transform the earth-mind, or ego. When the cells in our bodies become so filled with light, we become what Buddhists call enlightened. In other words, we have healed the dark places of our personality into the light of divine love.

I believe that it is wise to sit in quietness each day and consciously connect with the still, small voice of indwelling divine consciousness. Listening to transcendental music also helps. Different sounds and tones in the higher octaves can heighten our awareness. We are advised to become still and know we are divine. I believe also that our own unconscious is revealed to us through the mediums of meditation, sound, art, dance, colour and symbols. The body is the vehicle for such healing since the body maintains the information of the wounding. It is not enough to meditate ON our wounding - the body has to feel it and express the feelings in order for the healing to reach the cells in the body.

We have all been given the great natural gift of sound and all feelings have a sound particular to that feeling. These sounds are natural and need expression through the body. When we have ears to hear the pain, eyes to really see our inner victim and sound to release the pain we will have honoured the earth body. Then, through the eyes of love and non-judgement, we will look upon the Universe and there will be no need for forgiveness, as we will see only love and harmony. Then all things will make soul-sense eventually.

## FROM UNCONSCIOUS TO CONSCIOUS

We have not come to earth to become spiritual beings - we already are. We have come to learn in the school of love what it is that we need to heal back into that love again. Let us look at how we may be helped to experience more and more openness to our own healing. I have suggested that by working on our own re-actions daily, being aware of our inner states of unrest and finding their origins, we naturally heal our past. This is of utmost importance. However, I also suggested above that being in the company of soulfully advanced others can help us in our evolution of consciousness. Asking help from the energy of highly evolved beings such as Jesus the Christ, C.G. Jung, Hildegard of Bingen, Mary Magdalene, Jean Huston et al., can help us here and now to see the places within us that are still in the shadows. These beings can witness our enlightenment as we attain further stages of consciousness whilst still in this body form. Because of my belief in the collective, I know that whatever we do and think affects us all. I also believe that when someone here and now has the courage to heal past unconsciousness into consciousness, we are all helped.

The Great Mother Earth is also going through great shifts in consciousness and we are also able to help here do so by our own willingness to transform the dross into gold in our lives.

When I speak of stages of unconsciousness, I mean stages that are as yet not operating from pure love energy. Let us look at these states within ourselves without judgement.

### 1ST STAGE – known as Survival Consciousness

This is mainly the amazing state of instinctual awareness with which the animal kingdom operates. Human beings experience it as the need to survive. It is a magnificent, divinely inspired, instructive mechanism that ensures one can actually survive earth existence, that one can "hold one's own". With this "beginners consciousness" one's inner world is concentrated on oneself, not yet in a holistic way, but in a self-absorbed and non-empathetic way. It is a life-for-a-life existence in which the physique is also as yet unrefined. The inner conversation may consist of words like: *I need to know, I need to be safe. I am afraid that others will have more than me, I have to survive, I need a lot of food and drink and my own territory.* The emphasis is on the survival of the material being, so we also grab all we can. We guard what is ours with great angst.

We evolve into consciousness when we begin to heal the unsafe self and its wounds that stem from childhood insecurity. When we can truly say: *I surrender to a beautiful all-abundant Universe from whence comes all I need*, we feel ourselves healing into consciousness. We begin to share because we know we will always have enough. Surrendering is automatic when we have healed the inner fragility of survival-unconsciousness.

## 2ND STAGE – Survival Consciousness

The emphasis is on our need to join with another, to be a part of another, but for the sake of self-gratification. As long as the other is meeting my needs, I am happy to include her/him. However, as soon as the other fails to create happiness for me I easily overpower them until they give in to me. The inner conversation can be, "You are here to make me happy, and if you do, I will make you happy too. You make me sad at times and this is your fault. I am also to blame for your sadness." There is also either a sense of shame concerning gender or one's sense of sexuality, or one is promiscuous. Images of oneself as unworthy are born here. We know we have entered into consciousness when we can truly say: *I am now a fully responsible human being and I am supported by a gracious universe*. We invite others because we can share together, without owning or overwhelming one another and with no need to collect victims.

## 3RD STAGE – the Consciousness of Defensiveness

I fear that you will intrude on my life so I am defensive even though no one is threatening me. I fear the unknown places within myself and so guard myself with states of isolation and red alert. This place of unconsciousness is a place of inner terror. Here we continuously struggle and yet do not know why. In this place we also feel that we cannot and should not do things that will draw attention to our faults, so either we tell others about all our accomplishments or we deny our own talents for fear of being found wanting. The healing lies in being able to risk life and live fully in the present. Then we are not attached to what others think of us and do not need their acclaim. We can walk on water so we take the boat! We can open up to ourselves and others and risk being in relationships.

**4TH STAGE – the Consciousness of Over-Emotionalism**
This is the place of the immature heart that is over-emotional and over-re-active. It has no container. This is the place where love gets confused. Only sentimental love and romantic love is accepted. "You love me, so do as I say." Others are loved because of what they can give us. It is the place of the broken young heart, the heart that is responsive to the love it thinks it needs and is re-active to what it considers to be non-love. One cannot understand that "no" can also be an expression of love. One either over- dramatizes each experience or one closes one's heart to all experiences.

In the immature place one's inner response could be: "If you loved me, you would do anything for me. I would do anything to keep your love." The healed state is when we can love fully without needing a reward. We do things out of love for love's sake. We are not dependant on the beloved for a reason to live. The over-emotional heart cannot yet experience compassion for itself and others, but sets up conditions and does not "care-give", but rather "care-takes". It uses bribery as a means of controlling another, where love is concerned. For example: "After all I did for you, you should ..." This heart is always in a place of subjectivity and not yet altruistic in its actions. A wise heart is willing to be broken and widened by grief and ecstasy. The love-conscious heart opens to everything, irrespective of what it might get in return. It has moved from personal love to universal compassion.

**5TH STAGE of Consciousness, Becoming Aware**
This is the place of divine communication when we begin to connect to our intuitive selves and rely more and more on this than outward data. It is a state of recognition, recognizing pure, indwelling love. The earth-mind is met with compassion and the body- mind is a clear channel for grace to flow through. The childhood self-absorptions and emotional re-actions are healing into the wise heart and so this stage is one of conscious meeting with the soul-self, without too much intrusion from

the ego. Judgement is not so strong and one begins to see oneself mirrored in all beings.

**6TH STAGE of Consciousness, Loving Awareness**
This is the stage of opening into universal consciousness, the stage of communication with other divine beings in other stages of higher consciousness. This state of loving awareness cannot be permanent, because at this moment in time matter is too dense to facilitate the powerful energy of divine love. But our energies are refining and as a result we are becoming more enlightened. As a consequence, one can experience this oneness with all beings for a while but then the so-called spiritual battery gets low and the output cannot maintain its flow. But in the not too distant future we will be able to maintain this full voltage energy. This expansion is happening more and more now to people as they clear their so-called lower stages of unconscious and begin to live from love.

More people are gathering together and sharing their collective inspirations. Our collective care-giving to the great earth mother is also a result of a shift away from materialism and a movement towards the heart of creation.

**7TH STAGE of Consciousness, Evolution Consciousness**
This stage is about our evolution as beings imbued with grace. This stage of consciousness is difficult for human beings to live with since it opens up the eye of perception so that one may see through the veils of illusion. These persons may sometimes appear to others as uncaring. Since they have been able to see clearly the work of soul in action they will not be thrown into chaos or display over-emotionalism at the news of disasters in the world. Such perceptive humans are not involved with the drama of life and this enables them to stay centred. They may even find the whole story of life funny and laugh at what the rest of us call tragedy. Death holds no pain for them and so the material world diminishes, as the world of Spirit enlarges.

At this stage, human beings will be able to manifest what they need more quickly since the so-called Kundalini Energy is rising fast. The electromagnetic impulses of the brain will not be able to hold the infusion of consciousness and as a result, the person, if not trained and helped at this stage of openness, will have a difficult time staying grounded. As long as the other channels are cleared and the ego does not create drama or distraction as a way of taking the glory, then all will be well. Often, the ego likes to claim: "I did this and I did that and see the amazing work I have done". It sometimes likes to take on the archetype of Spiritual Drama Queen in its last struggle for recognition, in order to gain some glory. It often puts on a performance called: "See the phenomenal work I have achieved!" If people open up too quickly to this stage, because of deep meditations or too intensive out of body experiences brought on by drugs etc., they will find it difficult to be centred again. If the other channels have not been cleared these types will overpower others and act from a place of spiritual arrogance. Then they will literally "fall down" into the lower stages again. Then "the last stage of the man is worse than the first".

**8TH STAGE of Consciousness, Enlightenment**

At this stage one is changed for this lifetime and cannot go back. This stage is known sometimes as the Christ Consciousness or Universal Consciousness. Not many human beings have reached this stage up to this point in our human evolution but many are doing a lot to heal their past conditional victimhood and thus are clearly on the road to truly serving others from a place of healed, loving energy. These people naturally bring in light and love to all they do and seem to be able to retain a sense of inner calm, no matter what is happening on the outside. They operate in all dimensions and live divine creativity and inspiration.

## 9TH STAGE of Consciousness, Source Consciousness

This stage is where one unites one's soul with Spirit before death. This is the stage that the Christian church calls sainthood. The earth-mind is totally absorbed into love. In Buddhism it is called the Buddha nature. The earth-body has also become much lighter. At this stage one often feels the help and the great guidance of amazingly loving souls. They may be so-called dead or may have evolved whilst still here on earth. They also visit us in dreamtime. They can bi-locate and often bring healing to others simply by calling on them. Since souls are not attached to time or space it is easy for such inter-being to happen.

This radical spiritual evolution is taking place in many parts of the universe. As human beings believe more in the power of collective consciousness, we can create more love and joy on the earth. Of course, the opposite is also true; we also create fear and wars through the medium of our collective unconsciousness. Now is the time to choose between pure love or fear, struggle or peace … the choice is ours today.

We are therefore urged by the great ones to clear the re-active, judgemental forces within us NOW so that we may contribute to loving, creative and joyful community-building here on this planet earth TODAY - in other words, creating a heaven, whilst still on earth.

## 10TH STAGE of Consciousness, Joining with Formlessness

In this consciousness, humankind is no longer on the earth as we know it. The energies have literally lightened and all is in a finer attunement. To enable human beings to co-create on the earth-plane, earth herself has to transform. This means the earth's energies will have to become lighter too. We are the ones who influence the earth's energies. Fear and judgement keep the earth bound in unconsciousness. If one can imagine our first incarnation as being the note of low Do (C), then this $10^{th}$ stage is Mi (high E). At this stage, one co-creates out of love - pure divine love. We cannot understand this love yet because of our reliance on brain activity as the chief controller. When we reach the point where we rely solely on intuitive awareness, not on ego re-actions, we will not walk so heavily on the earth, we will also be able to travel throughout the galaxies and contribute to evolution there too. We will have contacted the mind of the creator and will have broken the code of universal wisdom.

## 11TH STAGE of Consciousness, Spiritual Adeptness

This has to do with the mysteries of creation itself. Jesus, or Issa, became the Christed one after his so-called death experience. He was able to function on the earth-plane as an ascended being with pure love-consciousness, since after his awakening he had a new body. He could not have done so with the electro-magnetism of the old form. He no longer needed to eat or drink, nor did he need to sleep. When he met the Apostles on the way to Emmaus after his resurrection, they did not recognize him in his new bodily form. He also asked Mary Magdalene not to touch him because he had not yet fully taken on his new form. Since Jesus had the ability to go beyond form, he could walk through the door of the Upper Room, where his friends, who were so frightened after his death, had gathered. He was no longer dependent or reliant on form. Although the earth herself had not transformed to accommodate him, because the people were unconscious, the Christ showed us what is possible whilst still in bodily form. We will also take on a more refined form when we have cleared the energetics of the lower form. This new body will enable us to accommodate to living in a Universe that is more light infused.

## 12TH STAGE of Consciousness – The Mind of the Creator

This magnificent stage is reached when we have transformed into pure love and pure energy.

May we all, you and I, help one another to keep clearing our past wounding so that we become clear channels of love and light.

### CONSCIOUSNESS, THE STUFF OF MIRACLES
*So we ask, what is this "stuff" and where does it come from?*

Much is spoken these days about consciousness and the raising of consciousness. My belief is that consciousness is everything that is and everything that appears not to be. That might be confusing to some and yet it is truth. The important sentence is that consciousness is everything that appears not to be, because no-thing is in actual fact empty or without energy. When scientists look at what we call nothing they find that it is full of energy and power. In other words, it is full of the stuff of which the universe is made. It is full of light. Nature abhors a vacuum so there is none. An ancient Taoist poem tells us about the Tao, or what Jung called "prime cause". I believe that it may also be called soul, that particle of the hologram of life force itself.

> *There was something formless yet complete*
> *That existed before heaven and earth,*
> *Without sound, without substance,*
> *Dependent on nothing,*
> *Unchanging, all pervading,*
> *Its true name we do not know;*
> *Tao is the name we give it.*

Today in the 21$^{st}$ century we give it the name consciousness. It is formless, yet complete and all pervading. This formlessness that existed before creation itself was what we might call electrical- magnetic energy that, although it is complete in itself and depends not on another, interacts with that other and affects it. The ancient ones knew about this life force, they just used another language to describe it. Rumi, the Sufi poet, also referred to consciousness in his poem

> *Out beyond the boundaries*
> *Of like and dislike*

*There is a field.*
*I will meet you there.*

He is saying that when we get away from judgement and blame, we will be able to meet in that field of consciousness, that place where self effects and meets with self.

When the great scientist Vladimir Poponin took a clear glass tube and placed some human DNA in it in 1992, he was surprised at what he found. His question was, whether or not the DNA had an effect on the photons. Clearly, he was asking if we as human beings effect our outer environments. He found that when he removed the DNA from the tube, the photons had aligned themselves with the DNA. They actually moved in the presence of the DNA. When the DNA was removed the photons behaved as if the DNA was still present! We can see, therefore, that we human beings affect our world. That is, the electrical field in one substance is affected by the electrical energy in another, and this relationship, once made, does not end. In 1993 the Institute of Heartmath in the USA performed experiments showing that there is an energy field around the heart that extends for many miles. As the heart changes its emotions the field also changes in response. Positive feelings like love, compassion and laughter expand the field whilst so-called negative feelings such as envy, hatred and fear cause restrictions. Positive emotions, therefore, relax the DNA whilst negative emotions contract it. Clearly, one can see which emotion is healthier.

To know that we affect our environment is one thing, but to truly believe that we actually affect our own bodies through our feelings is astounding. Some time ago a man said to me: "There is nothing in my life; it is just boringly dull". This reminded me of a poem by T.S. Eliot:

*When past and future are gathered,*
*Neither movement from nor towards,*
*Neither descent nor climb.*
*Except for the point, the still point,*
*There would be no dance,*
*And, there is only the dance.*

Yes, there is only the dance - all pervading, unfailing. Nowadays, scientists are showing that we create our lives by the thoughts we habitually think. These thoughts become emotions that move (or do not move) into the heart in order to express a feeling. It is from the heart, the wise heart, then, that we co-create. In 1952 Neville Goddard wrote in his book, Power of Awareness, "Not what we believe in the mind but what we feel in the heart creates our worlds." Still, one needs to have the thought before the feelings can arise in the heart. As an example, the dear man who saw his world as boring and dull was the creator of this very situation.

Whilst our industrial and scientific cultures are less than 500 years old and our own civilization has existed for only around 5,000 years, we have a lot to learn from the great magnitude of the other world's cultures and civilizations that are actually close to us here and now. Naturally, we know more now about the universe than our foremothers did and so we are continuously evolving, continuously dancing in and with the stillness. The great goddess Brigit was said to have remarked, "Nil muid criochnaich go foill"- we are not done yet! We have a limited understanding of the complexity of what is around and about us and how we are all continuously co-creating. We become the dancers of the great dance. What, then, is the other with whom or with whose energy we humans co-create and what outcome are we dreaming up? Even more important, we ask, as the poet asked, "What if the dream comes true?".

Einstein believed that we are simply observers of the universe and that we could not and cannot affect it. In other words, we simply observe the dance without taking part in it. Dr. Wheeler, the well-known scientist of Princeton University, U.S.A. believes that we are not just observers of the Universe but, rather, are participants. I quote from the book by Malcolm Hollick Ph.D., *"The Science of Oneness:"*

> "Meaning comes from deep participation in the cosmic process. It is found in the purpose of the whole. The deepest meaning is thus to be found in our capacity to co-create our planet and the cosmos". This is very different from Einstein's observance. This

gives us relevance, a certain power and along with it, responsibility. Since we are all interdependent and inter-related, whether we are aware of it or not, then how would it be if we began to act in a positive and healing way as opposed to a negative one? Supposing we could choose to dance with joy and act for peace, instead of dancing the rages and wars of the old age of confrontation and overpowering. Consider the possibility of co-creating with consciousness when healing disease.

The old belief that cancer kills has been around for centuries because science has not yet found a cure for it. If we believe that we affect one another, then we should not question why science and modern medicine cannot cure cancer, we should be asking why we can't cure cancer ourselves! Of course, the primary question would be: "Why does cancer inhabit human beings?" That is another topic altogether. As long as we hold that cancer cannot be cured, then we are affecting the outcome. A belief possesses a very strong energy that is the result of thought patterns, emotions and feelings. The English word comes from the words "by" and "life", meaning I live by it, I bring it into my everyday life. To believe in something, we first have to have a thought about it. The thought is then sent through our already well-installed cultural, religious and societal belief filters. Judgement soon sets in and beliefs that have been there for centuries may cast the new thought aside with ridicule and disbelief. Then the heart closes to the possibility of even hearing more about the new belief. The emotions say, "no way", so the feelings do not get engaged. Whilst the feelings do not engage, the belief cannot filter through. The feelings from the heart have the great power to initiate change or to block it. A belief that has not gone through the process from thoughts to feelings will not create change. My personal belief is that *"we can only heal what we can truly feel."*

As long as our thoughts say something cannot be done, our energies, our inner vital components, support and agree with them. A thought is composed of particles of electrical energy that become a mass of molecules when patterns of the same thought occur. The thought "It cannot be done" derives support from all the other thoughts and beliefs that say...that is impossible, that is not right, that is irrational etc. - when the majority of thoughts agree, then the majority rules.

Supposing there is just one small thought present that says, "Maybe it could happen, but not yet." Then this thought gets lost in the other more dominant ones that deny such a possibility. However, if that thought gathers up other beliefs that say, "You know, I never thought I would fall in love again, but I did" or "I did not think I could live alone, but I do" etc., then the heart opens again to those possibilities. When similar positively imprinted thoughts from the past join this thought and they fall down into the cave of emotion, the feelings engage and possibilities emerge. The heart opens to this new belief and a new energetic impulse is born. If I have decided that we do not have to wait until science creates a cure for cancer and that people have the healing power within themselves, this belief becomes a reality for me. If enough people say it can be done and they outweigh the ones who negate the thought, if the critical mass without has been reached, I do not have to wonder what the outcome might be; I know what it will be.

In the year 2005 I was living in Scotland. A German woman who had been living with lymphatic cancer for some time came to visit me. Her daughter, who was 3 years old at the time, told her she was going to Scotland to get rid of the cancer! I thought, "Ah, yes, out of the mouths of babes comes wisdom!" During her week long visit we had a session together and I was led to ask her to take some herbs that I had mixed together beforehand. I advised her that she would be sick and that she had a ritual to perform. She took the herbs and immediately had to vomit in the bucket I had already placed beside her. I asked her to open the earth outside with her fingers, and let the "putrid acid" seep into it. She covered the earth saying that her cancer had at that moment been taken by the great earth mother and she had been healed. She believed from that moment that she was healthy. So did I. One week later when she visited her doctor and tests were done, she was told her cancer was gone. She is still without cancer six years later.

So my question is ... Does the Universe or collective consciousness actually support our decisions in life and if it does, why have we never been informed about this? The answer is yes the universe supports all our decisions. As science was always only interested in the evolution of form, the stuff of consciousness was not a viable study for them. Now it is.

Regarding the story above, the woman in question believed that she would be healed. I also had no doubt that healing was present there and then, not in the future. I have other stories like this one. When two or more are in harmony with the belief, then that belief is strong and can become reality. I truly know that the Universe is a living organism, as are my thoughts and emotions. Thoughts are alive with the electrical melodies of light beings in the space between spaces. Thought is that stage that is pre-form. The melodies move at a particular speed in the body, creating sound waves throughout the physical being. Energy gets transmitted from one organ to another, from one system to another and all are inter-related. We know when the melody is slowing down; we know when the rhythms are not charging as they used to. I believe that cancer has its own rhythmic effect on the electrical field in the body system. Somehow, by looking at a person one can feel into the field of energy and know, as in having an intuition, that there is a rhythm out of sync, so to speak. There is a discord. I love to look into the physical body and feel the great harmony created, the great orchestral harmonies and melodies in a sound body i.e. one that is well and in which all systems are cooperating with one another to keep the homoeostasis. All of us are inter-beings, creating sound waves and coloured wave patterns not only throughout our biological systems, but throughout the entire Universe. Galaxies and tides, star systems and space itself hold within them the blueprint or the template of the physical human geography. If we are 75 % water, then we are simply floating in a cosmos that is more like us than not. I sometimes see us humans as small worlds floating, as the larger world does, in a magic web of coloured music.

In the Celtic tradition we believe that our thoughts are the stories that light beings listen to before they transform them into reality in their worlds. So thoughts are already beings in their own right that can become reality later on.

I see it thus:

> *We have a thought: "I can be healed."*
> *We have an emotional response, not a re-action.*
> *It becomes a joyful feeling.*
> *It becomes a habit.*
> *It becomes a belief.*
> *It manifests as reality*

If the thought pattern says, "I am going to die, I cannot get better", then the Universe in its interaction with individual and collective molecular energetic impulses, gravitates towards that belief-being and unites with it. In other words, the magnetic attraction of the electrical fields finds harmony. Everything is seeking harmony, oneness, and unity. We were all connected in the beginning; we are all growing towards this connectedness all the time. There is fusion in nature. If the egg remains an egg and does not fuse with sperm, life cannot follow. All energy flows home in the end. It is not the Universe's or God's fault that we die. Our own energetic impulses send the message to the higher cortex and it is answered in the great intelligence of the Universe. The heart answers by slowing down, so the word is released into the ether and our will is done on earth as it also done in heaven… Union has taken place, soul and Spirit unite.

When healing is longed for, is welcomed, when one's heart reaches out to it with the belief that says, "I can be healed", the right moment comes. When the right frequencies are present, the Universe supports our beliefs. Often it supports us by sending someone as a catalyst for the healing to happen, but frequently healing also happens alone. So one can say, "My own strong feelings and beliefs brought this about." All reality dwells within us, waiting to be born, to bring itself into the here and now. We simply find support in the ether or in the fields of energy around us because the stuff of which we are made is the same as that of the Universe. Matter is the result of creative impulses in our Universe.

When we die, consciousness leaves the body and the body decomposes, goes back to dust, and becomes one with the minerals of the earth again. So in fact it is not dead matter! Consciousness, whose first home is without density, simply travels back to the ultra light, takes up residence again in formlessness. This new world out of body is again created by the beliefs of the one who embodied them whilst on earth plane: "As above so below." Life is not dependent on form. *Yet we love to be informed!*

(*"Celtic Book of Dying"*, Phyllida Anam-Aire, 2005, Findhorn press/Ennsthaler Verlag)

All form is the manifestation of LOVE on earth - not the sentimental, valentine love, which is based on emotions only, but the love that is the stuff of which our thoughts are made, the stuff of which healing is made. And this "stuff" is pure consciousness.

*It is*
*That which never left*
*It sings*
*The between spaces*
*Of its own breath*
*That was and is*
*And always will be*

(PHYLLIDA ANAM-AIRE, 1989)

CHAPTER 3

# Beliefs And Love

**ACCORDING TO YOUR BELIEF**
*You can and are able to heal your lives with your intentions.*
*You can and are able to heal all your lives in one breath.*

If your belief is that your thoughts are at this moment becoming lighter, then all is possible because for too long you believed that your life and previous lives were ruled by some unknown force, call it God or Universe, Higher Power or Buddha. This was a false belief and you were conditioned in this false belief. The Universe et al supported all your intentions later to become beliefs. My daughter Anthea very wisely said to me the other day, "We are all born relatively free, but we enslave ourselves with every unconscious belief."

You believed that if you were good, your needs would be met and you would be happy, so you were as good as could be. And yet you suffered pain and helplessness. You were unable to heal your life alone because you thought you did not have the power to do so. This power is stronger than ever on the earth plane and is the overwhelming force on other planets. It is the very same power is in you and me.

It is the power of manifestation that beings without ego minds can call on naturally. With this power we can decide here and now to heal all past dysfunction in one breath; but our programming has been that we have to wait a long time. Our healing will come in accordance to our beliefs. The Universe hears and supports our intentions. The Universe gives us exactly what we ourselves project into our world. We are the power behind our realisations. We are the power behind our visions. We are the power that creates love and joy, harmony and bliss. We are also the power that creates the opposite! If we truly lived this belief, we would live joy; we would feel the streams of divine grace flow in our entire body-mind.

> *How then do I change my programming?*
> *How then do I insert a new programme?*
> *How then do I live by the new intention and not keep referring to the old one?*

It is not difficult. It depends on our own inner longing for freedom and soulful living. What keeps us back from loving our own life is exactly what keeps us back from total healing. Listen to the internal judge that dictates your state of mind. It says:

> *You have no power.*
> *You are not good enough yet.*
> *You have no right to think you can do anything.*
> *You are not healed enough for the light of pure love!*
> *It is God's will that you suffer here and then have heaven as a reward.*

> *Is this your programme, or something like it?*
> *Then, dear one,*
> *Sit quietly,*
> *Close your eyes*
> *Breathe in slowly and out slowly.*
> *Do not be distracted by the world around you.*
> *Concentrate on your breath.*

> *Now imagine as clearly and as deeply as you possibly can that there is a golden light streaming down from the top of your head, from the fontanel.*
> *It streams down into your eyes, lighting up your internal sight and giving you inner vision. It streams into your throat, giving you creative language to dispel the learnt language of fear and self-hate.*

## BELIEFS AND LOVE

*It streams into your lungs allowing you to take in the light and breathe it into the whole of your being.*
*It streams into your heart, opening it to purer love and self-compassion.*
*It streams into your inner organs, cleansing and purifying them of inner conflicts and fear.*
*Now it streams into your kidneys, leaving you washed and cleansed in the purifying waters of grace and joy.*
*It streams into your legs and feet, strengthening you for the journey ahead, the journey you are now embarking on.*

*It is time now to accept who you have always been.*
*You are a divine spark from the flame of truth.*
*It is time now to accept that the past is past.*
*It holds no more power over you.*
*It is integrated into love.*
*Have no care for the future.*
*Care only for*
*This divinely inspired moment,*
*This inspired breath,*
*This inspired now.*

*Now, where in your body-mind is healing needed?*
*With the breath of love and compassion breathe into that part.*
*See it coming alive with love.*
*See is sparkle with health and life.*
*See it and feel it coming into a state of healing and joy.*
*Feel the joy in your bones.*
*Keep filling up with the golden light throughout your entire body-mind.*
*Your thoughts are now filled with golden thoughts of healing.*
*You are now being healed by the power of love,*
*By the power of joy,*
*By the power of your own beliefs.*
*You are now healed.*

*Feel it and see yourself full of joy, singing a new song and dancing a new dance.*

*Stay with the healing.*
*Stay with the joy.*
*Feel the belief streaming through you and know that healing has happened.*
*Now open your eyes into a brand new world.*
*Drink water all day.*
*Do this spiritual practice at least twice a day and feel the healing.*

It is easy to go back to the thought … this is crazy; I am not healed at all. Know WITHOUT DOUBT that healing is forever happening in your life and accept this truth without fail.

May all beings be in joy now.

## HEALING IS ABOUT LOVING

When I speak about healing, I am talking about emotional healing which includes the psychological emotional healing of the personality. This may not sound like healing to anyone who has cancer or a terminal disease. One might say, if I am healed emotionally then that is fine, but I am still ill. The body may still hold the sickness, but when we are emotionally healed we can see the real situation of the illness more clearly and go about healing it. We see the origins of dis-ease itself. When we enjoy a state of freedom in the mind, we no longer have re-actions to outside stimuli and there are only responses to our interactions with people and with the environment. When one can happily see all experiences through the eyes of universal consciousness, or love, one knows the healing it brings to the whole being.

The dear body is the recipient of all our emotional disturbances and tries in its own way to heal. But it falls short because it cannot ask the questions that are necessary. It is the silent carrier of the pain in the physical form and often feels very helpless. Indeed, sometimes the disease becomes a habit and the body gets so used to being a victim that cannot let the illness go.

Imagine for a moment, if you will, that you live life from soul consciousness only, with just enough ego or earth-mindedness to help you stay grounded on the earth as a human being. Imagine how gently you would walk the earth without judging or condemning yourself or others. Imagine how you would know that no matter what happens externally, all is well internally. Imagine how your life would be if you viewed yourself and each and every situation through the heart of love and compassion, no matter what the circumstance. Imagine if you would not be heartbroken by so-called disasters, but would immediately see the true reality through the eyes of the soul. Imagine if you could see everything that happens from the perspective of balance and harmony and realize that there are no accidents and no coincidences, that all is seeking equilibrium. Imagine no matter what so-called problems befell you; you would immediately see the divine design in all. Imagine that you were so healed emotionally that your spiritual dimension had opened up completely and you could see the perfection of all things. Imagine if you did not have fear in your psyche, neither past, present or future fear. Imagine living without fear. Imagine being free of rage, guilt and envy. Imagine living in peace with all beings. Imagine seeing yourself as a divine being worthy of all love.

This is not easy to grasp, yet it can be our experience as human divine beings. Somehow, when we think of healing we immediately think of being cured of a disease, and yet the soul sees it differently. When we live more from our souls, that is, from a place of freedom from fear, without suffering, we live more congruently with ourselves and all beings. But we are still far from that and yet we have been journeying in this direction these past years. Each person journeys in their own way; each to the capacity that is right for their own soul's learning this time around. Some people will not have as much to learn about loving unconditionally as others and that is fine, no judgement at all. We are all at different stages of our soul's growth and so we will have different routes to take; that is the way it is with Spirit. When we reach a stage of inner awareness and have grown more in the consciousness of expanded love, we will know the effects in our own beings. We will feel the healing it brings.

This does not mean that we re-act to the ones who are not learning the lessons in the same school as we. They will have different exercises to do, as they will have different teachers, with various ways of teaching, each according to their own abilities to help the student. Our teachers are soul-chosen for us, so we do not have to worry about not learning enough! Neither do we have to worry that the teacher may not turn up for lessons!

We need much compassion for our soul's journey. Compassion is not pity or sympathy. Compassion is looking at your self through the eyes of truth without judgements of any kind. You are a divine being, becoming your divinity. Maybe you have grasped that, maybe you haven't. It is not important. In time you will say: "Ah, I know that now, I am a divine being." And you know it, because you will have experienced it in your being. Now you may say: "I will never reach that goal!"

Being a divine being is not a goal to be reached. It is the reality of who you are, but you have not earthed it yet. It is nothing you have to reach; it is something that is already part of who you are. You have to grow into it, like your new pair of shoes. Imagine they are too big for you at the moment, so you have to wait until you grow into them. But they will be there waiting for you to wear them when the time is right. No one else can wear them; they are made for you alone. They have your name inscribed on the sole (soul!).

Impatience with yourself does not speed up the journey; rather, it slows it down with every judgement and criticism of yourself. So, learning the gift of self-love and self-honouring is a large step on the journey to self-healing. The next time you start to re-act or you start to judge something or someone as good or bad, or right or wrong, just notice your inner feelings, your inner comfort changing from ease to not at ease. Judgements, whether they are of yourself or of another, always lead to unease because our energetic bodies are not meant for judgements, they do not do so well with the conflicting energies. Whatever takes us out of our centres will cause unease in the human psyche and the human energy field. When you experience situations that annoy you and you struggle to change them, you are choosing in that moment to invest your energy in the struggle instead of letting it be. When someone does something that annoys you and you try to change them by judging them, your energy will leave your body and dissipate while you try to transform them into who you wish them to be. Instead, try seeing them as also hurting, like you. Can you imagine you have inner wisdom that says "Ah!" to everything, and all situations, almost with a smile and a laugh? "Ah, death! Ah someone is dying at this moment! Ah, someone is being killed at this moment! Ah, someone is coming into life at this moment!" Ram Dass, the illustrious Western Buddhist teacher used to say, "Ah life, ah death, ah so!" It does not mean that you lose your sense of compassion. Of course, you still have compassion but this compassion does not hurt you, it does not take your energy away. You do not suffer because of it. What happens when you are anxious about someone is that you suffer because you are full of sympathy, and that is not compassion. You are feeling at your heart's immature attachment level. In time, your dear heart will grow into the universal unconditional heart of the Universe, the heart made sacred by self-compassion and empathy.

Can you imagine a state within yourself where your sympathy is changed to universal, non- personal love? You will see that you simply ARE compassion. You don't have it. You don't feel it. When you ARE compassion it is not a burden. At a feeling level of experiences you have no unpleasant charge within you. It is part of who you are, part of your breathing. That breath that is coming in, ah! Compassion, going out, ah! Compassion! You are not taken away from your centre – you are just simply compassion.

Re-actions become habits of interacting, especially when they are so-called righteous feelings. For example, we re-act with deep sadness to the news about killings in Libya and we become overwrought by the pain, or we re-act with anger to someone who did not do what we believe they should do. If the child in you was not allowed its instinctual, natural expressions, your re-act buttons will be pressed later on. Imagine, if having heard the news about the killings in Libya you responded with: "I feel so sad that so many are being killed" and allowed the sadness to flow through you. Or: "I am raging with anger toward my man." And then you allowed the feelings to flow through you. You may decide later to do something about your inner rage and channel it into changing something in your environment that no longer serves you or another. This is natural anger that has no charge of rage or wanting to hurt another. It is simply saying: this is not OK. If we can see all emotions as fields of energy flowing through us, we will see that we do not have to name them as acceptable or not acceptable. We will just notice that we have emotions and then invite them into the heart for feeling. Fear is always looking for love and love is always looking for expression.

The personality is so amazing in the subtle ways it judges. The more preferences you have, the more judgements you will have. Sometimes so-called spiritual people will have great preferences, e.g. I have to have the room perfect for my meditation, I need to have just the colour white or I cannot do my practice. I do not like the energy of this place, therefore I cannot teach here, etc. We know we have healed when we are not concerned with the surroundings. We can teach anywhere and we can meditate anywhere. When we are attached to having our environments just right, we lose the sense that the sacred is that which we name it, as the sacred is in the soul of the beholder. We know we have healed when we feel at home anywhere, because our centre is at peace.

Human nature is such a complex landscape. It gets very worried about its state of non-consciousness. Just be conscious of the fact that you are not yet fully conscious! Don't suffer because of it. Just say: "Ah! That is interesting. I was not conscious about such and such." You see, no suffering. But if you say: "Oh, I am not conscious enough, I am not good enough, I should be more spiritual", then you are suffering. You are attaching yourself to your non-consciousness. As you move onwards on your journey to yourself, you can begin to move more into the state of non-preference and deep gratitude to yourself for all you are willing to learn.

When you are grateful, the heart in you grows and widens all around, the soul in and around you expands deeper into the world. And that gratitude opens up the hearts of others also. So make it a spiritual practise to say: I thank you. I am grateful. Your heart cannot stay closed and be grateful. It sounds so simple, but these are difficult spiritual practises. It is easy to sit and meditate, but if your meditation does not bring you deeper into the world of form and cause you to reach out to help one another - then your practice is not working.

Some results of your spiritual practices could be the following:

- *You have patience with yourself and others.*
- *You have fewer judgements.*
- *You respond rather then re-act.*
- *You encourage others to live the divine they are.*
- *You have compassion for all beings.*
- *You create a world of gratitude around you.*
- *You have fewer preferences.*

I believe that cultivating gratitude is a wonderful spiritual practice because everything IS a gift. Let your heart be grateful. See all of who you are, ego included, through the eyes of your heart. Then you will see your own innocence. Open your heart wide for your self and for all beings, so that those who are coming into body may be enriched by your wisdom and those who are leaving the earth may be enriched by your love.

As you enter into this New HalleluJA, may you delight in the ways you have healed your life.

May you rejoice in your healing here and now.

## FOCUSING ON LOVE
## MEDITATION FOR THE HEART

It is recommended that another person should read the following words to you slowly and with feelings of loving compassion.

Whoever reads these words will also be blessed. When you focus your attention on something or someone, changes occur in energy between that which is focused on and the one who focuses. Distinct flows of energy affect your quantum field and when this happens changes within the subatomic levels occur. Remember, dear one, your natural state is love; your natural state is joy. You will need this little meditation more and more as your outer world becomes stressful.

### MEDITATION

*I invite you to sit comfortably and we will begin to focus.*
*Now you begin to focus on your physical heart.*
*Breathe your heart into your imagination - see it.*
*See the physical shape and colour, that rich, dark, earth-red, purple colour of your heart.*
*Feel it pulsating in your chest, pulsating the whole of your body-mind.*
*Thank your heart for being with you day and night, night and day.*
*Now imagine pure love flowing into your heart.*
*It flows like a fountain of the clearest crystals.*
*Focus this love now; focus it into your heart centre.*
*Feel your heart widening and growing to receive it. Let love in.*
*Now feel each breath flowing with more and more love to your heart.*

*This love becomes compassion for your heart.*
*This love becomes joy in your heart.*
*This love becomes companionship with your heart.*
*This love is a blessing to your heart – now.*
*This love becomes appreciation for the work that your heart does every moment, every second of every day - pulsating for you.*

*This appreciation becomes grace.*
*This appreciation becomes the heartbeat of creation.*
*This appreciation becomes an honouring of you.*
*This appreciation becomes a song.*
*This appreciation becomes an echo of love.*
*This appreciation embraces all of you – now.*
*This appreciation is now a celebration of you.*
*As your heart celebrates you,*
*pure love is now focused on the cells in your entire body-mind-systems.*

*This love brings healing.*
*This love is pure joy.*
*Your heart is one with the divine.*
*Your heart is one with the sacred heart.*
*Love has imaged this heart into you.*
*It is the image of whatever you see God to be.*
*Focus on that now.*

*It is all embracing light.*
*It is all embracing joy.*
*It is all embracing love.*
*This love is who you are.*
*You are not separate from this love.*
*All the worlds of creation sing a love song to your heart now.*

*One heart beat. One being.*
*One light. One love.*
*Feel joy now in all your being.*
*Feel it flow in and through you.*
*Feel it heal your sad places.*
*Feel it nurture your neglected places of love.*
*Feel it heal your angry places.*
*Feel it heal your not-good-enough-places.*
*Feel it heal your places of fear and doubt.*

*Let joy in – now.*
*Let joy heal - now.*
*Let joy be who you are.*
*Now... Now... Now...*
*Focus on now.*
*Focus on this breath now.*
*Here in this blessed now.*

*Let it flow.*
*Let it stream from you into all the earth.*
*Let it bring in a new vibration - now.*
*This is the power you are.*
*This is the power of love.*
*The earth sings it back to you now.*
*This power of focused love*
*At this moment.*

*All the cells in your body-mind have received this energy of love.*
*You have opened your heart to receive it.*
*You are powerful.*
*Love is your power.*
*Love is the power that heals you now.*
*The more you are able to open and receive, the more you will receive.*
*It flows in and through you.*
*Focus on love that heals you now.*

*Now you can heal. Now you are healed.*
*You have become love.*
*Now very, very gently and very, very slowly take a deep breath into your body-mind.*
*And let it come out slowly.*
*That's right, a breath of pure love!*
*Very gently without moving the rest of your body, open your eyes.*
*The more you focus on love, the more you will be able to see through the eyes of love.*

*May we all learn to*
*Be love,*
*See love.*
*Live love, so we can*
*Give Love.*

Do this meditation each day. It does not take long but your whole being will benefit from the vibrations you will create – because you are love.

## LOVE AND RELATIONSHIPS

When we talk about love in relationship to the world i.e. to other people, to children, animals, love in relationship to one other special being, then you really have to look at what love is. Of course, your definition of love will come from your own background, childhood, upbringing and your own experiences of love in your life. So what we are saying here is that our experience of human love is subjective. Love is the individual experience of one person and their connection and interconnectedness to the world around them. How you yourself were loved as a small being will, of course, influence how you, in actual fact, love. If you were loved on the conditions of being good, being intelligent, becoming what your parents wanted you to become, then that has been downloaded in your mind as the definition of what love is. So your impression is: if I am to be loved, I have to be a certain kind of person. That is conditional love, love based on conditions.

It is surprisingly easy for people to have children. A licence is necessary in order to marry but not to have children. There is no law that says you must go through a learning period first and then pass an examination to see if, in actual fact, you are psychologically ready to parent a child. It could be called Conscious Conception. Instead, what often happens is that a couple decides it is time to have a baby, in hopes of saving their floundering marriage, thinking a child might distract them from having to look at the reasons for their dysfunctions. They will have already chosen a partner whom they believe loves them because they are kind, or loving, or good, or a hard worker etc. There are many expectations ... e.g. I expect my partner to prove they love me by behaving in a certain way. And that means they must never stray from that path, because love is forever and ever, amen! Some typical conditions are as follows: "If you love me, you will not do this or that. If you love me, you will do as I say. If you loved me as much as you say, then you would certainly do/not do that." If the parents don't love each other unconditionally, how are they going to teach their children about unconditional love? This whole question of love is a very deep one, because when you talk about loving somebody, what you are saying is that you are investing your energy in that person. If that person behaves and acts according to your standards of what love is then you are satisfied that you have made a good investment. If they don't do that, then you are unhappy because you have expended a lot of your energy on someone without getting anything in return. So all your energy has gone for nothing! If you happen to separate, what you are actually missing is the energy that you invested in your partner. You are missing your own love!

After a separation we often say e.g., "Why did you leave me? I need you back with me." By that we are actually saying: "I need to have the energy that I invested in you back. I gave it to you but it is a part of me. I don't feel whole any more. It is as if I am only half a person and you have gone away with the other half. Come back and bring me that missing part." I have also noticed how love between people who have been together for a while can become just a habit. The following dialogue expresses what is meant here: "I wake up in the morning. There you are. I may not like you, but there you are. I have invested 12, 13 years in you and I would miss that part of me that I directed to you." As one man said to me some time ago, "I would miss her if she left as we are together 26 years. She is like my old chair, I just expect her to be there." When does love become just a habit?

Many relationships deteriorate when the couple no longer honours each other as individuals but, rather, see each other as a part of themselves. Sometimes the songs are very romantic, e.g. "You are a part of me, don't go away. You will take my heart with you." So someone is walking around with two hearts and you have got none? That does not make sense! Romantic love alone does not constitute love. It can, however, be a wonderful part of the fallen state of being in love, where the beloved means everything to us and we want to keep showering them with love. Romance also helps to make difficult times more easy to bear because love itself is not easy. It is a difficult path at the moment for couples to commit to being together for the rest of their lives. The passion and tenderness they show each other will also help any children they parent on their own journeys to loving themselves. So when people come together who have conscious-filled ideas of parenting and have worked on their own childhood dysfunctions that came from issues of conditional love, they are ready to give their love to a child, to give good energy to a child and that is wonderful. Such couples are helping the evolution of consciousness on the earth and their children will feel loved. These children will not have to take drugs and abuse themselves later on because they will have a sense of self-worth. Conscious parenting provides a safer world for people to live in. Young people will not become addicts if they have been brought up with unconditional love and good discipline at home. This combination is very important. If they see love mirrored for them in the relationship of their parents, they will copy this behaviour.

Now the love of God is a different thing - or is it? First we have to look at what love is. What is your definition of love and what do you mean by God? The catechism of old said one had to love God and also fear God. But that does not make sense because love casts out fear. Love and fear cannot co-exist. So we have to take fear and love it into love, into the safe place of the heart. When you love God, what do you love? You love the image you have created of what you think God should be. It is an earthly image, an image of a being with a personality like yours, with emotions and feelings, with a past and a future. You have created a being made up of your own projections. That is not God. That cannot be God. God is formless. God has no personality. God does not know how to love the way you love. God does not know the how of anything. God is love, the energy that has created everything. God has got bad press. It is a name that has been very much misused within and without religion. God, the father in heaven, is said to condemn some humans because, e.g. he does not like gay people, does not like Jews, etc. We hear that he loves all his children as long as they do what he tells them. So we have created God in our image and likeness, but that is false God. Yet we have been taught to create false Gods ever since the very beginning. We pray, "Our father who art in heaven…". The word father in the old Aramaic means Beloved One, beloved energy, beloved being and beloved creator. This definition of father is without gender, but the Christian and Judean churches etc. attribute a male gender to God. We feel more comfortable knowing we have a father in heaven. This father will look after us if we are good and if we are bad he will send us to hell. In this way we have created a punishing Father like the earthly one, perhaps. If he has a personality, this God must be very limited. This God sounds human and therefore must also have an ego.

We humans love the image we have made of people we love. When that person does not live up to the image we have created, then we don't love them. They have shattered our image. If God does not live up to the image we have created of him, then God is not a good God. He gets the blame for allowing storms and tsunamis, earthquakes and terrible deaths of children etc. Of course, adjectives like "good" and "bad" do not apply to God because God is not human. God is a formless energetic being, not a human energetic person. The more you can move away from this idea of a God with a personality, the more you will live your life without fear, the more you will free yourself into responsibility. You will have self-authority and self-control that will not allow anything outside of you to control you. No being outside of you will control you, not even God! You will have tremendous power that you never before realized because it had not been revealed to you through your normal channels of education, like church and school. In the old books of the scriptures, especially the book of Essenes, we read about the power given to human beings. It is our right and our divine innate state. But this "Gnosis", or inner knowing, would not have served the institutions of Church and State.

Now we are all re-calling our sense of inner authority and we are reclaiming our righteous power. This new dispensation, this New HalleluJA is singing now in all of us and we are awakening this God-self that has been in purgatory far too long …

HALLELU - JA!

## LOVE ILLUSION

If ever we humans reach an understanding of the meaning of life (another term for love) we will have broken the code of creation. On that day we will have reached the point of comprehending the vastness and complexities of the oneness of so-called opposites and paradoxes, of divine intelligence and spiritual science. Then we will have reached the stage in our consciousness where we will understand, not from an aspect of our intellectual logical left-brain reasoning, but rather from the mindset, the intention of this vast creator or creators. This is where we go beyond all language and beyond anything we have ever experienced whilst in physicality. Being in form has denied us access to such magnitude of comprehension. We have to bow to a vast Akasia record of all knowledge that is too intense and too immense for our limited minds to currently comprehend. When the soul-self is freed from all traces of ego and is reunited with universal energy, when the two become one being, a being of pure love, we will have access to some of that magnitude of comprehension. Then we have access to the mind of the Christ.

The aim of all true understanding is to reach the truth of something, not only through the medium of the intellect but with also with help from the deeper understanding of the wise heart. But this is somewhat unobtainable in one lifetime because as we evolve knowledge and experience evolve with us. Therefore, to get to the ultimate truth of something one would have to wait for centuries of discoveries, centuries of integral evolution.

For many the inherited D.N.A. of our ancestors dictates the limits of our understanding. Many great enquirers of course have gone beyond such confines but none have actually touched on the full meaning of life. They have isolated particles and have produced theories and then ran tests to qualify their hypothesis. Theologians are as limited in their comprehension as the most eminent scientists, which means that when they get together to debate, they stop short at the point of mystery. Science is too young to comprehend it and theology too old, too stagnant to think differently. When habitual thoughts have rusted at the altar of patriarchal theories the soul gets lost and spontaneity and inspiration are just memories in the heart of intuition.

With such handicaps how may we then ever reach the truth of love? I suggest we may not be able to in this lifetime. We can, however, try to radically transform our thinking and our understanding so that we can at least accept that there is a missing link in our comprehension. Then with humility and great gratitude to pure love itself, whatever this elusive being may be, we simply open to the possibility of either fresh radical thinking processes or to the possibility of no thinking processes at all.

I personally have come to experience that what we call love is often a dilution and disillusion of the powerful energy that directs and propels all creation. We have reduced love to the level of subjective emotionality, which has little or nothing to do with pure love but, rather, in many cases is an example of what love is not. Maybe we are not supposed to fully grasp the meaning of pure love whilst here on earth; maybe we are here to experience the antithesis of love. Maybe that was The Fall: the disappointment from a true definition to a falsified second best. So do we then come to the depressing conclusion that all our attempts to define love have been in vain? Maybe as we grow older on the journey to love we get glimpses, beautiful glimpses of what it is to be loved and to love with no conditions and no judgements - just simple devotion. But it is not so simple!

Maybe love expresses itself in myriads of ways - even in the antithesis of love. We talk about being lifted emotionally, having the heart open to joy, feeling at one with nature, being in the presence of a dear friend, being in the presence of children and babies. There seems to be a feeling of being transported to another place in ourselves, a place, perhaps, where the earth or ego mind are stilled in the presence of this other. This is certainly the case in sexual orgasm where both beings blend together and the two become one. I believe that what Abraham Maslow called *peak experiences*, were moments of bliss that were akin to being in love.

Pure love (non-personal because it is ego-less) has nothing to do with fulfilling the expectations or dreams of another. When we have grown in our consciousness we will also have grown in our definitions of love. The uplifting of consciousness is all-important; otherwise we will not rise above wars, violence, rape, poverty, terror or fear. In other words, at this time we are all working together to form a new consciousness, one that brings us closer to the mind of pure love whilst on earth plane. Perhaps we have to really consider what the words, "Love your enemies, do good to them that hate you" mean, since loving a person because they are "good" and hating another because they are "bad" is ego love. Sending one human being your hatred and helping only the victim is not the way of love. That, again, is personal judgement. Love does not wish that another should have pain or suffer in this world or the next. Love is a messenger of soul; soul is the messenger of Spirit. Spirit does not project feelings, as it does not have them! We are human beings and with functional feelings we can project more of this divine love to others, whether they are "good" or "bad".

The expectations we have of a loved one, if not fulfilled, create judgements that can lead to separation and sorrow. Our evaluations are based on our personal and cultural constructs. When someone says they love me, I feel good. I want more of this feeling. All is well. In actual fact, what I am saying is, I feel good when you say or do that! It is totally subjective. Now I have expectations of the next time we meet. When these expectations are not met, I feel sad. I do not feel you love me because I do not feel the way I did before. As the song says, "Bring back that loving feeling." the heart then grieves the loss of the feeling. We have to grieve the loss of the feeling until we realize that pure love cannot die. The soul uses the heart as a means of purification where feelings can be stirred into healing. But this stirring does not feel like healing - it feels like suffering and pain, and according to the ego mind, pain is bad.

The purity of love can easily be seen in its interaction with nature. Nature does not have expectations, she simply experiences. The seasons bring their transformations in her and she does not complain. She experiences all as part of divine outpourings, the great being of life naturally unfolding, opening through her. All happens in the now. There is no other time. The past and future are all contained in her being. Time is a concept of expectations; it is the result of being in a body-mind. This emphasis on time and judgement brings sorrow, brings separation. The uncluttered presence in which love abides is the state of perfection… mindlessness.

The leaf falls to the earth, the sun comes up, the snow freezes the little animals, the lightening kills humans and the rain drowns trees. All is here and now, no expectations, no value judgements, and no sorrow. So it is. Not so it was, or will be. Disasters befall human beings. Death can bring sorrow. Pain wrecks dear bodies and we are in despair. Many take their own lives, as the thought of a future full of pain is just too much. Others use people for their own benefit in the commercial world. Wars and violence sweep over our earth and we become deeply depressed as we feel God has left us, has deserted us. This is the old, old story. God should stop it all since it is somehow his fault. Why do we think this? We think thus because:

> *We have been sold the story that God loves his own and the just will be saved. We believe that hurricanes, diseases (e.g. AIDS) and earthquakes etc. are results of God's judgement of sinners. The God of wrath delighted in punishment.*

Again we give Spirit the attributes of a personality and so refer to these attributes in difficult times like this, saying: "If God loved us he would not send us these trials". Let us look at this statement for a moment and see the difficulties it creates for us.

According to Christianity, God loves us so much that he sent his only son to die for us so that we could be redeemed and saved from hell. One can deduce by this that God loved us more than he loved his own son. The idea of sacrifice is as old as time itself. Gods were inclined to demand sacrifice (to boost their egos, one might think!). Our catechisms tell us that Jesus died to save us from an afterlife in hell. But the catechism forgot to include that Jesus, whilst he carried the collective unconsciousness of the pain-body, said these wonderful words: "Now it is finished!" At that point he was ready to receive his new light body. When we can read symbolism into the death of Jesus we will be able to live without the inappropriate guilt we have carried.

I have worked in my psychotherapy practice with so many people who carry this guilt. My own belief is that Jesus was a great soul who contracted to take on the collective unconscious, and that only in the end did he really understand consciously what it was all about when he said: "If this has to happen, then so be it" (paraphrased from St. Matthews gospel). Many people since then have also made such a contract in their time. Many men and women have died so that others could live in a freer world, for example, Gandhi, Martin Luther King, the wise women who were stoned and brutally killed in the time of the inquisition in Europe. I said to a dear woman last week, "Why do you continue to suffer if you really believe that Jesus took on the suffering of humanity?" I did a ritual with her so that she could release her need to carry the cross for the collective.

Our souls, like the soul of the Christ, like the soul of Buddha, like the souls of my dear friends here in Germany, have chosen to be on earth with a personality, developed from a strong, or not so strong ego, or earth mind. We have all come to heal and to love. That is the great mystery of love. We come to heal into love and continue to do so until we are absorbed into unconditional love. Our perceptions alone judge something as good or bad. Everything is part of a wise and wondrous story that has no beginning and no end.

> *No one had to die for my sins.*
> *I am responsible for my own lifetimes.*
> *Love is not about feeling happy all the time.*
> *Love is about equilibrium; but often the earth-mind judges this process, attaches itself to the pain and thus creates suffering.*
> *Love is about creating oneness and uses whatever means necessary to do so.*
> *Love is not personal.*
> *Love destroys as much as it builds up.*
> *Love gathers as much as it shatters.*
> *Love dwells in opposites and if we are incapable of accepting the shadow as part of the light, then we will have problems with love.*
> *Love is perfection at work with imperfection.*

To love someone is to see them through the eyes of the lover, no matter how they appear. We may not like what they do, but their essence is an expression of life and as such is worthy of honour.

Putting this into practice is not easy when it comes to perpetrators and murderers.

> *They are also souls full of divine, creative energy, or Spirit.*
> *Their deeds come from their misguided personalities.*
> *Love does not make things happen in our lives, but it facilitates all actions stemming from thought, in order to balance what needs to be balanced.*
> *When we are attached too much to a love object we suffer.*
> *Our own expectations create our pain.*
> *To love someone is to allow them to be free from your judgements.*
> *Holding all lightly is grace, is love.*
> *Love is the greatest force in the Universe.*
> *Love is not about feeling nice feelings - it is about being love.*
> *To live love is a personal choice.*
> *To be in love is a constant choice.*
> *To know love, is to be with what is here and now and to go beyond all concepts of what love should be.*
> *So, this moment, as I am experiencing writing this down, is love.*

May I learn from the wisdom of love and learn to be in love moment by moment.

My I go beyond the immature heart of my human experiences and enter into the universal heart of soul.

May I be willing to be the love I am and not search for the love I think I need.

## EVOLUTION AND LOVE

Be not afraid when you feel that everything is too much for you to endure in these times. Remember, you have taken on a lot more spiritually in this life than in any other. Still, each incarnation was important, as it led you to this moment of grace. You had to evolve from a lower being without the gift of free choice, to a higher being on the earth plane – a being with human needs and a more refined physicality that serves your expanding intuitive awareness. You advanced from worshipping crude earth matter of which you were afraid, to worshipping with love the creator within yourself. This took many comings to earth. You had to adjust to a world that was also advancing in material ways. Your new human self was often times unable to take the strain of being human and you often reverted to animal behaviourism in order to have your needs met. Often you had to kill in order to provide food for yourself and your family. Often you had to tell lies and steal from your brothers. This is not a judgement but is, instead, an aid in awakening you to the facts of your evolution, in both the material and spiritual worlds. You have advanced from the earth energies of survival and self-preservation to self-discipline and self-compassion. Honour yourself for all you have experienced so far.

You are now entering into the stage of self-knowledge and self-awakening that will lead you into love consciousness and total healing of yourself and the planet. This is an amazing step for human kind to take within such a relatively short time, and you know that time belongs with the earth-mind, not the soul. According to the soul, everything is happening simultaneously. All lives are being lived in the Eternal Now.

Many of you are also aware that as you live your life in one dimension, you are also living a life in another dimension. When you can live with consciousness and awareness on this earth plane, then you can rise to another dimension in the other planes of existence in other worlds.

In these other worlds you are working and helping many others to advance in the ways of the soul. Perhaps at times you have a feeling or an awareness that you travel at night to other spheres. This is possible, of course, and many who are dying are being helped by your willingness to assist them during the night. Many of you are also experiencing tiredness at this time. This could be due to the fact that you are energizing other worlds with your breath of life.

You have no idea how important an awareness of breath is.

> *It is the powerful Holy Spirit of love amongst us.*
> *If you direct your breath to a person they will feel a sense of movement in their field of awareness.*
> *Your breath gives life to other beings all around you, yet you are totally unaware of this gift you give.*
> *For the next moment take a breath deep into your heart.*
> *Now breathe it out slowly whilst consciously directing it to the pain in the world at this moment.*
> *This breath may be just what another being needs to help them to remain on earth.*
> *This breath of love may be what another needs in order to endure the pain of disease.*

As you breathe remember to do so as consciously as possible. It has the greatest benefit to others and to yourself when you breathe deeply from the breath of life. It is a free gift you can share with all beings at all times. As you become more aware of your own soul journey, you will adopt an attitude of self-compassion and non-critical awareness of yourself and others and you will experience a surge of unconditional love flowing through your breath. At times you will not be able to stand it and feel weak. Do not be concerned since all is well and you will feel much more in touch with your soul's purpose. Breath connects you with soul. Conscious breath makes you more aware of pure love. Many have experienced this already and many will experience it in the near future.

As you earnestly seek healing in all the rooms of your precious lives, this will be your experience. Take time for all things that are sacred. Do not be anxious about time. Remember that time is just the judgement of your earth-mind telling you that you must keep going as fast as possible since time is running out. It is not running out. It is just that you are advancing more quickly towards you own awakening and that will cause everything to vibrate at a quicker frequency. This then gives the idea of time running out. Rest and take your time - not the time that another says you should take. And know that you can use time as you will. Time cannot use you. When you feel that you are not advancing as quickly as you would like in your awakening, then please take a deep breath and see where you have come from in a short time ... then bow to your own soul and its wisdom.

Always know that as long as you have a desire for total healing, this can happen in the wink of an eye. But first you have to look at your definitions of healing. Maybe you think you are not healing fast enough.

Remember when you used to feel trapped as a victim, and now you no longer feel that? Now you feel more inner autonomy and more compassion for yourself and all beings? It is a great step in healing to live this. This is a huge step on the way to more consciousness and freedom.

Do not measure healing by the amount of pain you still have, or by the insights and freedom from fear you have gained.

> *Healing is about freedom.*
> *Freedom is about choice.*
> *Unconscious choice brings fear.*
> *Conscious choice brings love.*

So healing is about how much love you allow into your life and how much love you are willing to share. Quantum healing is about your faith in love, total faith, that love the size of a mustard seed can feed the Universe.

## TRUE REALITY IS LOVE

True reality is love and love is life and life is consciousness which manifests itself in form or out of form. What an amazing miracle of creation that our bodies, our forms are equipped to facilitate the journey of our souls this time and our physicality serves soul in all ways. As we change our consciousness the body changes to facilitate the transformed soul's journey. A handicapped body serves the soul just as well as a perfect body. We shape our individual lives to what we believe is real, and these beliefs change and reform and re-create our outer reality.

*Yes, we shape life to our conditioned reality and then blame life!* We have to give shape, form and meaning to our lives and it is the ego-mind that shapes the personality, the feeling, functioning persona. Eventually, with more consciousness, the soul shapes our reality and we are then free from the great illusions created by the dear reactive self, our ego.

It is awesome for us to realize, to really believe, that we have the power to shape life as we wish it to be! Imagine, at this moment I am creating my life by my attitudes! It is difficult for our intellects to absorb this knowledge but as my friend, the poet Tony Ramsey from Derry City, Northern Ireland, advises: "Let the heart go swift to where the eye cannot see." When our hearts are open to this possibility then change happens. Remember, you can relearn anything you have learnt. You can open to new knowledge when the heart engages, not before then. Your heart has the power to shape either

> *Innocence or guilt,*
> *Love or fear,*
> *Traumas or peace,*
> *Friendships or enemies.*

You can shape yourself as light and purity or darkness and sinfulness. So, you can shape your world now in accordance to your own will and emotions. But make sure that you shape from the wise heart, thus bringing yourself more soul power. Make sure you shape from a will that has been led by intuition. Otherwise, you will shape it according to the dictates and preferences of your ego-mind. Remember:

> *Life is neutral.*
> *Love is neutral.*
> *Soul is neutral.*

They have no great so called success-orientated agendas for your life except that you should live life fully. You bring the agenda with your heart and will. Life is non-judgemental, and therefore love is non-judgemental. But you shape your present life according to the beliefs of the past and so you live the past instead of the present. Thus you live in illusion.

Your contribution to life, your perception of your life is either contributing to the healing of other beings on the planet, or not. If all beings left the planet, the planet would still exist because love is limitless and cannot die, just as life will never die. Your energy is important in the building up of loving consciousness and healing. Your life is important, as it is part of the whole. No matter how long it takes for individuals to heal, life will go on. Life is pure presence.

You are an individual expression of the whole. You may feel like you are an absolute individual, separate from all but whilst you experience life and love differently from others that does not make you separate from them. Thinking you are, does, however. You are not one soul living out your existence alone. You are a wonderful paradox: whilst individual, you are part of the collective. Nothing will ever change this reality because you are part of the Over Soul. Are the rays of the sun separate from the sun's energy? Each ray falls on a different expression of life. Some rays fall on mountains, others on the oceans, on trees, on your face etc. When we do not feel the warmth of the sun it does not mean it has disappeared. Our particular global geography prevents us from seeing and feeling it, that is all. It is the same with love. It is always there but our particular inner environment, our inner geography prevents us from feeling it at times. Shape your life, live your life close to soul so that your earth-self may be infiltrated with its force. Then you can live joyfully, creatively, consciously, always knowing who you are, always recognizing your particular contribution as a particle of and channel for pure love, pure reality.

Then, dear one, when you leave your form behind you will have left an aura of pure joy and love. Your soul can soar into the spirit of love itself out of which it shaped itself on earth. You will be made whole again in the fullness of love. And when the time is right, your soul will shape a form for this great life again and will experience all it has contracted to experience - each time with more consciousness and infused with more love.

## MARY MAGDALENA AND HER DEDICATION TO LOVE

Maria Magdalena holds the archetype of the ancient mother. She holds the secrets of the eternal feminine. She lived the true feminine in her dedication to living from soul, in her love for the Christ energy, in her personal dedication to her soul friend Jesus of Nazareth whom she called Issa. It was she who tried to show the Apostles what he really meant in his stories, his parables. She knew the deeper meaning of which he spoke because he spoke in symbols. Indeed, she was his muse in many ways as she used her intuition at all times, which inner knowing the Apostles were not able to understand. The Apostles could not grasp the inner graces of Jesus' teachings and in many ways the four gospels that we now believe to be the true recordings of the times and life of Jesus bears little resemblance to truth. The stories which Magdalene recalls in her own books that were not allowed to be added to the Bible were full of her conversations with Jesus. Through them one can get to know his humanity in a way the gospels never showed. When Mary Magdalena tried to explain the hidden truth within Jesus' stories the disciples criticized her. The so-called chosen Apostles maintained she was the favourite of Jesus and was fabricating his teachings by her strange translations and her insistence on the use of symbols. The Apostles did not approve at all of her relationship with Jesus and often times they told him of their disapproval when they were alone with him. He dismissed their rebukes of Magdalena by letting them know she was an inspired muse who held the wisdom to which one day they also would have to bow.

The truth was that she alone, with the exception of John, the man who loved Jesus deeply, understood Jesus not from the ego or patriarchal stand, but from the soul. When Jesus said, "I am the way, the truth and the light!" he meant the divine "*I am*" that is in all things. In other words, the "*I am*" that is in you, your own indwelling divine being, your soul, is the path you must follow. "*I am*" is also truth itself, as it is the light. So the meaning was: *The divine in you is the way, the truth and the light for you.* Jesus did not mean himself personally as the way, truth and light. Because the four Gospels are linear accounts of the life of Jesus that have been translated so many, many times before actually arriving at the English version, we have only a much weakened and absolutely biased male articulated version. Like fundamentalists of all religions, the translators took each word literally and so lost the deep soulful meaning. Jesus was a story teller, and not an academic. Jesus was a lover, not a pragmatist. Jesus was an evolutionist not a traditionalist. Jesus came to live love, just like us all.

As I interpret Jesus' words:

> *If you follow love*
> *Then release anything*
> *That prevents you from soulful living.*
> *Release old beliefs*
> *That no longer serve you.*
> *Like old beliefs that hold you back,*
> *Like materialism that becomes your god, etc.*
> *Whatever stands in the way of your soul's journey,*
> *Lovingly release it.*
> *And when you have released all*
> *Make a feast and rejoice together,*
> *For nothing has been lost,*
> *Just lovingly released.*

Jesus' teachings must be heard in the heart, not as dogma, not as scriptures, but as truth. He said: "I love you with an everlasting love." This was not a personal love. It is the love of the divine in all. This is not personal. When you can see the meaning behind the stories, you see the gem hidden in the setting. "I and the father are one"; the creator is always one with the created. Not that he, Jesus, was the same as the father. Jesus was the incarnation of the divine as you and I are. Remember, in the old Aramaic language father means beloved.

Mary Magdalena was also a beloved of Jesus. She cared for him dearly and loved his stories of which she alone knew the deeper meaning. Peter in particular did not approve of her since he was jealous of the love they shared. He called her "this woman" which was meant to belittle her, and tried to separate them after she anointed Jesus' feet in Simon's house. Judas also disapproved of her femininity and her extravagance. Jesus stayed with Mary Magdalena in her home with her sister and this was met with disapproval by some of the Apostles. Peter had left his wife who was ill, in order to be near Jesus. Now here was another woman in the company and this made him unhappy. Peter also did not like children, as he imagined they just made a lot of noise and were a nuisance.

Why is it necessary to invoke the spirit of Mary Magdalena at this time? It is because her earth energy was that of soul. She had integrated her sexuality and her spirituality and was a woman of great holiness. She was spontaneous and had a wonderful sense of humour, which also caused the Apostles to dislike her and claim she was not serious enough. She took herself lightly and was often heard to sing as she walked the beach with the master. She heard his words with such loving acceptance and was always ready to massage his feet and body at the end of a long days' teaching. Jesus was very attracted to her openness and her sense of inner wisdom. She embodied the energy of Sophia.

He was always attracted to the openness of the heart, because his own heart was open. Magdalene and John were soul friends and his own sense of wonder and innocence had never been lost. Since he lived from compassion and surrender his open heart also was attracted to Jesus.

Being close to the energy of Jesus Christ was not a guarantee of holiness. The Apostles still lived from selfishness and frailty. Their earth minds were not healed into their souls. Their hearts were not opened and they could not find the real meaning of Jesus teachings. Jealousy and rage still abided in their hearts, which kept them closed. And because of their unwillingness to surrender to soul, many of them turned to pride and power in the end. Many times Jesus said: "How long a time have I been with you and you have not heard me." In other words, "You still have not opened you hearts to my words. You only try to hear what I am saying from the outer, not from the inner ear. You have not integrated them into your own experiences." When we do integrate his words into our experience we will find a whole new way of being in the world. Jesus' way was the way of love, of living from love and living love in all circumstances.

Many of us have tried to live love. It is not easy. You may have mistreated your neighbour. Look at that action again. Why did you do this? What was your need at the time? You will find that every mistake you have made or misdeed you have done stems from an unfulfilled need in yourself. You overpower another because you need to feel secure. You take from another because you need to have something, yet the need springs from something deeper. There is a belief behind it. Why do you misuse another? The obvious answer is that you need to overpower, but your underlying belief is that you have no power. So under each answer there is another one, there is truth, and you have to find that. Jesus expected his followers to look deeper into their own lives to find the answers, the real meanings to the stories he told. Find the belief beneath the action and you will find the reason why you have behaved as you have.

Beneath the obvious, the material presence in human beings is Spirit residing. Beneath the obvious in humanity is Spirit. Beneath the obvious in words are messages for you that lie in wait. Live soulfully so that you can live your life at a subtler, deeper spiritual level. You live a surface live if you live surface beliefs. Surface life is about living at the gross material level of existence. Jesus said: "I come that you may live fully, that you have the abundance, the overflow of life in you." This life lies in the deeper parts of your psyche. As you live soulfully so you live these deeper parts.

You see, everything around you is symbolic. Everything is waiting for you to UNVEIL it. If you live from your earth-mind only, you will only find surface friends, those who live surface lives.

Find the truer, deeper meanings and there you will find your divine self.

CHAPTER 4

# Forgiveness Revisited

**FORGIVENESS AND ILLUSION**

We can carry the illusion that someone has hurt us for a long time and because of this illusion we are hurt. When somebody goes against our beliefs, when somebody does something, to annoy us, when they seem to overpower our will, then we are hurt. We are hurt because we carry within us seeds of illusion. If we connect too deeply with the hurt, then we suffer. If we carry within us the thought pattern "nobody has the ability to hurt us and make us suffer", then we cannot be hurt. If we believe that other people can hurt us, then that will happen (self-fulfilling prophesies). But if we believe that no another person has that power over us, then we will not create that illusion.

There is a part of us that has never been hurt, part of us that has never been abused and part of us that has never been wounded. That part is our divine self. It knows no illusion – and the more we live in and with this divine self, the less we will live in the illusion that somebody can hurt us. The more we live from the part that says, "I cannot be hurt, I cannot be abandoned, I cannot be forsaken", the less we will suffer, because suffering comes from connecting ourselves to the illusion, others can overpower us. You say: "That person has abandoned me." Yes, maybe they have left you. Maybe that person has told lies about you. Maybe that person has opposed you. That is painful, but you don't have to suffer. You suffer when you give power to another, as I have already said. Power is energy and YOU CHOOSE HOW TO USE IT. That is not easy to learn; it can take a long time, or it can take one moment, one breath, one second.

This idea of choosing how to spend your energy also applies to forgiveness. If you say: "I forgive you for hurting me", that is an illusion.

Instead, say: "I forgive myself for abdicating my power, for allowing this to happen. It is not that they have hurt me, rather, I have allowed them to have power over me, and in so doing, I have become weak and moved away from my centre." So, this idea that *I forgive you for hurting me* is without substance. A truer statement would be: "I forgive myself for having given my power away."

How does one know that one has truly let go of so-called past hurts? One has truly let go when one truly no longer has a need to blame.

In other words, when I no longer have a need for the other person to suffer because of something I believe they have done to cause me suffering, then I have let go. When I carry around the need for someone to feel ashamed or guilty, then I have not let go of the past pain i.e. the illusion that they caused me hurt.

Remember, too, that the things that cause you pain may not have the same effect on someone else. We all carry "hurt buttons" within and when another comes along and presses one of these buttons we re-act with an electric charge and the underlying unhealed hurt comes up again for recognition. If you could then say to that person, "Thank you my friend! I see I have not healed this old pain and I am re-acting to what you have said/done", then you would be free from your own inner pain. Imagine if you could truly do this with love and gratitude! One of our greatest teachers, one of our dearest spiritual leaders lies within our own psyches. It is called our re-actions.

May we all be free from the need for another to suffer because we believe that they have the power to hurt who we are.

May we heal this belief into love because we see the untruth of it. Please remind yourself:

People can kill my body, but they cannot hurt me.

They cannot hurt me because who I am is divine and the divine can NOT be hurt.

This means we have to take responsibility for our inner journeys.

I knew I had moved on the path to self-knowing and self-love when I did not need to have someone to shame, or blame for my so-called misery!

Our dear ego is often hurt because it gives power away in order to be liked. It also overpowers others because it feels insecure.

Love is the only power we ever need. May it fill us all with joy.

## PERPETRATOR AND VICTIMS

When we do not own the shadow self that is, when we do not own our own jealousies, our own sense of competition, our own inner aggression, spiritual arrogance, sarcasm, fearful feelings etc. when we don't own what the world calls "negativity", then, of course, someone else will have to carry it all. This can also happen collectively within families and even between different countries. For example, Germany was an appropriate place to lay the dark shadows of Europe during the Second World War. The debauched persona of Hitler acted as a perfect shadow carrier for the collective, for the mass. This is not to say that he was right in what he did - not at all - it just demonstrates how we can be distracted by the rages of another country whilst our own homeland is full of discrimination, fear, hatred and bigotry. Hitler, because of his internal states of insane hatred and revenge, acted for the collective at that time of unconsciousness.

Can the shadows of one man really produce such violence, such terrorism, such systematized killing, such brutality? Can one country produce such utter poverty of soul? Germany became the perpetrator. That is too easy; surely the rest of Europe complied with the terrorist Hitler through their collective unhealed hatred. The Vatican was also guilty for its part in aiding Hitler in his insane and revengeful slaughter of the Jews. Some months after the Third Reich was installed, Pope Pius XII Eugenio Pacelli stated that the parish records of the twenty-three million Roman Catholics should be made available to the Nazis so that it could be clearly seen who was racially pure enough to "survive endless persecution under the Nuremberg laws" (Christopher Hitchens *"God is not Great"*, Atlantic books, 2007). One wonders why this pope did not intervene on behalf of the Jews. In other words, did Hitler also carry projections from the Catholic Church at that time?

When I, who am also part of the collective, do not own my shadows here and now, children suffer, generations suffer and countries suffer. What happened in Germany was hell - hell for the victims, because everybody was a victim. When we see the story through the eyes of the soul, no one escapes his own inner state of being. When we tyrannize other people we are actually terrorizing ourselves. The energy of hatred has to flow through my own psyche before it reaches the other so I am, in fact, the receiver of my own hatred. It seems as if we always need to have the positions of perpetrator and victim. But when we look with the deeper consciousness we see that everybody in Germany was a victim. This is difficult to understand. We have to see it all through the eyes of a different consciousness. I lived through 26 years of war in Northern Ireland. The killers, the bombers, the terrorists shot their own people because they did not share the same beliefs. These men were just as much victims as my husband and I who had to leave our home with our small child because the terrorists said, "we will get you". Anyone who terrorizes another is not happy, is not peaceful; they are in fear themselves and that is the state of victim hood.

When you watch television and see the victims of terrorism and see the families in grief, of course, naturally, your emotional heart will support the families, the ones who are maimed, the ones who are suffering in hospitals as a result of bombing and shooting and terrorism.

But when we allow ourselves to be led by a deeper consciousness we realize that the terrorists also need love. As we watch the television and see the results of violence we send our prayers and love and sympathy to the poor victims. This is very important, but please do not believe in a separatist gospel. If you send love only to the victims and their families, you are not seeing the deeper cut of humanity in the perpetrator. The wound in the terrorists is just as deep as the wound that has been inflicted by these terrorists on the victims. If they do not heal, then the war will go on and on and your children's children will suffer. When we come to a deeper consciousness of what hell is, we understand that the lives of the terrorists are full of fear. Do you think they would commit such tragedies, such acts of violence on other human beings if they were free in themselves?

I know it's easy for me to say: look back to the lives of the terrorists and see what happened to them as children. Of course I also know that NOTHING is ever an excuse for hurting another being, either mentally or physically. When we see only one side of the story we are making a mistake. As we move deeper into our own consciousness and as we become more aware, then we will see that our love does not stop at the door of the victim but also has to extend to what we call a perpetrator.

If we want to create a heaven on earth, we can't have places of hell. We cannot look into hell and not want it also to be heaven. Look into the eyes of the terrorists, see what hell is, then send impersonal loving and universal deep compassion to those places of hell in those beings, or else they will create more hell externally. There is never an excuse for murder or violence. We all have choices; we are all responsible. But before we cast the first stone, please let us look into our own lives and our own subtle ways of terrorising others, of creating fear, the ways we hold back our love, our subtle jealousies, our feelings of ownership, our ego-driven ambitions in the workplace. Thousands of companies, institutional hierarchies and hierarchies in institutionalized religions terrorize people that are under them. Mother Superiors and Father Superiors all have to have inferiors and in many cases they use their superiority to abuse others.

My friends, if you are to create a heaven on earth, your love must also reach out to the terrorists. Maybe tonight when you light your candle for the victims of crime and war, you might also light a candle for all the terrorists in the world. Send out a conscious light of compassion to all those at this moment who are holding bombs in their hands, who are holding hatred in their hearts. For out of this hatred comes rage, and rage is the accumulation of anger that has never been expressed.

If you could do this: include all terrorists in your blessings, you would create a safer place for your children's children to the seventh generation. Your compassion would be unconditional, like the compassion with which the Christ loved.

### *One*

*I am one,*
*One with the mothers grieving.*
*I am one,*
*One with the child in shame.*
*I am one,*
*One with the one who's leaving.*
*I am one,*
*With the one who remains.*

*I am one*
*With the victims as they shape their lives in freedom.*
*I am one*
*With the perpetrators' pain.*
*I am one*
*With the homeless, who are drugged into destitution.*
*I am one*
*With the men who deal their chains.*

*I am one,*
*One with the starving children.*
*I am one,*
*One with the killers' rage.*
*I am one,*
*One with the young man cursing God.*
*I am one*
*With the nun who prays.*

*Alleluia*
*Shalom A Hiah*
*Namaste*
*Anam Arun*
*Tu Tare*
*Magdalene*
*O Mane Paedme Hum*

(SONG BY PHYLLIDA ANAM-AIRE FOR HER NEXT CD)

CHAPTER 5

# The Hidden God

**DISGUISES OF THE DIVINE**

It is such an awe inspiring practice to really look beyond our physical reality and, with the eye of perception, feel through to pure presence, the sacred in all things. I believe the word sacred not only refers to that which is holy and divine, but also that which holds a sense of secrecy, that which is hidden and has a certain vulnerability. Mystery holds within itself the code of creation, a code that has never been broken. When we contemplate the various forms that shape consciousness we awaken to the sacred, that divine being hidden in our own physicality, which is pure consciousness, pure love. To be allowed to experience this love is amazing grace, yet we so easily get distracted and move further and further away from what is sacred, hidden in the depths of our own psyches. When we move away from our own vulnerability we lose something vital. It is so easy for us to look into a child's eyes and see the love of the creator in them. We look into nature and see spring budding into summer, beauty tentatively peeping into life, everything greening, colours abundant. We look to the majesty of the snow-capped mountain, reaching to the sky. We see and feel the sun shining on our skins. We delight in sunsets and sunrises. Singing sacred songs and contemplating the divine in poetry and verse widens us into a sense of awe and appreciation. We feel the oneness of creation, the innocence of our own fierce, yet magnificent fragility. How beautiful our Universe is! How magnificent the creator! How we all love to experience the purity of love. This is natural.

On the other hand, we see and hear of disasters in our world, we empathize with the peoples who suffer earthquakes and the total destruction of what they thought would last forever. We see and feel the devastation of tsunamis and some people wonder where the sacred in all of this is? They feel it is not fair, that God should have intervened. These are again the child's feelings i.e. nothing is fair, these dear people did nothing wrong and still this suffering has come. Eventually we realize that God does not decide who will suffer and who will not. But as was said before, we have made a God in our own image and likeness and created from our own projections a persona around God and by doing so, confined IT to our limited imagination and understanding. With this limited consciousness, or rather with this unconsciousness, we try to grasp what pure consciousness is about, but our definitions from the past no longer serve us.

How easy it is for us to judge the outer appearances of things and forget that we cannot define reality by applying our confined linier understanding to it. The soul has her spiritual wisdom that the ego will never comprehend because the dear ego does not appreciate the hidden code of creation, the God code, so to speak, and only wants solutions and answers now.

Having spoken some days ago to a friend whose five-year-old child is both mentally and physically handicapped, I was awed by her answers to my questions. I asked her what it was like for her to be the mother of this child. Her answer was immediate and clear: "I realize only now that I have been truly blessed with this child. When I look into her eyes, I believe that she came just to show me how to open my heart and become more conscious." We also discussed the physical problems regarding caring for her daughter, and they are many. However this dear mother maintained that her child was not the problem, the problem was how she as mother sometimes got into a state of real fear. Now, with practical help in dealing with her daughter, she said she allows the love to flow, unhindered by her own fears. When one continuously offers unconditional love to another being, one lives more from soul than ego. When we have the eyes to see through the mask of a terrible physical or mental disablement and sense only the presence of pure love, we will have seen beyond one of the disguises of the divine. I have learnt much about unconditional love from being with parents of handicapped children. They have shown me how to go beyond so-called tragedy and see the face of love.

Celtic consciousness advises that everything and all in this beautiful Universe is there because we have called it consciously or unconsciously into our lives, so that we may use it creatively or otherwise. But you might say: "I have not created pain - that would be crazy." Yes it is, but we have made some great choices from an unconscious place in ourselves and thus we have had consequences that were not so happy for us. When we see that all is a disguise of the divine, we can learn from the mistakes we make and eventually see that we really are divine beings having a human experience. Divinity is deeply impressed, deeply impregnated in each life form. It cannot be otherwise - only our judgements blind us. We have to learn to see with the inner sight, hear with the inner ear, see and feel with the universal heart. We have to heal our conditioning regarding value judgements in order to be able to truly see the divine imprint on our world of form each day. This is not easy for us to grasp with our habitual preferences and judgements.

In 1994 I worked with Dr. Elisabeth Kübler-Ross in two prisons for men in Scotland. We had to stay for a full week in the prison and live amongst the prisoners. Our cells were beside the men and we slopped out each morning in the queue with them. We had requested that we be given no privileges and so we had first-hand experience of how the men lived. At one stage during our expressive therapy with the group of forty five men (all of whom were in prison for life) I got the distinct feeling that we had all come to earth to heal past lives and that our common humanity united us all. Most of the men had been very badly sexually, emotionally and physically abused as young people and they had done what they had to do in order to survive. That is not an excuse for having killed someone since that is an act of revengeful rage and, as such, is never righteous. One man told me that the moment he killed his father he thought, "Thank God he is dead; he will never hurt another person again." (I wonder if this thought was also given as an excuse for killing Osama Bin Laden. But, then, when the command to kill is ordered by the head of a state it is different, it is legal. Or is it?). I remember feeling sadness when I left the second prison since I felt that the men could have achieved more by training to help young men who were violent. Could I find the divine in a prison? The answer is: *"Yes"*.

When I started my journey to becoming more conscious I had to draw back the curtain of my own blindness and see the face of the divine in myself, in my mistakes as well as my achievements, in my falling down and my rising up, in my tears of sadness and tears of sheer joy. I sought and I found but I had to seek with an open heart that judges no one and was willing to find the pearl of great price, especially hidden in the clay of my own earthing. I had a hunger and a thirst for the quest and I was filled. Do not let go until you have found the gem within the setting of all situations and circumstances of your very precious life. This is an amazing spiritual practice that teaches us not to judge the outer appearances, the mask of things or the so-called presenting reality. As an Irish comedian used to say ... "Look, there's more!" and our quest is to find the *more* and not rest until we have found it.

Here is an exercise that might help you discover the real truth behind a painful appearance. You may believe e.g. that life is all about suffering. You may like to blame God or a circumstance or another person or your parents etc. That is fine.

**EXERCISE**

1. Write down all the difficulties in your life right now.
2. Now take a look at these situations, one by one.
3. Feel the anger and the frustration and also the sadness in you.
4. Honour each feeling.
5. Notice which emotion is the most prominent in each situation.
6. Say out loud, I feel so... name it.
7. Now imagine the person or thing you want to blame is in front of you.
8. Tell them how hurt you feel, leave nothing out.
9. Now breathe very deeply.
10. Take time and see how you feel.
11. Stand up. Walk around the room.
12. Sit down again.
13. Breathe in deeply and breathe out with the sound of AAAAAAAA

14. *Notice how you feel.*
15. *Stand up and breathe fully in and out.*

Do the same with each feeling, going through the above stages.

When you have worked through each prominent feeling, bring the arms straight above you. As you breathe in say out loud the word … "I" (say your own name). With the out breath bring the arms down quickly with the word, "release". Do this for the next five breaths.

When you do this spiritual practice with full consciousness you will experience a state of inner freedom and peace.

The next stage is where we find a blessing from each hurt.

> *Write beside the hurts whatever blessing you believe they brought into your life. Naturally, you will not see the blessings immediately, but if you really look in stillness and peace and ask for inspiration to see clearly, you will eventually find the gem.*

Many people tell me that forgiveness is a natural result of having honoured the so-called negative emotions and having found a blessing in them. Soon you will be able to naturally see that all was a *"blessing in disguise"*. As one woman said to me: "Well hidden under the pain was a great blessing that I was not able to see at the time."

Premature forgiveness and prematurely searching to find the blessing does not last because we need time to feel the feelings and honour their wisdom. Usually, we were never allowed to take the time to honour all our so-called negative feelings because we were made to feel less spiritually evolved when we expressed them. Feelings are fields of energy, nothing more. Of course, the strongest and most powerful feeling is love. Some spiritual people are very afraid of their so-called *negative feelings* and will do anything to *get rid* of them. In this new Age of Aquarius we are beginning to see the tyranny of not having been allowed to express feelings from childhood. Much disease and many mental problems are a result of having had to repress feelings.

Ponder these thoughts for a while and notice your feelings as you repeat them.

*I am a being of divine grace and love.*
*I am a beautiful disguise of divine love.*
*I am the very mystery on which the whole of creation is built.*
*I have the power to create joy and love.*

*Like all beings, I am amazing grace.*
*Like all beings, I am worthy of love.*
*Like all beings, I am not alone.*
*Like all beings, I make mistakes.*
*Like all beings, I need love.*
*Like all beings, I need support.*
*Like all beings, I am vulnerable.*

May our disguises fade with each passing day so that one day the essence of who we are i.e. pure love, can be made manifest on the earth. On this day God will have come out of hiding.

## I AM THAT

You often say you have no choice. You don't have a say in how you live your life. You are not involved in decision making - life makes the decisions for you and you just follow blindly. You say your life is mundane, without success, and that it probably will remain so in the future. God also gets blamed for your horrible existence and you claim it is really unfair that you suffer while others get it easy. But that is not the truth of your magnificent life. The truth of life is that life is neutral. Life just is. It does not make choices for you and it does not create problems for you. Life is that impulse, that energetic world in which you and all beings live and move and have their being. It is the very force, the strong movement and impulse of creation, the same energy that lives in the leaves of the trees, in the whole of creation. Life calls everything into being. It is the law of creation. All created beings are kept in motion, activated by life force. Thus we are all part of this energy, this great field of consciousness.

The great truth is that whilst we are an important particle of life, nothing is personal and life does not have preferences. In the world of the child, everything and all centres around the individual. The moon shines just for them etc. Every experience is subjective and personal. Everyone else is responsible for what is not OK in their lives. But an attitude that is natural for a two-year-old is rather immature when adopted by an adult of fifty.

The Divine Natural Activator (D.N.A.) is the nucleus of divine light activating everything, seducing all to its own individual place in creation and each species is accountable for its contribution to the Over-Soul. Every aspect of creation knows its purpose on the earth, its space within the family of things and knows exactly how to fulfil its potential. The tree will always own its own energy. It has no desire to be a mountain or a frog! It *knows* that it recycles itself naturally through the seasons. Each created phenomenon *knows* from innate wisdom that change and transformation are essential impulses in nature.

Earthquakes bring great sorrow to human beings. Whilst nature is adjusting to an inner movement that is necessary for her next evolutionary shift, we suffer and many consequently die. The great alchemist, which is life, balances, harmonizes and brings all her creation to order, an order that is not predictable nor is it without sequence. The seasons create what we humans call upheaval and confusion whilst nature herself is merely following an inner breath that brings everything into balance. It acts independently of our emotions, our desires and wants; it is doing its own thing by helping in the overall evolution within nature.

When nature does what is necessary to bring about balance and order, she is helping humans too, though dear human beings often die in the transformation process. This is sad for the ones left behind and our compassion helps them to recover their own equilibrium after such so-called catastrophes. We say that nature helps us to grow and evolve; this is not easy for us to understand since we always view evolution and transformations through the eyes of suffering. Nature does not suffer in her transformations because she does not have an ego system to deal with. The love nature shows for humanity is not the personal emotional love that we know; rather, it is expressed in chaos, peace, harmony and so-called disaster, in order for us to reach a state of equilibrium.

If we were to love with equilibrium and unconditionally what would that mean? It would mean that we would no longer act as a result of hurt over emotions from the past. We would no longer re-act from the inner wounded child, no longer act from the place of unfinished business. We would respond to everything and everyone without judgement, without re-action. We would see the *Is-ness* of everything. We would see the *Aha* of things; we would see things the way they are, new and wonderful, without our past associations and judgements. Love, in relation to nature, is sometimes a noun and sometimes a verb. Nature loves, independent of a love object, as such. Love experiences itself in nature and nature experiences itself in love. Love experiences itself in everything and in everyone without judgement and is, therefore, our great example of unconditional love.

How can we humans see that e.g. love experiences itself as a tsunami and also experience itself as pure joy? Love has to live the antithesis of all experiences. It does not name one experience *good* and the other *bad*. It experiences all as a flowing of energy that it is able to harmonize and balance when the energies get out of order. Can you imagine that this love, or life, experiences itself as a wind blowing through you hair, as a hurricane, as a flower in your garden, as water in the seas, as thunder and lightning? It can very wonderfully disguise itself in human form e.g. in the form of a baby child, just come to earth, an old man, limping or as a young girl and boy falling in love. It is disguised as the soldier going to war to kill. It is also disguised in governments that show young people how to kill. This love is also disguised in the sick and the needy. It is masked in animal and plant form, in water, fire, earth and air. The disguises of life, or love, are too many to name. Look around how all is manifesting this sacred life. Someday we will have learned the skill of how to express this love with pure intent. Until then we will use it in inappropriate ways. How amazing that even when we misuse this loving energy we are never judged or condemned! That is why it is called unconditional love.

This divine energy experiences itself in all creation at the same time, forever and ever, in one breath, creating itself over and over again. The human template, the human form is one of unbelievable beauty and variation. No two forms are the same. Even so-called identical twins have differences. The only agenda life has for us is that we experience it in the fullness of our own chosen experiences.

Whilst we have a personal sacred contract to fulfil as human beings, one that balances out our own experiences, it does not mean we have to fulfil it in this lifetime. We have a choice as to how and when we will live out this personal contract. It is not the responsibility of life itself to make sure we fulfil this contract. God or Jesus or Buddha cannot and would not be able to dictate to us how we should live our own chosen lives. Our lives and how we choose to live them are our own business and, unfortunately, there is no one to blame when life seems mundane - not even ourselves. Because of collective consciousness we can call on the loving energy of the Universe in our ancestors. Likewise, the angels are willing and happy to help, but we have to make the move and ask.

It is important to always remember that our own habitual thoughts and feelings create our moments and our futures. I will reiterate this thought, this truth throughout this book. If we look around us we see our own self-created images in the world. This is an amazing thought, a powerful thought, a thought that might fill you with dread. But there is no reason for you to be afraid. All is well, since you have the power to change what does not serve you at any time. When you hear this long enough and really believe it, you will begin to realize the truth of it. Can you imagine that everything in your world right now is there because you have unconsciously or consciously called it in? Take a look inside your heart at this moment.

- *Notice the thoughts you are thinking right now.*
- *What are the feelings in your heart?*
- *How is your body right now?*
- *Do you believe you have the right to choose your life?*
- *Can you see how you have attracted all your experiences?*
- *What do you see around you at the moment? The place you live, your friends your family, your work or vocation.*
- *Are you at peace with all beings? If not, why?*
- *Can you imagine that you can say no to what does not feel right and good for you?*

- *Are you afraid to say what you feel in case you might no longer be loved?*
- *You can still choose through the fear.*
- *We make choices all the time, from morning until night, and we blame life or whatever for the consequences of our decisions.*
- *We say, "I do not like the government", but we are part of the collective, so we are also part of the government. We do not like the community but we constitute community." We say, "God is not fair!" but we have forgotten that we have made God in our own image. Whether we like it or not, we are part of a collective Universe, a collective consciousness or unconsciousness and we contribute to all that we experience, whether it is good or bad. We can then take this theme further and notice that we also are part of the love that streams into the world and the joy that fills it. We are one with the compassionate one and the one who cares for others. Like the healer, we are also full of grace and are as gentle as the raindrop on a leaf. We are part of all created phenomena and that is our power and our joy. If we are one with all beings then we are also one with the antithesis of all love and beauty.*

Can we also see that we are one with the soldier who is going to kill, ready to shoot from a place of fear in order to defend himself? Can we feel how we are also one with the young man who is about to be shot, full of fear, not knowing if he will live or die? And can we picture ourselves as the older man introducing the young man to the skills of shooting at his target? Of course, we are also one with those who give their energy to help others in need.

The above was not written so that we carry guilt. Rather, the words are there for us all to consider. I learnt in my life that when I can see myself in all beings and in all creation I am less judgemental of myself and others. Seeing ourselves in all beings helps us to reach out and help one another and to realize that in this way we are, in fact, helping ourselves. When Jesus the Christ said ... "If you give a drink of water to someone in need, you give it to me", he was talking about collective consciousness of which he was also a part. He contributed to the awakening of all beings through his own living and dying experiences. Of course, we contribute to the overall unconsciousness when we do not consider what consequences our actions might have.

Give yourself encouragement each day and give yourself thanks for all you are willing to learn and share from your heart. Allow yourself to love yourself unconditionally, so that you are free to make conscious choices in life. Let go of all criticisms of mistakes you made in the past, as regrets eat away at self-love. When you cannot love yourself unconditionally there are no free spaces in you to make good decisions.

For many years I followed old patterns of thought, those of my unhealed ancestors, with the agenda to control and to be good and strong so that God might love me. We were indoctrinated from a very young age that Catholics were going to heaven, so we prayed the rosary for the poor Protestants. We learn at a young age to create a separation between *them* and *us*. I also learnt that to be self-loving was to be selfish and that was not good. These are some of the lies I lived for so long. I also know that the teachers themselves did not know any better at the time, and they gave me what they themselves received.

What were some of the lies you lived?

Now you can heal your own life as you learn different beliefs, yet you will always be connected to your family of origin by the strong impulse of birth. This impulse can be transformed into unconditional love for them and for all the teachers that you attracted for your own healing. As you begin to see your own goodness, your own divinity, you might even see that your life can be good, can be creative if you make just a few different choices. Here are some questions you can sit with for a while and then answer for yourself on a piece of paper.

> *What is important to me in my life?*
> *What does it mean to heal?*
> *What does self-love mean?*
> *What are my fears?*
> *What delights my heart?*

When you have worked on the above questions and answered them on paper, then leave the paper on a small altar with a picture of yourself and maybe even a small candle and some flowers. Read your answers daily and then put the paper back on the altar. After a while you might want to change some of the answers and that is fine. May your very wise self help you in your great quest and great inner search for your own way of life, for what truly serves you.

Please know that whatever serves your awakened self, also serves the collective. Then maybe God will not get "lost in translation"!

**IDENTIFICATION**

Your belief in suffering is conditioned by being in the world of matter. Your continued belief in struggle and suffering keeps you bound to earth.

Suffering and struggle are mechanisms that the earth-mind adapts in order to escape the responsibility of being here and now. It cannot hear the messages of soul that knows when an old fear is about to become an attitude and the attitude is about to develop into a way of life.

When you cannot seem to be able to stop your mind from creating worries and stresses, your body takes on these energies as illnesses. You continue to stress because you have body pain. This brings you annoyance with the body and you begin to see that now you are nothing but pain. The annoyance manifests as body pain and now both are affected, mind and body. You ask a person, "how are you?" and the answer you get is, "I am suffering from so and so." This identification with the stress is a mind state. It is a statement of victimhood. As if you have no control in what is happening, as if your total identity is just pain, a body and mind full of pain.

The mind creates the state and the body just manifests it. Natural stress, which is the movement of contracting and relaxing, is what keeps our physicality functioning. Movement is life force manifesting in all created phenomena. This movement has its own inbuilt balance and harmony. Whatever is not in movement is decaying, yet the very act of decaying is also infused with movement. Because we do not have eyes sensitive enough to perceive the movement, we say it is not happening!

Movement is a natural response to change, both seen and unseen. But we are discussing the constricted movement, the over-tensed movement, like an over-strung guitar string. This unnatural state, when accepted as normal movement by the mind, produces worries and overstress.

The very language we use is stress-full. We hear people say: "It is terrible what is happening in the world." The vibrations in the word *terrible* (from the word terror) are full of fear and, therefore, not healthy. We say, with added feelings, "Everything is so stressful these days." So we are actually creating more stress by making this statement. You say you cannot lie and say there is no stress even if you feel it. The thing to do is to recognize the over-stress in your mind and then do something about releasing it. It needs a counter action in the thoughts. When the stress is released from the thoughts, then it is no longer a reality in the physicality. There are many ways of dealing with stress. For example, we can detect the beginning of stress especially in our breathing. When we are more aware each day of how we breathe, then we will easily detect when the breath shortens and is erratic. Are you annoyed about small things in your life at the moment? Do little things get on your nerves? Then stop for a moment and breathe deeply into the centre of your body. Realize that at this moment you are allowing this annoyance to take your breath away. You do realize by now that if you live more in the past or in the future than here and now you are creating problems. Notice that regrets about the past or worries about the future interfere with your joy here and now. If you try and control everything around you, you are adding stress to your life. Simply noticing how these situations interfere with your breathing, without judging them, is so important in regards to your well-being. Always keep remembering that whatever feeds your heart nourishes your soul. When your soul is nourished your breath is full and gives you energy.

You can allow your thoughts to help you enjoy a more abundant life.

Tension happens when we are not conscious of the breath, how we take in information and how we release it again.

People can have much physical pain. And because they do not identify themselves fully with it, they have no suffering. Suffering, I believe, is the result of seeing the world through the eyes of struggle.

Imagine if you had great pain in your body and you could say with all truthfulness, "There is pain in my body and I am well." If we could use language like this, I wonder how different we might feel regarding suffering, stress and struggle. The inner story seems to be: I have pain, I struggle with the pain and then I suffer because I struggle. When you are asked to pray for someone who is ill or in pain it is good to always visualize them feeling very well, smiling and full of life. Never visualize them suffering or sad. Your thoughts affect them too. Thoughts produce outcomes.

In our so-called progressive society we are encouraged to rush and multitask. We act like automatic machines without consciousness. When we achieve goals set by others, we are then asked to set even higher goals. This is stressful as we then begin to compete with ourselves. Self-judgement creates great stress. Trying to be perfect in all things leads to great nervous tension and when the body can no longer hold the tension, it becomes ill. Prevention of illness does not begin by taking more vitamins but by looking at our belief systems. If your beliefs serve you and delight your heart, and open you more and more into life, then they are healthy. If they stress your heart and prevent you from sleeping and nourishing yourself, then they are unhealthy and need to be lovingly examined.

CHAPTER 6

# Experiencing Soul

### EXPERIENCE

Our clay form, the physicality of our individual soul, is moisturised by experience. The physical body is not always ready to allow active experience to move in the rivers of its clay. When we, because of old fears, no longer welcome new experiences the clay dries up and we are left with the rigidity of the dried up form. We also need the wisdom to know when to move into experience and when to wait in the between spaces. I believe the experience of non-doing is as important and necessary as the experience of activity.

The body is such a flexible vehicle of sensuality and movement where all experience can feel at home. Soul uses physicality in which to move and have its being. We often think that in order to experience one must be physically involved. That it must be something big and eventful, something full of adventure. But the soul does not have such expectations. Whatever moves us, whether it is grief or joy, the soul calls it experience. Breathing in brings inspiration; breathing out brings the inspiration into being. No need for drama, no need for judgement, just the experience of being.

To experience presence is to experience soul because presence is the sacred space where no outer landscape distracts and no outer voice can rob the moment of its total commitment to truth. Presence is witnessed only by breath and breath always attends the consciousness of experience. Indeed, breath is the subtle monitor of our emotions and feelings. It watches with the experience and flows authentically with its inner movements. Breath can inform us as to whether we are in fear or in love. It invites also the watchfulness of the heart in all experiences. Heart is in charge of the emotional levels and does not judge but, rather, becomes intimate with experience and allows feelings to express themselves when the will allows.

Creation herself is longing for us to experience her deepest nature in fullness. Trees have a longing that we truly see them and know how they guard us so lovingly. It is as if the trees themselves have a dream that we become conscious of our own inner strength by communicating with them. As they carry the experiences of all seasons without judging, without seeking another way of expressing love, they show us how to express our essence. They show us how to be on the earth. When we can unite with the essence of tree, we know our belonging, our unique place in the family of creation. If we look only to the material, the man-made parts of our world for our inner security and stability, we will be disappointed because this will be taken from us. It was never meant to shelter our souls. True security may be found in unity consciousness, our oneness with all creation. We cannot possess nature, we can only experience her in all her various forms. When I want to possess a tree then I am no longer experiencing it. I do not see it as it is, I am not conscious of its self-ness, I am only sensing my need of it. It is the same with people - I cannot fully experience them if I am distracted by my inner clinging to them. If I have drifted into the ego space I will want to possess them. My language becomes one of personal ownership e.g. "*my*" tree, "*my*" friend, "*my*" life, "*my*" child etc. This inner self-dialogue leaves me bereft of pure experience, which could be grace and delight for my soul. Our sense of oneness lies in the belief that although we are separate as individual expressions of divine being, we are also united in our essence of pure love. Any sense of loneliness can be cradled when we truly feel this unity, this belonging, this homecoming to our self and to the other, the beloved.

When the time is ripe the leaf detaches from the branch of the tree and slowly, with the witnessing of the whole tree, it drifts downwards toward its earth home. If we were able to let go with such consciousness, without the suffering brought on by our tendencies to ownership and attachments and could let go of our false sense of security, we would realize that what we think we own is only on loan. To belong is to be free; to be at one is to also feel our individuality. To feel that sense of gentle awareness of the magnitude of our soul and at the same time to know the minuteness of our own contribution is to know joyful humility. We know we have a place in the family of all beings and that we count. When the rose bush falls back into the earth we say it is dead, no longer able to beautify our table. Nature knows, however, that it is not the end of that expression of life. It knows with the knowledge that is embedded in all nature that it will undertake a process of transformation. It will become the compost, the rich mineral soup for the next rose bush, maybe for many generations. Human beings likewise become the rich compost for the following generations.

All our experiences on earth are the ingredients from which our successors will learn and live. Just as the story of the rose bush is hidden in the seed, so the story of our lives was hidden in the rich soil of our ancestors. There may be much that we have to heal regarding the compost left to us from the unhealed parts of their lives, but their experiences were and are the soil of our becoming. Theirs was the earthed home from whence and in which we took form. Their experiences run in our blood, as do their beliefs, preferences and also their thoughts. Still, we had to individuate and now have our own inner landscapes to hoe and to plough, to seed and to harvest. The ancestors are no longer responsible for the contents of our individual harvesting or for the experiences we choose.

Whilst self-discovery is necessary, sometimes we sift too much and too long until the gifts of remembering and resourcing get lost in too much hoeing, too much scraping at the sacred foundations. We need to make spaces for mystery and the unknown, the as yet uncalled in us. I feel that at times there is a self-tyranny in too much revelation. We need also the dark brown red earth of our belonging in which to set the seeds of that which is unknowable and mysteriously sacred. Filtering off too much from our own stories leaves us barren and we lose our sense of the wilderness. Neat green lawns where no weeds are allowed to grow are simply exhalations to our satisfied ego that loves to name things good and bad, to judge the appearance of things. Then it feels important and worthwhile! The dear ego spends long hours in the garden of our stories solving the problem of weed overgrowth, whilst the soul experiences them as different varieties of flowers. It is easy to forget that life is not a problem to be solved; rather, it is an amazingly beautiful experience to be lived in each moment.

If you can see your life as an extraordinary example of the beauty of the creator without looking for the extra experiences, you will not wait for the big adventure in order to awaken your awareness of the magnificence of life as it is. When you can gaze with love and awe at a tiny flower and see its place in the order of love, or look into the eye of the horse and be taken beyond concepts and biology and experience the presence of beauty, you will feel only love. We need time to just be and not do or think, but to know that we are journeying beings on the earth and we all share the same inner vitality. This knowing will help us to walk the earth with joy and a deep sense that we are richly blessed, both in times of so-called joy and so-called sorrow.

On this day, we will have allowed the great wind of truth to reveal what needs to be revealed regarding her mysteries in us. On this day also, we will have come home into the welcome of our own soul and we will run with a song in our throats and a blessing for all in our widened hearts.

## SOULFUL LIVING, LIVING LOVE
*What is it to live from Soul? What is the alternative?*

Many good and reasonable questions may be asked regarding the above title. Reasonable questions are always required if one is to follow a path that is purposeful and conscious. That being said however, the empirical mind with it's insistence on logical debate that leads to logical conclusions, often gets in the way of deeper inner discoveries. Since soul is synonymous with paradox and synchronicity, the empiricist cannot expect to find a definition of soul that submits to left-brain cognition. Therefore, we immediately have a problem if we cannot go beyond predictability. This problem may, however, be overcome if we can see that the scientific mindset is still in a state of childhood when it comes to unravelling the mysteries of the Universe.

Scientists like Louise B. Young and Deepak Chopra would agree that the ordinary mind or linier left-brain has to eventually bow to mystery if it is to gain any real knowledge of unseen phenomena. I dare to suggest that indeed not only must left-brain eventually bow to mystery, but it will also eventually have to submit its left-brain language to that of the mystic or the poet because they possess a deeper Gnosis of the mysterious.

What the scientist might call unsolved phenomenon, the mystic and poet names mystery, the very essence of life, which is consciousness itself.

## ▪ What then is soul?

According to ancient wisdom, soul may be described as that life power or essence from which, in which and through which all creation lives and moves and has its being. I dare to call it pure original D.N.A. That is: Divine Natural Activator, the primal force, through which life continuously creates itself in and out of matter. Movement is synonymous with life, with energy and so all movement, seen and unseen, is activated by this never-ending energetic dance.

Energy is incapable of annihilation; it flows in a continuous rhythm of contraction and fusion. It is through this dance that various forms emerge. Trans-formation, not annihilation, therefore, is the nature of energy. This very fusion and contraction is the stuff, the vital stew of soul that creates the breath of life itself. Fusion creates a mechanism for rapid revolution i.e. egg to sperm. The egg and sperm are not of themselves alive but life flows from their union. It seems that life is forever moving towards union/at-one-ment: towards an internal *hieros gamos*, a full and total integration of all of itself. It is a return to the consciousness of unity that existed before the so-called Big Bang.

In a human relationship, one meets another special being, soul is attracted to soul and from the fusion love is born. The process is reversed when separation between them occurs. That is, contraction takes place and in the contraction creative juices are stilted. This is the time of transition wherein nothing seems to be happening and there is seemingly no movement. The love dynamics would seem to have been put on hold and thus emotional work has to be done. Indeed, in this space, this place of seeming aridity, the soul is gathering her harvest from the last fusion and is transforming the dross into gold for that life form if the person so wishes it. This is known as healing.

No experience is ever lost; no experience is ever without significance.

No thought, word or action can ever die. The energetic components of these variables interact with one another as they are stirred, melted and interwoven into a mass of what we can call vibrational vortexes. These vibrations float and move through our environment like unseen beings, ever ready to influence our particular D.N.A., the collective consciousness and unconsciousness. This continuity of electric and magnetic influences bears witness to each thought pattern, like each creative brush stroke of the artist. Nothing is new under heaven and earth. All is recycled. Nothing is lost; nothing is too insignificant to re-emerge as a singular or collective pattern of perfection. Imagine for a moment that the insights we now delight in may have had their origins in the brokenheartedness of a deep loss experienced two years ago. The gold of this moment may have had its origin in the clay of yesterday's compost.

The infinite extravagances of nature clearly show us that nothing is ever wasted or worn out. Nature herself builds on order and beauty. Indeed, the orderly manifestation in Nature is her beauty, her deep, intelligent beauty. She builds beauty from form to form, from excellence to excellence. She produces a profusion of creations, each one built on the death of the previous form.

Death of form provides further inspiration for even more magnificence.

> *And in the dying of the leaf*
> *Is not the tree grown?*
> *And in the reshaping of the pupa*
> *Is not the butterfly born?*
> *And in the splitting of the heart*
> *Is not the life made full?*
> *And in the final letting go*
> *Is not the union with soul?*

This natural progression is within us all. The manifest difference is that in nature contraction is seen as a natural phenomenon, whilst in human relationships it is seen as separation, which is synonymous with grief and suffering. This natural evolutionary process as viewed from a creative perspective in nature assures that life will continue, though transformed and transmuted. When we have reached a certain degree of wisdom in our spiritual intelligence, we will clearly see how pure intelligence is pure love. Divine Intelligence assures unlimited creativity.

When we are in a place of love we are at our most creative, our most beauty-full. When we are "in love" we shine through the Universe like stars at night, lighting up the darkness wherever we go. To see all creative phenomena through the eyes of love is to live soulfully and in the presence of the holy (the whole: non-separate).

To live from soul is to live in communion with grace; it is to live love. This is not to be confused with romantic love that contracts when the beloved is not receptive to one's advances. That is conditional love. The love of nature is without conditions, therefore free. Nature is free and I, who am of nature, am free, therefore we are free to admire each other without needing or expecting. This makes all the difference! It is *Namaste, agape* love without personalities getting in the way.

But sometimes on a rainy day I often feel, *"Not on that kind of love alone can woman live all she is!"* Whilst in bodies we also often have a need for down-to-earth human relationships. The love of pure beauty itself is to go beyond the ego expression of love. When we live that love, we simply are love. This is the love that sees the perfection of grace in all creative phenomena.

This is love without preferences. This is the love that sees the perfected order of love in all events of one's life. This love is not dependant on form, but senses the beloved in the wind, the vibrations of a song, the breath of a child, the flutter of a butterfly's wing. This love is captivated, is enraptured by one raindrop on one petal of a rose. This is the love of which poets write long and ecstatic poetry. It is the music of the cosmos, the Song of Songs, the rapture of Rumi, the poems of

Mary Oliver in their longing to belong. This love is also to be found in the pulsating of the widened heart, widened and strengthened by the very pain of longing itself. This longing is, however, closer to understanding the mind of the creator than the empty soundings from theological debate about the existence of God. Though it suggests a longing, a holy longing (Goethe, "Holy Longing") for the union of love within themselves i.e. enlightenment, it extends a total acceptance of the beloved in all form without exception. Thus one lives in love with differences and judges not, as pure love does not judge. When we can live thus we are truly living from, in and with soul.

Living from soul necessitates risk-taking. In the science of nature, quarks have to risk rejection when they attempt to fuse with nucleons; atoms have to risk rejection when they attempt to fuse and make molecules and crystals. Rejection is seen as a necessary process in the dance of evolution. Entropy is seen not as a state of death, of nothingness, but as a passageway to enlightenment, a longing for further creative development.

### ▪ How can we live thus?

Mostly we live from our social and collective conditioning. Our parents did not have the knowledge we have. Their beliefs were tribal; therefore they believed that security was the most important element of existence. Whilst personal security relied on staying with the known, with the past as our guide for future choices, the group or tribe provided the "known" network within which boundaries one was safe. Fear creates restrictive movement and even creativity is challenged by its insistence on mediocrity. Fear is the dull stifling insistence that life is a struggle, that we are victims of fate and nothing and no one can actually rise above the given of their existence. Courage tries to make an inroad but the past ensnares us, as our hearts are closed to possibilities and our minds are closed to any inspirational thought.

When we dare to follow the soul's song we risk living in the abundance of life. Then we live with nature as our mentor and pure joy as our inner guide. In order to live thus we have to change the language of the sceptic to that of the poet or mystic. We have to decide whether life is a long walk from A to B and then The End or life is here and now and full of surprises.

What kind of life are you choosing to live here and now?

Every thought is the result of choice, so begin today to direct your thought patterns away from the cold, arid air. Run like a gazelle, float like a dolphin on the fresh winds of your own creative thoughts and remember: nothing is lost in the story of your precious life. Not one tear or sigh goes unnoticed by the breath of creation. You are guided by the Great Oversoul of creation itself, guided back, back home, to your individual imprint of D.N.A., to your individual expression of divine nature. At this time in our precious lives, all is being danced back into love from whence it came. This can take centuries but it can also take one breath. Your own timing is important, so remember: *You can choose to live love from this moment on.*

May you and I and all of those who dare to live the creativity of their souls know that we are growing into the order and beauty that we are. We are not afraid of chaos, as it brought forth the harmony and order of love itself. In this river we can swim into eternity and bless our lives.

May you and I and all of us be blessed because we are the stuff of the magnificence and the terrible beauty of the divine.

## A GOD WITHOUT SOUL

It is amazing that no matter how advanced we are psychologically, no matter how far we have individuated as adults, no matter how scientifically and spiritually evolved we seem to be, there is still this insistence on holding on to the *"Our father up in heaven"* God. At least the father/son/daughter relationship of the Christian God is less terrorizing than the tyrannical soulless God of the Old Testament. In the story of Abraham we read that God asked him to slay his son. Later on God changed his mind and let the child go free. This is a story of an overpowering, emotionally abusive dictator playing with the minds of men. But then, God the father treated his own son even more abusively by allowing him to suffer violence and agony without intervening. Strange God, one might think. One wonders why the father did not at least send an angel or speak a word of comfort to his son. These words of Jesus: "Father have you forsaken me?" have been reiterated many times by young men suffering from an abusive, soulless patriarchy ever since.

The offering of one's will to God was a very important aspect of religion. Man's will had to be broken. We have a saying in the Irish language that translated means, "When you break a man's will you own his spirit." After speaking with some men who had been in the English army, I was appalled to hear of the brutality involved in the way their Spirits were literally owned by their so-called superiors. How can a young man find inner authority when he is indoctrinated into the false belief that he is of no worth? Seemingly, in the military one's worth is gauged by how many of the so-called enemy one has killed. This is an abusive philosophy and belongs to the Old Age of *"an eye for an eye."* When we forget the soul we forget our humanity and our Spirits become robotic and re-active. We can then easily, too easily become immune to the suffering we inflict on others. Institutions that control through fear, rather than lead with compassion must be seen in the light of what was acceptable and common in former ages but no longer serves us as men and women.

## LIVING THE SYMBOLIC LIFE

*What is symbolic living?*
*Why would one want to live thus?*
*How does one live a symbolic life?*

Our Celtic relatives believed that when we live our days in close relationship to nature we live a more symbolic life. They also believed that when we watch with the dying, or when we work as midwives, we also learn to live symbolically. Being with children also brings us into the realms of symbolism. How can this be?

When we are in close contact with nature, we adapt to her rhythms that contain vibrations and frequencies different from ours and are often rather erratic and driven. Nature shows us with her endless patience and centeredness how to live with paradox and be content with confusion and conflict. She also knows the timing of things that we have forgotten in our materialistic worlds of progress and an orientation based on so-called achievement. Nature lovingly manifests intensity and integrity in her ever-changing seasons and allows us to share her symbolism and deep spiritual relationship with all beings. She shows us the meaning of life through her watching, waiting, allowing and opening into transformation and non-resistance. She does not speak a word, yet she teaches like no other educator can because she teaches from the ancient wisdom of symbol and sense.

I find the same deepening of intuitive learning when watching with the dying or being with a woman giving birth. These two life situations show me how to be with beginnings and endings and still be centred in that place of gentle natural symbolism that transcends words and movement. It is like a dance that dances itself in the cells of the body; cells that communicate without any sounds other than the sound, the natural sound of life coming and life leaving this form to join in another dance of formlessness. Soul shows herself in both situations and we have to be very conscious of the subtle changes and nuances that move and open into the internal landscapes of both mother and child, dying person and the one watching with them. These life occurrences demand an awareness that transcends all language of the head. The reasonable mind has to bow to a deeper, older knowledge that tries to instruct us. Then we are always available for the instruction. Soul is the instructor, the informer and is always answered by intuition, by the immediate and unquestionable inner tutor that knows the minutest timing of the changes in the dance of creation and the music of the spheres.

If I believe that everything in my world is there for my edification and instruction then I begin to see the significance of symbols, the hidden, unperceived, pure educational qualities in everything around me. I learn to discover the masked messages and teachings of which I am usually unaware. As I have already said, awareness is the key to symbolic living. Symbolic living leads to a deepening of consciousness and a widening of our souls' experiences. For example, my physical eyes are drawn to a beautiful tree. I see tree, leaves, bark etc. If I simply notice tree, leaves, bark and leave it at that I am missing an inner significance, an ocean of personal information. The tree informs me of much more than simple physical existence, no matter how beautiful it may be. We can begin to listen to what the tree says to us personally. And this is the wonder of symbolic living. The symbols are personal to the perceiver. No two people observe a tree in the same way. Each of us experiences the tree in a way that is significant to us. We bring all of our past experience of tree to our observations.

When we are aware of the many facets that tree manifests, our internal senses awaken. Many people actually say that the tree talks to them. Of course, I mean this metaphorically since a tree, by nature, does not have physical vocal cords. However, what many observe is that the tree conveys, as if in spoken form, information and instruction in a way that one might reserve for humans only. If all created and inanimate phenomena can convey information to us about our lives then naturally it would seem important to tune into this form of instruction.

C.G. Jung believed that our souls speak, so to say, in symbols. Symbols, according to his findings, are universal. Certain symbols carry within them universal meanings e.g. the circle is a sign of never ending continuity. Indigenous people often refer to the deity in symbolic representation of circles and spirals, the tip of the spiral being the highest point of ascendance. Celtic Christians also depicted divinity in forms of spirals and interwoven knots and crosses. Shape was important and the triangle denoted the triune, the three beings in one, each independent and yet co-existing in a spiralling form.

**SPIRALLING LIVES**

Because of the effect of continuous spiralling lives in timelessness, there is a part of you that is looking on, the objective sacred observer in you that we call soul or divine elemental. The soul sees that you are already healed. You are already your divine self. Looking back on this spiralling timelessness through the eyes of time, you see all that it has taken, all that it is taking and all that it will take for you this time to reach that place of divine love. It is difficult to understand from the place of time; it is difficult to grasp the mystery - such an individuation you are, such a divine spark of the reality you are, forever the true love. It is God itself, it is divine being ness, travelling through space, from timelessness, to the earth dimension, back into timelessness again, continually spiralling itself, continually moving, experiencing itself over and over again.

We are caught in time; therefore we are caught in conceptual language, caught in the language of time and space. That is the way it is, and it is to be accepted in the here and now, but it is not truth, not pure reality because pure reality, or truth, is without time. We say: "I know," but we only know from this tiny spark of individuation and believe that knowledge is something we acquire. Pure knowledge cannot be acquired - it can be accessed but not acquired because it is not without your own soul being. The cells in your body-mind hold the wisdom of ages and just as the Book of Akasia records, the book of life is within the sacred DNA of all beings. Each one of us holds within our own particular structure the knowledge we need to survive upon the earth, and when the time is right, we have access to a deeper knowing. This is part of evolution. The organism knows when to evolve to its next stage of growth, as the caterpillar knows when to emerge from the old shape and evolve into its next stage of life. Human beings mostly depend on outside data for their knowledge, when a limitless library of knowing lies within the soul structure of their own lives. We receive data from the external; we receive data from past experience. But data from without is merely partial knowing until one decides to delve into the unbelievable depths of one's own inner resources. So we wait until someone else gives us the answers or explains to us the adventure of life. We are not used to finding the information for ourselves.

It seems quite strange to say that we are growing daily into who we already are. Sacred life seed operates in all places at the same moment but there is only *now* with the soul. You say, "I am growing towards my divine self." This is true and this is not true. You are growing into the love you are and the love you have always been. That does not make sense to the linier, logical mind because we live in terms of past, present and future. But within the soul atom we are forever love and, at the same time, growing into love here and now. Future and past are synonymous with soul.

The part of you that is eternally love is inspiring your earth love into greatness, wholeness, into its own state of purity. Soon you will be able to speak in the symbolic language with which your soul speaks in you. Your soul is forever speaking symbolism, the symbolism of love. In order to understand that language, the earth-mind has to go through stages of purification, so that it can eventually find the love it has always been and always will be. It is difficult to put this into words.

What we are saying is:

> *In this moment you are ALREADY your divine self and BECOMING who you are. That's the paradoxical expression of love. At this moment you are becoming who you already are.*
>
> *Accept that!*
> *Accept who you already are and allow the becoming.*
> *Accept who you already are and allow the becoming.*

At this instant in your time frame you are not just one being, you are many beings. You are one fragment of the whole and in timelessness you are living many lives. You are living life on the earth plane and also on other galaxies. In other spaces you are other beings. Earth life is not the only existence you have at this moment. You are also in each other, part of each other, becoming the whole. You are part of collective consciousness, a part of the collective belongingness. As you have individuated you also have remained part of the collective – this is the paradox.

Do not try to understand, just hear the words and let them be part of who you are. Let the words be part of who you are and eventually the words will become beings.

*I am individual and I am also the collective.*
*I am one and I am many.*
*I am the beginning and I am the end.*
*I have no beginning.*
*I have no end.*
*I am eternally becoming.*
*I am the eternal becoming.*

*Let the love that you are reach deep into the earth so that others around and about, all beings, all kingdoms may breathe out as you breathe in.*
*They are coming into being as others are leaving.*
*This being takes form.*
*This being goes out of form.*
*As one leaves form*
*I also leave.*

*For I will forever be one in my self and one with all,*
*As I am forever one eternal,*
*Without beginning,*
*Without end.*

*I am the formless in form.*
*I become the being of my individuation.*
*I am the being of the collective.*
*I am forever being,*
*For ever.*

## WALK LIGHTLY ON THE EARTH

At this time in our spiritual evolution it would seem that those who have not done their emotional cleansing i.e. those who are still holding on to bitterness in their personalities, regrets about their lives, remorse, inappropriate guilt from childhood, those who are carrying shame and jealousy, inappropriate anger expressed as rage, those who are still expressing passive aggression and fears of all kinds will find it difficult to stay centred until they have done healing work. As we get to the end of these years, what is hidden will ask for transparency and what is not clear will ask for clarity. And of course as we are talking about a time scan; we realize that with soul there is no such quality as time or space. But since we took on the garment of time when we took on an ego- mind at birth, we have to live in time and deal with it the best we can, and yet not be ruled by it. We have to hold the idea of time and timelessness in graceful paradox.

Now is the time for gathering and now is the time for healing ourselves as well as our environment and for co-creating with nature. When we reach the point where we respond instead of re-acting from past hurts and past bitterness then we will be able to create our lives with joy and with abundance. We are always creating - even when we are not aware of it - for each thought is a creation. The time is coming for us all when we will no longer be so preoccupied with the grosser problems of our daily lives, when we will no longer be so fully immersed in density and materialism. Our bodies are becoming more lightsome - also in regards to the shapes of our bodies. They will no longer be burdens for the energy of our own hearts or for the earth to carry. As we become lighter in our thought patterns, no longer burdened by past dysfunctions, our physicality will also change. Thoughts create reality so moment-by-moment we are creating wellness or unrest, and unrest becomes dis-ease. When we truly understand that and when we clear our emotional dysfunctions, our bodies will get lighter. As we move from the denser colours of our auric systems to the lighter ones, we expand ourselves more easily into the Universe. The beautiful hues of violet, blue and turquoise are some of the colours I experienced in my N.D.E. (near death experience). No artist could ever create or recreate these colours. I understand now that these colours are produced by an individual's auric or electromagnetic field that, without the body, becomes lighter and more love-infused.

The time will come when we will be able to communicate through the medium of the aura. Communication will sound more like tones. As love creates a different vibration than hatred and fear, our communication will create a beautiful rainbow of energetic patterns. Fear fills us and others with heaviness, due to the colour and vibration of its thought patterns. In the end, when we gather together words will not be so important and moments of stillness and energy sharing will be. Stillness creates its own beautiful auric patterns and when we are still and know the beauty of inner peace and inner joy we will create these vibrations wherever we go. Start practising joy and stillness now!

> *May there be peace in the hearts of all beings.*
> *May joy radiate through the eyes of all beings.*
> *Let your words be of joy and love.*

When you meet together have times of stillness between your words, so that the soul can speak her wisdom through and in you.

## A SOUND MIND ... A SOUND BODY

As we are preparing at this time for transformations within our own beings there is a dramatic shift going on from our present state of unconscious to one of becoming more conscious. Naturally, our nervous systems and other physiological systems in the body will go through a transformation also, as nothing works in isolation. Do not be disturbed by this. If you have always been in good health and the regulatory systems of your body have always functioned well, but you are experiencing disturbances at the moment, do not be alarmed. Since you are on the journey of self-healing, everything will be stirred up inside you. Psychological and physiological change is now happening and this is natural.

Everything is preparing for and awaiting the new birth. As your thoughts change, your beliefs change also and as your beliefs change so do your actions. That is really the dynamo effect on the whole body-mind system. I recommended that you spend a great deal of time with friends and uplift your minds from the mundane to the lighter things of life.

- *Do things together to bring out joy in each other.*
- *Joy is hidden under the heaviness of your thoughts.*
- *Allow laughter and tears to express themselves without judgement.*

- *Do the natural things that are good for you, like walking and dancing.*
- *Exercise your physiological body, just as you exercise different thought patterns in your mind.*
- *Singing brings in a strong healing vibration - so sing loudly and with joy.*
- *If you cannot find sleep at night, please do so at some time during the day, or rest undisturbed for at least a half hour.*

This is important as it helps the body to resuscitate itself, especially at the moment with all that is happening. Please care for your bodies. You have not yet realised the importance of rest for your nervous systems. Your other physiological functions will be able to operate better when you take time to rest. You may also find that your temperaments are changing. The mood graph will be quite erratic for a while. You will be in a state of euphoria for a few days and then you will reach a depth of depression and inertia. Please know that this is natural. Things will begin to harmonize and then you will be in a state of inner peace where nothing can disturb you. You are heading for these times so do not worry. Know that this is totally natural. Soul transformations are causing great stirrings at the moment. Everything is being made transparent by the great transformer called life. You are either re-acting to what is coming your way to be healed or you are responding without resistance. One day your emotions are high and you feel you are reaching your goals, whatever they are; the next day you will realise nothing has changed, and you are back at the beginning. But, my friends, you are never back to the beginning. There is no beginning! Each step you have taken since you decided to in-body has contributed to this very precious moment. You have been born for this moment, not a moment in the so-called future. All your life is this moment and it is constantly in flux, in change, in movement, so you are forever changing and transforming. The difference is that now you are noticing these changes more quickly since the end of an era has come and everything is transforming together. But you will never reach your goal since there is no goal to be reached! The goal is now - here and now. The illusion of the earth-mind is: "Oh yes, I will reach my goal, even if it kills me!" The earth-mind loves setting goals. It feels important: *oh yes I have goals to reach, how amazing I am!* And when you do not reach these goals what happens? Your ego gets annoyed with you and judges your actions. Goals are about projections into the future. Supposing there is no such thing … the future is now!

Whilst there is truly no goal to be reached there is, however, a precious life to be lived, every day, every moment. The soul sets no goals for you, she asks you to live your life – here and now, to experience each moment fully without judgement of yourself or one another. You are all doing your very best - no blame and no arrogance. Spiritual arrogance is an emotion and state of being from the unhealed earth mind, or ego. All people are experiencing their own salvation in the way that is right and in the right time for them. No one is higher on the path to pure love than another. Here and now is the place of eternity. Here and now is the path. It does not lie in the future.

On the physiological level remember to rest your body. When you exercise the body do so not as an addict where you drive your dear body to extremes, but as one who dances each sinew and each muscle alive with the vibration of love. You are also learning moderation and that state of inner stillness that consciousness brings to the psyche.

Eat natural foods with awareness and gratitude, but do not worry if you cannot find certain foods. Drink clear liquids, free of sugar, but do not judge yourself if you need a glass of juice every so often.

Breathe deeply as often as you can and clear your lungs many times during the day, but do not set yourself a target.

Help yourself to maintain a healthy and enthusiastic physical immune system, but watch how you judge yourself when you do not keep up your routine! For those of you who are eating red meats at the moment, be aware that there are also changes in the animal kingdom. It is sometimes better to eat only what comes out of the earth, not from the flesh of the earth. This helps you to become lighter in your thought patterns. Your bodies will remain light on the earth even if they seem otherwise. Eating the flesh of animals at the moment will cause a disturbance in your digestive tract. As you are changing your old systems, please know that you affect the other beings of the earth. But if you really feel it is better for your body type to eat meat, then do so with humility and ask forgiveness from the animal and eat with joy! It is better to eat meat with joy than to fast from meat and be irritated! There will come a time when the animal kingdom will also be more refined in their psyches and therefore in their physicality. Just as dinosaurs are extinct, so there will be a time when the animals we know today will also be extinct and other beings that are lighter in their physics will walk the earth with human beings.

Grasses and herbs are in abundance to heal our bodies but we have not yet realized what abundance there is. In the times to come, there will be no need for other medicines. All that we need for our healing is there for us in the flora of the earth. We must not live with fear in our beings, as there is nothing to fear. Remember, the greatest antidote to fear is love, love, love - pure, unconditional, unemotional love. When we say "unemotional" of course we mean those emotions that are not attached to the past or conditioning. Clear love, by which I mean emotion without a dysfunctional pattern, brings joy, fulfilment and deep, deep harmony. The energy, or feelings, that come from those emotions are conscious and holy.

When the ego is so loved into the soul, fear is then transformed and we no longer live from the wounding of the past. Then we will have come out of the past and be grateful for each new day. Then we shall live in peace and in love with ourselves and with all beings.

CHAPTER 7

# Universal Heart

## EMOTIONAL VERSUS UNIVERSAL HEART

The over-emotional or re-active heart is the child's heart -the irresponsible and needy child's heart, wanting something here and now. This heart is truly appropriate to the child as it takes no heed of, nor does it have to recourse to a deeper wisdom or thought construction. The emphasis is ... *"I want it now"* and *"I need it now"*, with no thought to the consequences of the actions. This child's heart will grow in wisdom as experiences widen it into maturity. The whole idea of becoming congruent as an adult is about allowing the heart to grow within us through our experiences and feelings. And yet to depend only on feelings is also immature. When we can marry the emotions with the wisdom of the mature heart, then we are more congruent.

Let us look at some of the sayings of the over-emotional heart:

- *I want to marry that man/woman because s/he makes me feel happy.*
- *I want to help that person because s/he cannot do anything without my help.*
- *I just know I am meant to be a great singer but no one else thinks so.*
- *I need to be alone. People scare me. My heart tells me to stay alone.*
- *I have to be with people as I cannot be alone.*
- *Drinking helps me cope with problems.*
- *I want to eat now since I am so worried.*
- *Smoking helps me to stay calm, so I smoke a lot.*

- *I need a man/woman since I cannot live without sex.*
- *I need a partner so I can feel good about myself.*
- *I will give all my money away since I cannot stand the hunger in the world.*
- *I love to drive really fast as it makes me feel good and I forget all my troubles.*
- *My heart says I should get what I want since I deserve it.*

One can clearly hear the pain of the immature heart. One can also imagine the consequences in the fulfilling of some of its needs and wants.

- *If I am dependant on someone or something to make me feel good, then I am listening only to the emotional child's heart.*
- *If the person or thing does not make me feel good after a while, then the emotionally charged heart will find ways to blame. He/she is to blame.*
- *It is/they are to blame. It is never because I made an immature choice.*

The universal heart has another agenda that goes as follows:

- *I would like to have so and so but I can wait.*
- *I would like to be with a loving partner since I feel it is now time.*
- *It would be good to meet a loving partner. If not, I am happy anyway.*
- *I feel angry and I have to see where my expectations have hurt me.*
- *I would like to help that person to help her/himself in this situation.*
- *I need to see why I feel so annoyed with my friend. She touches an unmet need in me.*
- *I like that person but she/he is not free. I deserve to have someone who is free to be with me.*

The universal heart is the heart that has endured the storms; it has been widened by the trials it has come through. It has been strengthened by inner security and peace. It has healed much of its past conditioning. This heart has had much compassion for itself and so can reach out and touch other hearts in need. It does not need approval or acceptance and does a so-called "good deed" not because it wants something in return, but because it is the natural thing to do. The universal heart expands to embrace the entire Universe. Its loving energy reaches out to all creation. It feels complete within itself and can easily encourage and uplift other hearts.

The over-emotional heart is more ego-centred. It becomes self-absorbed when in pain and cannot seem to separate the personal from the collective. This happens when it has not opened to its own pain. Its boundaries have not been implemented and therefore it either tends to sympathize and over-identify with others in grief or it cuts itself off from another who is in pain as a result of not having had compassion for itself. Our intentions when helping others are important. Sometimes we do not like to refuse another out of fear of being unkind. This eventually leads to resentment e.g. "After all I did for her, look what she is now saying about me!" etc. Being aware of our own needs, owning our own insecurities and working through the old messages helps us to become more conscious.

If we use another or a substance or thing to make us happy then we are not being conscious. We are simply reverting to the child's heart, the immature needy feelings of the child. Childhood needs have to be met by the first carers, the parents or substitute parents. Emotions and the expressing of them in feelings are very important in the opening of the heart and keeping it open. But clearly, if we rely solely on emotions for our decision-making we are not going to grow in consciousness or in love. We need to have the internal marriage of feelings and conscious thoughts (i.e. heart and head) if we want to have congruency in our lives and wish to communicate with clarity and love. We can then look gently at our actions and see why we actually chose to do or say something, or behave in a certain way. There is no judgement, no guilt or self-blame. We just lovingly look at ourselves and our feelings.

*May our wise hearts be open to ourselves and all beings.*
*May our wise hearts sing for the sheer joy of breathing.*
*May the child's heart in us be healed into contentment and self-love.*
*May the wise universal heart in us keep expanding its consciousness, so that we live only love.*

### FROM HEAD TO HEART

Mary of Magdala, because of her open heart and willingness to hear the deeper truths in the words of Jesus the Christ, was the only real interpreter of his words at the time. Her story, "The Inner Light," has never been heard since the fathers of the church erased it from the books of scripture in the year 323. At that time women's voices were not heard and certainly not believed. The advice of St. Paul that women should remain quiet in church and be subservient to their husbands was observed to the last letter of the word and so "The Inner Light" and other books by very intelligent women at the time of the Christ and shortly thereafter were not allowed. As stated before, the Nag Hammadi library held many of the forbidden books and many of these gospels had been written by women. Mary of Magdala said we have to hear the words of the master as codes and as symbols and that we have to listen with the ears of the heart if we want to really know what Jesus meant. If you have the mind of a child, then you will understand as a child. If you have grown up in your spiritual life you will hear another message. Therefore, depending on your own growth, you will be able to hear the messages in the symbolic words of Jesus. When we use the gift of true interpretation with soul input, it deepens the teachings within and the inner light can show us the soul meaning. This way of knowing cannot come through ordinary intellectual pursuit. No book could possibly teach inner awareness and true wisdom; this has to come through the indwelling divine teacher. This does not mean that we cannot glean information from history or old documents. Information about the spiritual journey, then, is the external input that needs to be translated by the heart into living truths so that they may be lived each day.

There are many ways of understanding. The old teachers used books of scripture and asked us to use our intellect and remember the words so that we could deliver them back as an echo to the teacher again. This was not the way Jesus taught. He asked us to go into the heart and hear the words from there. He never used books when teaching. He taught a lot through the medium of nature, he told stories that everyone could understand and spoke from the fullness of his heart, not his intellect. He had an amazingly sharp intellect that was always aware of the deeper meanings hidden in words. He enjoyed a state of being always inspired or being in Spirit. When he needed to talk with the scribes and Sadducees he used their language, the language of the Temple, the language of sacred texts and scriptures, the language of the patriarchy in which he was also well versed. Through the help of our intuition, which is imbued with inspiration, we are able to get to the roots of the metaphysical or transpersonal meaning in his words and let them dwell within us. They are not just nice words for the intellect to remember and analyse; they are full of symbols and have to do with inner wakefulness.

When Jesus said, "No one can come to the father except through me" what exactly was he saying? He was the embodiment of Spirit, the grounding of divine love on earth, and we are also the creation of divine love. So, just as Jesus was inspired and put in touch with the divine through the medium of his physicality, so it is that we are also inspired or awakened or enlightened through our physicality. Jesus had to use the language of personality and relationship so that the people could grasp what he meant in those days. He said that some will hear his words and others will not, meaning some would hear the truths hidden in the messages and some would only hear a nice story. Mary of Magdala said that only with a wise heart that has been opened by life itself, can we truly hear his words. But the intellect has to learn to submit to the inner light for interpretation, in order for that to be transformed. The beauty, the sheer wonder in the inner teachings of Jesus are lost to those who try to argue his message or try to manipulate his words with fine language that the intellect delights in. If you can walk the symbolic path, then his words can come alive in you. We need to look beyond the written word, to look with humility beyond the stories that he told and find the truth.

## HOW DO WE BREAK THE CODE?

We break the code by living in the present moment and breathing into the wisdom of his words, not by struggling with meaning. Meaning comes when we accept with joy and with openness the sense of his words. He lived fully each moment; he invites us to do the same. He felt each word and he spoke like a poet; he used language in order to take us out of our ordinary, everyday translations into the inner Universe of real meaning and real connection. He said that the reason he came to earth was to show us how to live fully each moment. He said answers do not come from theory; they come from experiencing the opening of our hearts into ourselves and each other. That is the work of our souls, to open our hearts into now. Now is love and now is joy and now is freedom. The code for understanding, then, lies in our willingness to listen with the humility of the heart and not interpret from past information.

The heart that is open knows about connection and sharing. The heart that is open is willing to learn from all around. The heart that is open also knows that everything and everyone is a teacher. The more we have experienced our precious lives in love and surrendering to Spirit, the more we become lovers of life, rather than observers. Full participation in life demands that we surrender to delight and pain, knowing that the one holds the key to the other and that one is, at the same time, synonymous with the other. Soon though, we will see that all is just experience with no judgement of good or bad, holy or sinful... all is movement, all is the dance of abundance.

If we really want to know the messages behind the words of Jesus but we do not have access to the Gnostic gospels in which his true wisdom is revealed, we just have to ask him in Spirit and in humility to teach us.

The loving relationship between Mary and Jesus must have also included sexual encounters as she was called his "Koinonos" (Greek word for true partner). The church, the patriarchy, was not happy with such teachings and announced that the Gnostic gospels were to be labelled heretical. Jesus was not allowed the human adventure of a relationship with a woman. Having women friends like Mary, Martha, Veronica and Judith etc. seemed quite harmless, but the idea of a divine being engaging in sexuality was an anathema to the Christian church. Therefore, Mary Magdalene was marginalized and, again, we are reminded that her profession was anything but spiritual. When we go inside and touch the human heart of Jesus' teachings we can begin to realize the treasure store of heart-opening and life-changing messages that are there waiting for our souls to rejoice in. Maybe in this age we can tell the stories of Jesus in a different way to our grand children, so that they can also live a New HalleluJA, free from the bondage of a religion that denies the sacredness of the body.

May we all find the treasure of the inner light when we dare to live fully.

### *The Canyons*

*If you shield the canyons from the windstorms*
*You will never see the beauty of their carvings.*
*If you shield your heart from splitting open*
*You will never see the beauty in your life.*

*If you shield your daughter from leaving the house of the*
    *father*
*And if you wrap your heart too tightly around your son,*
*If you shield your children from falling and getting up after*
*They'll never know the victories they've won.*

*If you still stay closed to love and so to being loved*
*You will never know that grief and joy are one.*
*For the heart is made for opening*
*Or the soul gets crushed inside*
*And you'll have left the earth long before you've died.*

(PHYLLIDA ANAM-AIRE, SONG FOR HER NEW CD)

## NEW BOTTLES FOR NEW WINE

When did you have to learn that by becoming less human you become more spiritual? Were you ever told the truth of humanity that deep in the cells of your human self is your Spirituality? You came to earth to live your divine-ness through your physicality, as God needs to manifest in all of creation. Becoming totally conscious of your beautiful, vulnerable humanity is the way to a deepening of your Spirituality.

"Oh! But," you say, "I am not very holy and I am not a religious person." That dear one, is a conditioned reflex. You learnt to put yourself down but that is not your natural state. The good news is that you can relearn anything you have learnt!

> *Jesus himself had to learn to become who he was, the Christ, meaning, he had to ground divine love as we too must do. He also had to grow into the Christ Energy from his humanity, from his longing, from his vulnerability, from his not-knowing, from his pain, from his heart-brokenness, from his grieving, from his jealousy, from his loneliness.*

These were the seeds that grew in him, the spiritual leader who became the greatest lover of humanity.

We are also growing in the Christ energy, or universal love. As we become more and more deeply aware of our humanity, accepting every part of ourselves, accepting our jealousies, accepting our stubbornness, accepting our knowing and our not-knowing, then we will realize that the key word is awareness - just that. Self-awareness was all that ever was expected of us as human beings. And in that awareness of our divine humanness, we project a new consciousness on the outside. But this consciousness has its seed in the inside. What I inwardly hold to be true, I project to all other beings in all worlds.

Everyone and everything holds a mirror for me to look into. Then I have to look at the ways in which I criticize others, the ways in which I speak of others when they are not present, etc. In other words, my inner states of consciousness or unconsciousness are always being projected on the outside. The compassion with which I look upon myself will find its reflection in the face of another. The beliefs I hold about myself I will also see reflected in the outer world. I bring myself wherever I go. I look around and there I am in the faces and hearts of all humanity. Of course, I also find others on whose shoulders I place parts of my own unacknowledged burdens … "I am never arrogant, but he is!"

When we can reach the state of consciousness where we can find joy and peace all around, we will live in heaven on earth. While we still see strangers everywhere i.e. "Not like me syndrome", we are living fragmented lives, lives of separation from our own selves and separation from the world around us.

To be able to see ourselves in all of creation, in the so-called good, the bad and the ugly, is to be able to see from the soul perspective, without blame and with a deepening of compassion for our human state. Only then can we say we know about unconditional love, the love that just loves because that is all it can do!

---

Since the 60s things have been changing rapidly in our worlds of consciousness. We have all come to earth at this time to be part of an even more radical change. The spiritual teacher, Jesus the Christ, never taught that the reason he came to earth was to suffer and die a very violent death for our sins. He said: "I have come, that you may have life in abundance." He came into a body to build up a state of heaven on earth. And that state is about living in joyful abundance. It is a state of absolute peace, harmony, balance, love, light and compassion. This world has to grow in us first before we can share it with others. Heaven is an internal place, the place of peace, non-separation, non-polarity, joy and unity-consciousness. Do you think you have come for anything less?

Our fathers and our mothers came to provide a place for us where we could experience what we needed to experience, so that we could fulfil our own soul purpose. Indeed, many times we have lived the hell of our incarnation: a place where we experienced pain and separation.

Our parents did not consciously know their part in our lives. Until the early 1950s Germany was a place of hell on earth for many people, and even if you were not around during the Second World War you had to live it all through your ancestral line. Even though I am not German, through the line of collective consciousness and the line of indirect ancestry I too am affected by what happened then. The effects of the atrocities that happened there lasted a long time, as the ancestral shadow line infiltrated people's individual shadows. Northern Ireland, from the late 1960s until lately, also provided a war environment for my own children coming into the world. The inherited dysfunctional energetics of war include the hereditary feelings of hatred, grief, rage, fear, helplessness, blame and guilt. I personally believe that the damaging energetics of war can last up to four generations.

Now we are all part of creating a heaven out of the hell of the past. Now we have no so-called enemies, no place or shoulders on which to lay the blame. No longer is there the hierarchy of *them* versus *us*. It has to be you and me together, and we make us. This is the energy we can hand on to our children's children.

There is no need for us to have fear of the future; the energy of the sacred is with us until the end of all ages. As I have reiterated many times in this book, we have to rename the sacred in our everyday lives. The sacred can no longer be confined to a church or religion. It is the very breath of humanity reaching out to one another in peace and blessing. It is the mother feeding her child. It is the young boy leaving home with the father's blessing. The sacred is what you name it to be, not what a church proclaims it to be. We have to give the sacred a place once more in our vocabulary, the everyday vocabulary of the ordinary people living extraordinary lives. Caroline Myss, the American spiritual teacher, talks about "Mystics without Monasteries". This is who we are, those of us who believe in the mystery of life and the divinity in all beings. For we are all the wonder of God, the vast expanse of its creation and the vulnerability of its feet in the brown soil of life.

The Pisces age is passing over, the new has not yet appeared and we are in the in-between-time, awaiting the new birth. The age of harbouring secrets, of hierarchies and institutions, of hatred and international elitist communes, of patriarchal control and manipulation, of sexism and religious abuse, of materialism at the expense of the few, of slave labour camps, of legitimized child prostitution is passing and we are not mourning this past age. We are breathing a sigh of deep relief that we are here and now, that we have come through the hell and are now together, awaiting the heaven on earth. Yes, we had to confront the past in order to integrate it. But this is the age of opening the heart into forgiveness for ourselves and all beings. If we can truly say from the heart, "I forgive myself for all I have projected to the world. I let go into love", then we will have the energy to be of help to one another. Let yourself fall into love, for love is the only healer.

> *May all beings at this moment, at this out breath, open into self-forgiveness, for there is nothing to forgive – only ignorance.*
> *May all beings grieve their losses.*
> *May all beings be gathered into love.*
> *May all beings know the timing of things.*
> *May all beings know the time is now to reach out in love.*

But do not give your hand if your own feet are unsteady. Steady your own feet first. Make sure that your spiritual immune system is as strong as your physical immune system. Then breathe the consciousness that assures *I am now, at this moment living in heaven* and see the world in which you want to live. See the people you wish to have around you. Feel the love energy flowing from one to another in healing, in beauty, in life, in all of creation. Become the one and the many, the many become the thousands who stand on the mountain looking all around at the splendour and graciousness of a magnificent earth and Universe. Hear all voices join together in total harmony and beautiful overtones singing out a New HalleluJA to sound throughout all worlds of creation, awakening all to a new life in abundance. As you keep singing with the others, you realize that after a while the sound fills the entire Universe and the sun and moon and stars join in and the skies are ablaze with song and the New HalleluJA floats on the air and becomes one voice, one tone, one chord, one vibration, one frequency full of the colours of the cosmos, and the sound is called LOVE.

I do not have to become spiritual. I did not come to the earth to become spiritual. I came to the earth to allow my humanness to become more conscious; and that consciousness heals my conditioned mind into my divinity. For everything is possible with the open heart. Nothing is possible when the heart is closed to itself.

> *May your day be filled with moments of heaven.*
> *As these moments become minutes,*
> *The minutes become the hours,*
> *The hours become lifetimes*
> *That you will leave behind*
> *For the next generations.*

## INTUITIVE AWARENESS AND SPIRITUAL GROWTH

It seems that religious rules and regulations, dogmas, commandments, orders and decrees provide us with security and a sense of belonging. Until we can listen within ourselves for answers to life's questions, this external information is important. Religion has also provided this sense of communion. It provides us with a leader who will lead us, the flock, to the green pastures that we on our own seemingly could never reach. The priest or parson, rabbi or minister takes the place of mediator between heaven and earth and we put our trust in his deeper knowledge of God and wise instructions. For some of us who prefer to be more autonomous in our relationship with the divine, this poses a problem. We would rather follow the inner self, the inner tutor, or intuition, on our soul's journey. It is surely as Scott Peck remarks "the road less travelled".

The question about morality has been asked many times. Would humans really behave morally without religious instruction? Do we need more than the natural innate universal laws of humanity to "*keep us good*"? Perhaps we have not yet reached a place of collective spiritual evolution and therefore need outer controls to regulate our behaviour.

Self-guidance and self-regulation is surely an important stage in spiritual adulthood. If we remain children in our spiritual beliefs we will not taste the deeper waters from our own rich source, but will always have to appeal to another well when we are thirsty.

Though for the immature hearts self-regulation and self-guidance often culminates in chaos and anarchy, it also helps people to take responsibility for their behaviour and helps them mature psychologically and spiritually. Many indigenous communities have self-regulation as a rule. It stipulates that when a person digresses he/she must decide what the retribution should be. They seem to believe that humanity as a whole operates from original integrity, rather than from original sinfulness and can also decide its own retribution, for the good of the collective.

Jesus the Christ was the fulfilment of the old laws of Moses; therefore there is no further need for these outdated laws. Jesus realized that the dead letters of scripture could not pour balm on the human heart that suffered repeated condemnations. He mentioned the fact that loud prayers of "Lord, Lord", without the opening of the heart were useless. True devotion, on the other hand, is to be found in service to all, arising from a willingness to love.

Jesus said, and I paraphrase,

> *I have come to bring you joyful involvement with life.*
> *But you prefer to debate and argue scriptures.*
> *You hunger for the bread of life, yet you are satisfied with the stale crumbs.*
> *Read not about joy – live it.*
> *Study not my words – live them.*
> *Learn not about rules for living with your neighbour – love him.*
> *Worry not about what to say when you pray – open your heart.*
> *Dream not about the kingdom of healing - be it.*
> *Talk not about freedom - walk it.*
> *Try not to understand love with your intellect - flesh it in your body.*

*What are the "dead letters" ravaging your devotion, your creativity, your abundance of life? What "dead letters" need to be torn out of your book of life and burnt in the fires of pure passion?*

Dead letters create lethargy or even anxiety. They cannot give life. They are not creative. They cannot inspire, but are the result of man's manipulation of man. Many rules, dogmas etc. are too structured, too rigid and too analytical. They do not and cannot allow for the flow of symbolic interpretation. Intuition dies when we indulge in uninspired scriptures. A poem I wrote some time ago suggests:

> *Words cannot kill*
> *But tear the soul*
> *Leaving us naked*
> *In the winter cold*

### ■ What is uninspired scripture?

Uninspired scripture is written dead words that cannot and do not open the heart. Many books on theology, such as the tomes of Augustus and Ignatius, to mention a few, are books reputed to be holy. But mostly they create guilt, shame and self-loathing. They also leave a sense of hopelessness with the reader. "The Internal Castle" by saint Teresa of Avilla is also a self-denigrating book wherein she sees herself as an unworthy wretch and full of sin. Theological tomes are for scholars of literature who philosophize about God. The spiritually aware do not need such useless analysing; they know God in the heart of all created phenomena.

*What scriptures and prayers touched you, made you feel alive, loved, worthy, honoured?*

Bring out the scriptures from your own heart – you are the greatest book ever written. You are the greatest mantra ever sung, and yet you are driven by the past sad conditioning of indoctrination that deprived your soul, body and Spirit of the richness of creative verse. Believe in your own inner stories, full of mystery and authenticity.

Then live the scriptures you believe in. Live the religion your soul can be creative in. Create your own blessings, your own mantras.

Create the steps of your own dance with the creator. Sing your own "Song of Songs" until your soul, ecstatic from too much joy, arrives panting at the door of grace and falls into the arms of love. This is total surrender. This is Bliss, Nirvana and Heaven.

Imagine the divine saying to you,

> *"I have written the scriptures of all wisdom; not in books, but in the very veins in your body.*
>
> *Open up to the music in all forms and find therein my teachings for your day.*
>
> *Read the scriptures in the hearts of each other.*
>
> *Close the books of intellectual understanding; tear out every reason why you are loved and grow, moment by moment, into presence.*
>
> *For that I am."*

If the scriptures do not inspire you to love deeper, stronger and more purely then shut the book and help your neighbour, sit with the dying, help the old man, play with a child, eat a wonderful meal with joy. That will be the translation of scriptures for you in that moment. Sacred books, Holy Scriptures and most devotions were man's way in the past of reaching God. But they were someone else's way, not that of the readers. If the kingdom of God is within us, then there is no need for an outer King "up there" to rule us; our guidance comes from within.

## INTUITION AND DECISION-MAKING

One of the attributes of intuition is that it is here and now. If you intuit something today and you act on it, you have the guidance for today; you have the grace for this moment. If you choose to act from intuition, it may not make sense. This is an attribute of intuition. It may also be that you make an intuitive choice today and you find tomorrow that your decision no longer applies. Was your intuition of yesterday wrong? Was it simply your unconscious leading you on? Time is irrelevant in the world of Spirit, as time belongs with form. Regarding the divine, everything takes place in the graceful breath of presence here and now. Intuition is that spontaneous dance that creates a movement for this moment and is not meant to be forever. Someone might say: They got a feeling last week that they should e.g. sell their house and move somewhere else. The buyer of the house had planned to move in, but suddenly pulled out of the deal, or perhaps the mother gets ill and this person cannot possibly move. Was their intuition wrong? The soul often tests us to see if we are willing to make a change in our lives, to go beyond fear and get out of *"habit"* living. The fact that we say: "Yes, I will do it, even though I feel fear!" is often enough. Habit is one of the greatest escape routes the earth-mind takes in order to avoid change, transformation, risk-taking and growth. Habit becomes a strong container for our energy. The old adage, "It has always been so, and it will always be so!" is our security. This is what keeps us stuck. This is what negates joy. This is what stifles creativity. This is what blocks out intuition. This is what creates addictive patterns.

> *No risk – no change.*
> *No change – no growth.*
> *No growth – no healing.*
> *No healing – stuck in past dysfunctional habits and patterns of behaviour.*

Fear needs an ally and habit is such. Old patterns that later translate into addictions get handed down through our biology to the next generation. We become creatures of habit because of fear. Fear needs an escape route and finds it in habit.

## INTUITION AND CONSCIOUS IMAGINATION

Surely all decisions we make have input from the external world. Can we know something we have never seen, heard or experienced? Can a blind man image a star? Can a deaf man imagine music? Surely some kind of subtle associative recall is always happening in the mind, every day, all day, year to year. We are forever accumulating information. We bring the so-called filtered information into our awareness. The unfiltered still remains as information not yet admitted to awareness. It lies dormant until some other time. This information may never be admitted to consciousness. But in actual fact, nothing is really new in heaven or on earth. Some years ago when I had a near death experience, I was impressed that… we cannot learn anything we don't already know.

Imagination comes from the words *to imagine, to create an image,* so to use ones imagination is to be creative. To be creative is to have the mind of the divine creator itself. Intuition is also creative; it creates, rather than controls. It guides, rather than rules. It suggests, rather than demands and yet it takes our full and total attention. When we give it our attention, instead of following the dictates of our ego's insistence on behaving from fear, then we allow grace to flow and this opens the way for spiritual, divine guidance.

## THE PINEAL GLAND AND INTUITION

The pineal gland was known by the old yogis as "the seat of wisdom." Seemingly, it is the sacred anatomical location of intuition. It is close to the cosmic antenna. The pineal gland acts like a magnet for cosmic consciousness - another word for intuition. The pineal gland, together with the thymus, which had its previous location close to the pituitary but is now in the front of the chest, are the oldest and most unappreciated of all the glands in the body. Medical science believes that the thymus gland exists only in childhood and is irrelevant thereafter. Modern medicine has a lot to learn from the ancient medical men and women. The ancients knew also that the sacred space where the Holy Spirit resided was in the pineal gland. Sensitives were said to understand the sacred in our physiology. Popes through the ages have acknowledged this seat of wisdom in the body by guarding it with a small white skullcap called "Zucchetto". Rabbis likewise wear the "Yarmulke". Other spiritual believers grow hair from the centre of the back of the head to safeguard this vulnerable site. The Bindu chakra, in Yoga philosophy, which is situated at the back of the head, actually refers to the pineal gland. Some orders of Catholic priests shave their heads in recognition of this sacred place. This is called the tonsure. The ancient teaching is that from this spot we gain access to the wisdom of Solomon, and many shamans who go into trance in order to gain information from the ancestors connect with this place, the holy of holies. Dervishes dance it awake; chanting also contributes to its awakening. Many shamans use breath or pranayama to do so. A particular ritual with the dying helped them to leave the body with ease and consciousness. This entailed extracting the light energy from the gross body and drawing it through the energy centres up into the pineal gland, or highest chakra, out through the top of the head. This was said to bring the soul into communion with her beloved Spirit.

Intuition can be known as the collective creative consciousness in our world at this time. From here we all can draw guidance and blessings for our lives. When we are in tune with this energy we are said to be in our original nature, our original divine, creative nature. In this state of spiritual consciousness, all is possible. Our choices are more conscious. Therefore, the consequences are joyful and beneficial, not only for our own lives, but the lives of all beings i.e. the collective.

As we evolve in our consciousness, we contribute to overall consciousness. The very leaves on the trees are healthier; the weather is also affected by our choices (ozone layer, how we treat Mother Nature etc.). The animal kingdom can also advance in its evolution, so that it also can contribute to the uplifting of consciousness. We will use only intuitive knowing in the years to come but we need to practice now, today with this breath. The spiritual evolution of our planet also depends on our shifting from external input for guidance, to inner listening. The more we do this, the more we become proficient, and in the end we become more soulfully aware than earth-mind driven. The work of the soul is to seduce the earth-mind, or ego. This she does through compassion for the earth-mind with its struggle for power and external information. Compassion is one emotion that also awakens the pineal gland. It creates a space of open kindness since love is the only true awakener of humanity. The times are coming when we will better understand the complexity of our humanity.

Jesus said, and I paraphrase:

> *When you enter into the holy of holies within your self, you will have ears to hear and eyes to see... all that the world cannot show you.*
>
> *And there will come an end to external knowledge – all outer information will pass away, but what will endure is that gem without price, the wisdom of love.*

Thus, all things that have been veiled so far to our limited consciousness, all that has been left awaiting consciousness shall be revealed. We will see clearly, not through a glass darkly or through veiled illusion.

## INTUITION AND INSTINCT

Like instinct, intuition is innate, but unlike instinct, intuition is not automatic. It is not a conditioned response to an outward stimulus, such as the fight or flight re-action of Pavlov's salivating dog, our instinctual re-action to flame, or our self-defensive response to real danger. A young child will instinctively re-act to loud noises from behind. Self-preservation is instinctive and we share this with all other animals. We are careful not to touch a live flame. This is innate knowing and natural. On the other hand, we respond positively to smiles and go towards flowers and lovely objects. This is innate instinct. In other words, we re-act instinctively to danger and respond positively to life-enhancing phenomena. We are repelled by ugliness and drawn to beauty. This is automatic.

As I see it, there are four aspects to intuition.

## ▪ Four Aspects of Intuition

1. *It is grace for the moment.*
2. *It draws on information from the conscious collective.*
3. *It does not always make sense. Trust is the important ingredient; to trust, no matter how ridiculous the situation or the guidance is, that all will make spiritual sense in the end.*
4. *The more we practice using it, the more it influences our whole lives. It accelerates our spiritual growth because it is from the soul.*

### INTUITION AND DISCERNMENT

How do we know that we are actually following our intuition, as opposed to our earth-minds, our egos? Intuition is soulful guidance, soulful leadership. For ages the churches have preached the love of God, but have spread only fear and guilt. We were never told that the inner voice, the God within, was a voice of pure love that never judged or condemned us. How, then, could we possibly understand that intuition is the voice of pure love and compassion? Our instruction advised that the voice of the ego was the voice of the devil and it, therefore, had to be suppressed and overpowered. This is not the language of the soul. The soul loves the ego mind and has only the deepest compassion for its fear and sense of helplessness. As inner guidance is soulful, it is, therefore, not dependant on time. It has no interest in the future, though it does effect our futures.

The decision we make today has a long-term effect on our lives. Be assured that when you make a decision based on ego awareness instead of intuitive awareness, there will always be a question of fear. I may choose to do something out of fear, or not choose to do something out of fear. Fear will be the guide. Therefore, we know that we make the decision from the head only, from the ego mind. Soul does not guide from fear, it only knows about love. How many people can attest e.g., to being led by some unknown force not to drive on a certain night, only to hear later that a terrible accident had happened on the route they would have taken? Whilst soul does not have an agenda for you other than that you experience what you have contracted to experience, it supports you to go beyond all fear and take a risk for life, for love. Soul will honour each step you take in self-honouring. Guidance that advises you to re-act and judge, to stay fearful and closed is earth-mind guidance.

The inner voice of soul is always one of compassion and love. It cannot be otherwise. Even when you believe that you have done something terrible, the voice of the soul will not condemn you, but will gently guide you back to the centre of yourself again. The earth mind condemns, forbids, is harsh and makes you feel guilty and ashamed. This does not mean that the soul does not also "discipline" us. It does so with firm, unconditional love. It knows the road we have chosen and when we decide to go back to the old ways, it's helper, collective universal love, may give us a jolt, sometimes in the form of an illness or having lots of accidents. There are no accidents and when we know that, we can listen to the information in all that happens to us and learn from the soul before we experience consequences that are not so enjoyable.

Discerning the voices of inner guidance is always important. If someone says that their inner voice told them to sell their house and move to America, it may just be an impulse of fear that speaks. They may be running from something here. On the other hand, if they were to admit that they always wanted to go, but had hesitated because of fear about leaving home and now want to go beyond their fear and explore a different life that is more than likely a call from the intuition to go deeper into life. If someone is depressed and feeling self-destructive and says that his intuition has told him to take a lot more tablets because that will help his depression, this is an inner voice but not intuition. This is a voice of self-destruction that clearly wants this person to die. This voice, then, is the accumulation of all the voices that have been guiding him. This is the voice of inner hatred, the voice of unlove. This dear person is now not in a state where he will follow any internal prompting. His mind can no longer make good decisions for him, so someone else must do so until he has gained soul control again.

Many people seem to have little discernment regarding the inner voices or guidance that they follow. Many say that angels speak to them and they have guidance for others. Jesus said, "By their fruits shall you know them." In other words, how consciously do these people live their lives? Having messages for others may be a subtle way of escaping one's own work. On the other hand, there are people like Sabrina Fox from Austria, Dianne Cooper et al. who, because they are in touch with their own healing, are also allowed to help others on their journeys by bringing angel messages. Upon hearing Sabrina Fox speak in Austria, although I did not understand the words she spoke in German, my heart was touched and my soul sang. When my friend Mark Fox (not a relation of Sabrina!) prays his prayers and sings his soul songs, the earth herself gives thanks for one who has also contracted to be a carrier of inspiration for others. These people bring us inspiration until we ourselves can reach in and find our intuition. Many speak to, and with angels, but they will not speak with, or to their neighbour. Many hear the voices of higher beings, but they do not hear the voices of their children asking for help. Many say they channel the Archangels, but they condemn those who are not so "Spiritually advanced". By their fruits you can recognize who really hears angels and who hears the voice of their own need for attention and acclaim.

People who have been diagnosed as schizophrenic also hear voices. This can happen because of psychological illness. However, the more one listens to these people, the more one cannot be sure whether the illness lies in their mental instability or in our collective misunderstanding and ignorance of the phenomena of altered states of consciousness. Perhaps these people have access to other worlds, which we cannot yet reach because of our scepticism and closed hearts. My dear friend Peter Haeckl from Bayern believes that unless we work with the soul when helping people living with Schizophrenia, we will never understand the depths of wisdom soul brings. Perhaps they also have come to advise us to listen within more than without. We can learn from all humanity, the so-called sick and so-called healthy.

## EXAMPLES OF INTUITIVE GUIDANCE

In Northern Ireland, where I lived for twenty-six years, the collective unconsciousness carried bigotry and anger, resulting in war. One found it difficult to live with such strong energy of fear. The soldiers acted on instinct – kill before you are killed - because fear creates an environment of dysfunctional caution. Very few people can access intuition in such grave situations. There are stories of great courage, however. The following is a true story of a young soldier in Berlin during the last world war.

The philosophy of war is "shoot first, think later; think first, be buried later". As he entered the upstairs room in an old house he thought he heard a sound. He had his gun ready to shoot, to kill. Later he said, "Something in me said: wait, do not shoot. It did not make sense but still I did not shoot. I went against the orders from my superior. And then, out came a young girl 8 years of age with her younger brother. They were both so scared. I brought them outside and gave them to a neighbour to care for". This was truly acting on intuitive guidance and not from fearful instinct. The young soldier risked his life. When we act from intuition we cannot rehearse a situation. We simply make a choice from soul.

## INTUITIVE RESPONSES IN
## THE CHRISTIAN SCRIPTURES

At the marriage feast at Cana, Mary the mother of Jesus said to the servant, "Whatever he tells you to do, do it!" Mary had no idea what Jesus might tell the servant to do, but she knew he would act from intuition. Jesus was led by his intuition into the desert, where he was to spend 40 days alone. He was placed in isolation, detachment, away from the crowds, alone only with his soul self. Jesus knew the timing of things, a time to be with people and a time to be alone. When Jesus asked Peter who he thought he was, and Peter answered that he was the son of the living God, Jesus said to him ... "not flesh and blood has revealed this to you." In other words, *your inner guidance revealed this to you*. When the angel Gabriel appeared to Mary announcing that she would be the mother of the Messiah, Mary answered, "how can this be, for I know not a man?" Never the less, she said, *Yes, I will conceive this child; I will do the will of God.* It seemed senseless to Mary to become a mother, as she had not had a sexual relationship with a man. However she had faith that all would be well.

When an angel awakened Joseph and said he had to flee with Jesus and Mary, this seemed ridiculous, but he did it; he left Jerusalem and went to Nazareth. This was seemingly an absurd thing to do in the middle of the night with a young baby and his mother, but Joseph obeyed his inner guidance and was proven right. It seems that angels in the Gospel stories often symbolized inner guidance and intuition.

The way Jesus taught was purely intuitive. He told stories that just came to him in the moment. We never hear of Jesus preparing a lecture or a talk. He spoke in the moment, obeying the instruction from Isaiah: "Open your mouth and I will give you words." In other words, the teachings were intuitive and spontaneous. It may be seen that intuition and inspiration come from the same source – the divine. To be in Spirit i.e. to have access to the highest energy is also to be in-tuition i.e. to be instructed from within. If we follow the call or the impressions of the higher good in small things, we will build up a strong spiritual immune system that enables intuition to flow into us and out into the collective. Practise helps to awaken our intuition. It also helps us to go beyond fear and to surrender to the beloved, to love itself.

**THE CHAKRA ENERGY SYSTEM AND INTUITION**

The lower chakras, or the earthing chakras, are important for grounding us in matter. We need to be earthed first before we ascend, so the usual deep earth sounds and colours of red, orange and yellow associated with the earth chakra energy draw us deeper into the soil of our humanness. These energy centres are activated by involvement in the world of matter e.g. working, especially on the land, community building, experiencing our sexuality and dancing are ways to ground us and open these centres. The heart has to open in order for creativity to flow; so the fourth and the fifth energy centres have to be awakened. The colours of green and turquoise, together with the associative sounds help to do this. When one has opened ones own heart and begins to reach out to others, the colour changes from green to rose pink.

The actions required to open the heart centre include honouring oneself and others, going beyond our fears, taking risks for love, having compassion for oneself and others, experiencing great joy and caring for others. These actions not only open the heart centre, but activate our creativity as well. This opens into the intuitive-inspiration sixth chakra, the third eye centre or the Pineal Gland. The etheric energy that flows from the twelfth energy centre down through the eleventh and tenth chakras, through the colours gold, white, magenta and indigo, rests in the Pineal Gland. When the black colour of transformation meets the gold of illumination, then the union of soul and Spirit has occurred. Jesus seemingly had activated all twelve chakras; this created the halo over his Bindu chakra. (This was called the Lotus Flower in Buddhism.) Jesus was fully in contact with the beloved, which is the Aramaic word for father. Jesus said:

> *I and the beloved are one.*
> *He, who knows me, knows the beloved.*
> *You cannot get to the beloved except through me.*

So Jesus was speaking symbolically about the wisdom of intuition – inspiration. I believe that although we have to go through much transformation before we are healed, we can achieve the spiritual experience of the opening of the Pineal Gland into the eighth and ninth energy centres. When this happens, the internal marriage of soul and earth-mind, or ego, will have happened. May it happen before we die.

It is not easy to imagine living fully from soul, no longer attached to the materialism and dense energy of the lower chakras. The next years will provide opportunities for those of us who are willing to go through each initiation of purification into personal and collective transformative, unconditional love - the kind of love with which Jesus loved the world. The soul will be the focus, not the material personality. Then we will be able to heal as Jesus did since we will have transcended the need for approval.

### ■ What helps to strengthen the Spiritual Immune Systems?

Spiritual music that is not in the key of "C" is a great heart opener. I also include:

1. The higher octave colours of magenta, turquoise, violet and gold.
2. Joy, much joy and laughter.
3. Good food and lots of non-alcoholic liquids.
4. Exercise and brisk walking.
5. Art, creative writing, speaking with children, connecting with trees, flowers, plants, birds, sunsets, music, singing and dancing.
6. Pottery, celebrating beauty (like my friend Vera Bohlen in Findhorn).
7. Standing under waterfalls, being near rivers, swimming.
8. Walking in mountains and forests, building fires.
9. No artificial lighting or cloth from synthetics.
10. Change the language you speak, from coarse words to a language of healing. Use of poetry, use of beauty in correspondence.
11. Gratitude for all of life, grateful to oneself and to others, grateful for life, no matter how it seems in this moment.
12. Encourage each other, and lift each other up in love.
13. See the humour of your life.
14. Everything in your world is information for you. See everything through the eyes of symbolism. See what is not readily visible to the outer eye.
15. No judgements of anyone. All are where they are here and now until, like you, they find a different way to be in the world.
16. Dying every day to what we love - loving and letting go.
17. Taking time for time.

## A SUMMARY

Intuitive knowing is our natural state as human beings. It is the state of grace. Our nature is conscious knowing. Our nature is wisdom. We had to use our instinct in order to feel secure amongst other animal creatures but as we evolved and moved up the energy centres in each incarnation, we began to also move up octaves of Spirituality, from gross life and gross instinct to emotional fields and eventually to spiritual awareness.

As we experience the end of the Piscean Age and enter into the Age of Aquarius we will reach the place of co-creative living and respond to everything intuitively, rather than emotionally. We will be ready to use our discernment instead of unconscious choice. We are the co-transformers with nature, the fruit gatherers, the soul singers, the fire igniters, and the dream catchers. We, you and I, are the Second Coming of Christ, the ones to carry the Christ energy. We are intuitive awareness. We are the collective consciousness of the Age of Divine Revelation. What Jesus Christ called the "Kingdom of Heaven" on earth is being revealed in us. It is time for "The Lion of Rage" to lie down with the "Lamb of Compassion".

> *But these states of consciousness have to be sown in the earth of our hearts first.*
> *We cannot give water out of a well out of which we will not drink ourselves.*
> *How will others know the difference between fresh water and stagnant?*
> *How will we discern the healthy from the unhealthy if we ourselves are sick?*
> *If we ourselves have lost our own sense of what is pure and true, as opposed to what is conditional and illusive, we will not be able to enter the Kingdom of Love.*
> *Now it is time to dare to sing a New HalleluJA.*

## COUNT THE WAYS

Love holds the entire Universe and your heart in its flow of divine grace. This is the movement of boundless energy, the balancing of order and chaos, of constriction and relaxation with which Universes are held together. The resultant harmony is reflected on earth in a child's smile. This forms an energetic alliance with all beings from all worlds, of which you are a part. Love holds all, contains all with what we humans call perfect presence or compassion, with unswerving attention. This magnetic impulse draws all to itself and seduces all to its divine beauty.

Your particular reflection of this love on earth is important, for although you are one of many, you are unique and your uniqueness is your will to manifest this love in your subjective and individualistic way.

> *Your greatness is about*
> *How much you have opened your heart, in spite of the fear surging through your bones.*
> *How often you were able to let go of judgement, when your ego shouted "blame, blame".*
> *How much you could still remain true to yourself whilst allowing the waters of purification, to reshape you.*
> *How much you could share with others even though you felt your input was too small.*
>
> *Your greatness is about the times you still went on through the darkness and kept a tiny spark of hope alive in you and in others.*
> *Your greatness is about the courage it takes to actually get up each day and do the same boring things with dedication and honour.*
> *Your greatness is also about being able to see beyond external reality to find the sacred that is hidden in all things.*
>
> *Count not the ways you can achieve so-called success in the world.*
> *Count not the many ways you can win over another, but count the ways you have gotten up again after you have "failed" and have gone on with what you had to do to survive for that day.*
> *Count the times you did not let external forces dictate your emotional state - the times you trusted when all others said it was useless.*
> *Count the ways in which you are willing to let go of past conditioning that condemns you and others.*

> *Feel the willingness in you not to keep on carrying the guilt of the past, or the guilt of your ancestors. They will then support you in a way that is benefiting to you both.*

Soon you will begin to understand what you value in your life, what your special gifts are and how you are willing to say yes to them and bring them into the earth.

The love I speak about is not the love of the romantic; it is the love that sees through the illusions of your daily lives. It is the love that awakens you to look at your fears, rages, jealousies, etc. and, at the same time, honour all your feelings. Love is amazing grace that helps you to see the journey to yourself not as a long upward struggle, but as a moment-by-precious-moment, step-by-stumbling-step movement towards the centre of your self at last.

> *You may be the only one in your family circle who is willing to let go of damning religious beliefs that hold you all as victims.*
> *Be the one who dares to be different, and do it with a sense of freedom.*
> *You are not willing to go on living a half-life. You are not content with half-joys. You are willing to do what it takes to go the whole journey to inner and outer love, truth and peace.*

*May you know that you can never count the ways you are loved. May you know that you are loved by LOVE itself.*

CHAPTER 8

# Beyond Freud

## A LITTLE BIT OF FREUD AND BEYOND

It may seem strange that in the year 2011 a woman should write something about Sigmund Freud that seems to be positive! I personally believe that we have much to thank Freud for, regarding his study of human psychology and, in particular, his work on the defence mechanisms of repression, sexual dysfunction and the internal states of consciousness, to name but a few. According to Freud, when we find the root cause for our mental illnesses we can live a fuller life. Freud is the father of psychoanalysis, but in today's more advanced stage of psychological enquiry, his views are possibly too reductionist, too linier. They leave little or no space for spontaneity and self-autonomy. We had to wait until years later for such inclusion. Holistic well-being needs more soulful participation than the simple cause and effect regime.

But one must not discount the studies that Freud initiated, for they are from a wisdom that was innovative at that time. His perceptions have, like all other great thinkers, contributed to a certain amount of clarity in our understanding of ourselves and our interactions with one another. Roger Wolgan, a Jungian therapist, was later to say, "We are multiple beings. We have many personalities within us." Some of these are surprisingly close to consciousness and can be awakened quite easily.

The ways by which we awaken this consciousness are important. Each age defines its own expressions of collective knowledge. Perhaps it is now time for a deeper spiritual approach to psychotherapy and psychiatry, thus co-creating a more integral psychology of the human divine being.

From a feminist point of view, Freud was, naturally, for his time, patriarchal in his studies. This was the linier way of calculating, with no room for diversity; so clinical interpretation and a structured model, rather than a journey to awakening, was the norm. At that stage in our collective evolution that was helpful.

Freud was seemingly attached to his mother and viewed this relationship as a safeguard throughout his life. I believe that psychotherapists are governed by their own subjectivity, their own personal interests and beliefs; therefore in bringing their new insights to psychology they will emphasize what is important for them. E.g., my particular study was that of death and dying because of my own story around these issues. Freud, because of the time in which he lived, when fundamentalism in Religion and Psychology was the norm, seemingly viewed our psyches as basically dark and unattractive. He saw them as originally sinful, rather than, as Matthew Fox years later called them: "Original Blessing". This unattractive, melancholic state of being as put forward by Freud held no great treasure within it, but showed us the misery and the dysfunctional states which we inherited and inhabited when we incarnated.

In Freud's "Future of Illusion" he says: "Where questions of religion are concerned, people are guilty of every possible sort of dishonesty and intellectual misdemeanour." Perhaps he believed that the moralizing Super Ego would set one on his way to righteousness at last. Freud believed that healing could come when we were brought to a functional psychology again, whereby the Super Ego acted as a kind of saviour to our victimized unconsciousness, an overseer of our fallen state, keeping us on the good and narrow path to a personal psychological paradise. To go beyond surviving and to taste the exquisiteness of life in a creative and imaginative way was not Freud's forte! We had to wait for C.G. Jung for a more evolutionary psychology that is transpersonal and self-revealing. Looking back at Freudian theories one can see the many ways we have progressed in both the theories of the psyche and in our constant evolutionary experience of soul, or consciousness. But it is interesting to look at what Freud did bring to the field of psychology and be grateful.

## FREUD AND WOMEN

Freud attracted many sad and lonely women to his therapy couch. For the younger woman he was an attentive father figure who was, it seemed, a man with an understanding of feminine dreamtime and who honoured their "free associative speech." Perhaps his interpretations of their dreams opened up channels of energy in their psyches that had long been stifled by an overly strict and overly rigid religious programming. These rich women, needing the attention of a powerful man, lay on his couch and surrendered to him their dreams and, indeed, the contents of their fine purses. I am sure many received great help just by getting his absolute, undivided attention, since Victorian husbands and fathers were rather lacking in these qualities. At the time, Freud's advanced theories regarding sexuality provided at least an interesting platform for his listeners who were steeped in Victorian tribal taboos. Therefore, the subject of sexuality was not spoken about in high society, especially with a member of the opposite sex! Freud also tried to rid his patients of the religious delusions of the time that pronounced that the function of sexual activity was for procreation only. Freud realized that much of our sexuality is repressed and, therefore, appears later on, seeking recognition in inappropriate ways.

## THE ABSORBING PSYCHE OF THE CHILD

Freud expounded that all that was repressed, since childhood comes up again for recognition in adulthood. I believe this theory is still applicable today. I would even go so far as to say that whatever has been repressed in one incarnation will come up for healing in another, no matter how many lifetimes it takes. This, I believe, is in accordance with the natural law of the Universe. Everyone and everything must reach a stage of harmony within and without, as above so below. Each time I re-act I am re-enacting something from the past that it is accompanied by an inner charge. By contrast, a response is a clear here-and-now energetic impulse. So each time I am raging at something, each time I cry inappropriately at something insignificant, each time I feel an uncomfortable charge within myself, an unsettling feeling of, say, annoyance or hurt or fear, Freud would believe I am re-acting from a repressed scene from childhood. I then suppress it later on, by using a defence mechanism, such as hitting out at the person who annoyed me, sulking, acting superior /inferior or by shutting down and not feeling anything at all.

My dear ego-self, my conditioned, socialized, religionized, institutionalized self will do all in its power to prevent me from feeling the original pain. This is the job of the ego, to cover up my past and pretend all is well, so that I can survive. It can take on the role of either blamer or victim, i.e. "it was your entire fault!" or, "it was my fault; I am wrong." The latter re-action is easy to detect in so-called "good people" who always want to appear good and caring. It is not easy for us to accept that we are co-creators of our own reality; we attract exactly what we have in front of our eyes. This information was not included in either our study of psychology or religion; we had to wait until years later for this knowledge to download. To every age is given its own interpretation of reality.

**THE OLD TIME RELIGION**

The religious knowledge I received from the nuns in the 1950s was, naturally, patriarchal in content and instruction. Freud saw religion as a force for limiting and subduing the populace. For us, however, it was more like tyranny. To suffer with and for Jesus was holy, to cry for ones sins was holy, to feel guilty was holy and to be always resigned to God's almighty power and will was holy. Dealing with sexuality was not easy for young people. I, personally, had to build up within myself a whole new theology about my divine nature to include the physical, sexual expression of who I am as woman. I had to rename the sacred in myself and in all beings. To be able to see life through the eyes of the sacred is to live in joy and inner equilibrium. This is what this new age is heralding for us all.

Naturally, theology, like psychology, has evolved through the new experiences of the collective. Collective consciousness, as spoken of by C.G. Jung, is known as *the communion of saints* in Christian language. The mystical body of Christ is another way of talking about our shared Christ energy. We are pioneering a spirituality that our children's children will know about. We are learning that by not sharing our individual spiritual journeys, by staying locked into our individual religions, we are denying ourselves and our children's children a broader, more integrative, more evolutionary spirituality. Together, we are all creating a new force in spirituality and psychology and that is a force of the fourth dimension of the wise heart - the wisdom of the heart in spirituality and the wisdom of the heart in psychology.

It is interesting, however, that the Celtic Christians believed that we co-create with each thought and with each intention. Jesus said we could also do the great things he did and do even more that he did, and we are beginning to believe this truth. Freud was right when he said that we need to be healed from the illusion of religion. Our religious beliefs need to be brought into the sacredness of full consciousness and be healed.

**THE FIRST FORCE IN PSYCHOLOGY**

The first part of the 20$^{th}$ century saw the growth of psychoanalysis and behavioural psychology. We were caught between a so-called biological reductionism of psychoanalysis and the mechanistic beliefs about humanity that re-acted to conditioned reflexes from the environment, as put forth by behaviourists like Watson, Skinner and Pavlov. In 1900 Freud's book on the interpretation of dreams was published. He also saw the possibility of hypnosis and free association as ways of reaching the unconscious. Of course, the beliefs of the people in those times made it difficult for the psychology of Freud to be greeted with applause. The mass hysteria at times of national jubilation or collective grief was also indicative of the repression of collective emotionalism that had been the norm. When given the opportunity to express either grief or joy, the collective took the chance and did so.

This was seen very clearly during the emotive speeches given by Hitler in Germany and Churchill in England. Ancient wisdom states that whatever we believe also affects the collective. Modern day wise ones, including Amit Goswami, nuclear physicist, Deepak Chopra, MD, Kenneth Arnette, PhD., and Malcolm Hollick PhD. now agree that since consciousness is everywhere, whatever happens on the internal landscape of a human being, affects the collective. We are also given many situations today in which we can join the collective in our emotional expressions. Princess Diana's death allowed us to mourn together all the losses never expressed. The wedding of Prince William and Kate Middleton gave us the chance to joyfully express our delight. So perhaps Freud would agree that all the unexpressed grief and joy of childhood get a chance to be externalized when the collective is involved and the culture allows.

If we want to understand clearly how childhood experiences affect our adulthood, we only have to read Alice Miller's book "For your Own Good" in which she offers her assessment of Hitler in the trauma of his childhood. The patriarchal psychology in vogue in Austria and Germany at the time when Hitler was a child advised parents to use the strictest discipline and demand total obedience to the will of the father. This was later translated into the will of the Fuehrer. As most of Hitler's SS men had similar upbringings, one can understand how their rage had to find an outlet later on. This does not mean that everyone who experienced abuse as a child automatically collects victims later on. Hitler, seemingly, was very insecure as a young person and was abused by his father and schoolteacher. Later on he took out this unhealed rage on others. He needed to overpower. One wonders that if he had had help dealing with his feelings of shame, inferiority, aloneness, and rage towards his father, Hitler might not have behaved in such a brutal manner. The held in screams from childhood when he was being beaten by his father and teacher were perhaps externalized during some of his raging verbal demonstrations. One has to observe his bodily behaviour in order to get a glimpse of his inner states of agitation and madness. Perhaps his repressed and later suppressed sexuality was also the cause of his relationship with his niece, who later committed suicide.

## FREUD'S TRIPLETS: THE ID, THE EGO AND THE SUPER-EGO

Freud categorized the psyche in the form of a triune. The Id represented the unconscious, the Ego, the pre-conscious and the Super-Ego, the conscious. They held three particular aspects of the psyche and, ideally, could be integrated to form a whole being. This is the dichotomy, or trichotomy, that creates the split in us all. Whilst we give attention to one aspect of the triune we must also remember that it is not isolated from the others. The integration of all aspects of our personas helps us to live more congruently.

## ▪ The Id

The Id was seen by Freud as the impulsive unconscious part of us whose only interest is in itself and its own needs. Its behaviour is motivated by the pleasure principle and has no thought for consequence or responsibility. Although we are totally unaware of such internal structures, all our behaviour is seemingly governed by it. Freud also decided that we are governed by an impulse called Thanatos, or the death principal. The Id can be seen as the child in us that has to survive, and whose life often depends on a selfish ability to take from her surroundings. Street children seemingly have learnt well these inbuilt survival techniques. I have seen them on the streets in the middle of winter, cold and unfed and yet displaying an untiring spirit that still keeps them going, amidst the sheer misery of it all. I have also worked with gypsy children who, in spite of the abuse from the community, still kept faith in life alive, a life that contained very little of the pleasure principal.

If, as Freud has suggested, the Id is the instinctual self, totally without consciousness (which I believe he interpreted as awareness or the presence of an observing self) ever looking after selfish wants and needs, including the pursuit of pleasure, with no thought about consequences or responsibility, then this is surely a natural and necessary component of our growing up and individuating. If we survive childhood and then advance to a reasonably integrated adult stage, of course this Id self will have been included in the whole making of our personality, including the so-called lower and higher selves. If, however, the adult still carries the unhealed abuse of childhood and is still behaving like a street child, taking what she needs from whomsoever she meets and emotionally pick-pocketing from the community at large, due to existentialistic fears, then, perhaps, she needs to look at the inner street child and ask some questions about unexpressed childhood emotions.

When we look with compassion and patience at this treasure house of unmet needs in us, when we open our hearts to the inner hurting self, much can be revealed. I also believe that it is here where we contact the ancestors, in that cave where their ancient wisdom is held but rarely reaches consciousness.

The reptilian brain holds such great cosmic brew for the soul. Here we can taste the "origins of the species" within us; and from the rich dark place of the serpent self we can breathe out graces to the so-called more civilized pre-conscious self. In this storehouse, this library of ancient wisdom within us we can know things through symbols and sound. It is pre-language and, therefore, sounds its way into our psyches by means of the instinctual self. We need to enter here with reverence and with a sense of awe and bow to a deeper, more ancient knowing.

Patriarchies knew only to probe and excavate the interior self. The feminine, on the other hand, honours the rooms of the cave woman in herself; she also honours the dark rooms of ancient hurts. When the time is right, when trust has been established between the unconscious and the near conscious, the adult self can care for and nourish the child within. Inner child work is not a soppy excuse for not intelligently looking at our deficiency psychology and healing it, but a sure place where much can be uncovered and recovered and healed. Inner child work enables us to witness from the child's perspective, and that is all-important. By refusing to travel to the place of hurt animal feelings and emotions we also refuse, in a way, the blessing that comes from the ancestors. Is not the animal self also our ancestor? We need the help of a wise openhearted, unafraid other to help us access the deeper realities that lie within the emotional heart of the child self. Freud would have approved of this, I am sure.

When we rationalize our pain only, we talk ourselves out of our hurt self and then the child retreats in anger and fear. We often then placate the child by offering her the latest and most expensive programme in a self-development plan. I have so many times witnessed dear people being hooked on tarot, goddess beads or angel cards to help them heal the traumas of the past. All the while, the hurt child within them cried for the nourishment of being listened to and being allowed to express its feelings. The tarot and angel cards come much later, after the child has been allowed her say. But these artefacts are often times used as a means of healing instead of a gentle support later on. Until you can express the pain, the energy stays lodged in the internal castle and reappears to haunt you. In a therapy session, working with the inner child, the young child cannot and must not be expected to express in words alone what she feels. The adult self tries to interpret from an adult perspective. Art and drama, the use of sounds etc. are all very helpful tools of expression. When the emotional pain keeps returning again and again after years of psychoanalysis, we see that intellectualizing about it does not always heal. Those deeper hurts, which are often pre-language and pre-reason, need another avenue of help. Whilst I endorse the externalizing of emotions I also believe that that is not all. The next step is being able to accept ourselves as beings of love who are capable of great insights. Then we reach the stage where we accept total responsibility for our lives and all that we have experienced and recognise the events as graces along the way to the centre of ourselves. But that comes later! I believe deeply in the timing of things. In the Christian book of Ecclesiastes it says, "There is a time for all things."

> *"A time to be born. A time to die.*
> *A time to build up. A time to pull down.*
> *A time of war. A time of peace.*
> *A time of love. A time of hate.*
> *A time to embrace. A time to refrain from embracing.*
> *A time for all things under heaven."*

## ▪ The Healing of Abuse

When I worked with victims of abuse, I always had to bear in mind that the history of abuse goes back a long way. It seems to be almost endemic in some family trees. There is never an excuse for abusing another being, animal or human. However, we have to delve into the past and see where the conditioning for the abusive behaviour was learnt and never healed. I remember the feelings of helplessness I felt while working with the abusers. I realized that the wounding went back very far and that our personal and collective ancestral lines are full of the secrets of abuse. The secrets get hidden in the personal and collective Id and I believe that as we heal from there, our ancestors also heal. At my workshops, people have said how relieving it was to be allowed to express the feelings from childhood and to be witnessed and honoured in them. Here the ancient, unglamorous, prehistoric, instinctual self can be "seen and heard" and the gifts from there can be gathered into the psyche as graces for the rest of ones life. From here power and inner authority can heal into wholeness.

## ▪ The Id and the Stories around it

The Christian church also introduced us to the mystery of the triune. In Celtic literature we also hear of the three-in-one in the older woman and man i.e. maiden-mother-crone and youth-father- Wiseman, respectively. This integration of the many selves, or many aspects of the primary self, is both history and good psychology. Our rich inner fields of awareness can support life when seen as unity consciousness, all contributing to the whole making. As I have said before, when we view only one aspect of the Trinity within ourselves, we deny ourselves the rich pastures that are held within the energetic fields of the other two.

When the Christian church considers the Id, it is seen as the original sinful self, the evil, ungodly part of a person that needs a blood sacrifice in order to be redeemed. No wonder women have felt shame and guilt for centuries, as they were the means through whom and by whom the Id came to earth. Through the female dark womb suffering came to earth and human beings fell from grace. The message was that because of woman, God was angry.

In the homeland of the Id lies also the animalistic sexual self, the self that is base and crude and needs to procreate. According to Freud, no matter what the presenting problem was, sex was the reason. Sex was seen as the deep, unconscious need in men to capture and own, to subdue and overpower. On the other hand, it was believed that the wanton female needed to be captured, to be owned, to be subdued. Some say it is too easy to blame sex for everything, as life is more then sexual problems. But Freud's reasoning was that because of the Oedipus complex in the male child (his jealousy of his father who had won the mother, and the prohibition of a sexual relationship with her) made difficulties for some adult men to have sexual contact with women. The same could be said about the female child and father. Of course, Freud was not inclined to look at his own sexual relationships with women, as he was too busy helping them deal with their husbands. Today we look upon sex as a powerful intimacy between people, as a spiritual expression of the union between matter and Spirit, male and female, yin and yang. It is that spiritual moment of out breath, where heaven and earth unite. Sex is often seen as that out-of-ego moment of orgasm when we transcend form and merge with formlessness.

In general, one may say that the dear Id has gotten very poor press regarding the human state. We are advised by church and tribe to go beyond the basic animal self and become angels on earth, bodiless creatures with only higher super selves. We have learnt well how to be accepted by church and tribe: by caring for all others whilst neglecting our selves. Freud led us to believe that our basic Id-self was at the root of all dysfunction in our lives. Whilst he had no love for religion, he agreed that we are all potentially selfish beings in search of pleasure at all costs.

I prefer to see the Id as a helpful inner being that is willing for us to take the lid off our too well behaved selves, to welcome all of our self into our hearts and see that it is grist for the mill of healing. I see it as the very rich undergrowth where the dark creatures of soil and brown stuff of healing earth reside. I see it as being full of good information for my healing. It only gets in the way of living a full life when, because of its hidden-ness, it becomes the hunchback kept in the black bag in my psychological cellar, never allowed the light of day.

The poem "Wild Geese" by that wonderful woman poet Mary Oliver, never fails to touch that alive human self in me.

When we can love what we love without shame and guilt, but with joyful consciousness, then can we begin to talk about unconditional love for ourselves and for others. If, however, we just abuse the pleasure principal and seek only its happy ways in our life, we then abandon all our internal riches to its addictive hands. We sell our souls for the forty pieces of silver and nothing outside us, in the end, satisfies our deeper hunger for the pure joy hidden in our deeper pastures. This joy is always there but gets covered over with the hurt and wounding of the past. It does not need an outer stimulus to engage it; it asks us to uncover it in our own deep inner belonging.

### ■ The Ego

Ego is the name Freud gives to the part of us that deals with the world around us. It is the interactive element of the psyche, its socializer. It acts as the middleman, so to speak, and performs the balancing act between the hedonistic Id and over-moralizing Super-Ego. Not a happy place to be…in the middle! This Ego self is, again, not approved of because it is fed by its lower neighbour, the Id. Whilst the Ego is somewhat higher than the Id, it hovers none-the-less in the preconscious. It is the means by which the mind becomes the enemy and is an intruder on the purity of pure mind. It distracts one from all that is meditative and contemplative. In Buddhism the ego mind is called the *monkey mind* because of its continuous flittering around, bringing only distraction. Christians believe that it was the means through which an innocent Saviour had to come to earth and suffer. We have only to look at the devastation that the inquisition brought in order to see the havoc that such beliefs can bring. There is such a great fear of the Ego in the minds of the patriarchy, a fear that, if left unhealed, can ruin the psyche.

My Celtic soul accepts Ego as a firm, necessary base, a strong psychological grounding out of which the soul can flourish and the sacred can be expressed. The sad damnation of Ego is seen in the smothering of creativity and the damming up of the juices of expressive imagination. In actual fact, to deny the Ego is to deny a stage of life itself, as cathexis (attaching, belonging) socializing and being part of a tribe is the work of the Ego. Saint Paul, in his letters to his students, confesses that the things he knows he aught to do, he does not, and the things he knows he should not do, he does! This, in a sense, defines what was meant by Ego, i.e. that which led me astray. This sense of guilt and shame follows us from generation to generation.

Maybe it is time to start accepting and loving the dear old Ego self and integrating it as a very real and authentic part of our whole self. But the Ego does not hold the control button! It has looked after us very well in the past, keeping us safe, whispering caution in our hearts and warning us of dangers real and imagined. Maybe we can dialogue with the Ego, thank it and assure it that we are now well grown up and know what serves us and what does not serve us, that we can take responsibility for our choices and it does not have to make them for us any more since soul will do that. Also, we can say that we may have to leave tribal values behind but that we are grateful for all that the Ego has taught us about these values. Here in the subconscious self lies great potential for our awakening. The information held in the symbolism of dance, art, song, poetry, imagination etc. can be gleaned from here. Here indeed is the red, warm home of the psyche with such potential for creativity.

## ■ The Super-Ego

The Super-Ego, then, in Freud's theory is the part that judges our actions and is the moralist that keeps the Id and the Ego in check! In German it is called "Über-Ich" the "Over-I". It is the essential, critical parent, the judge and the jury waiting to pass judgement any time our Id or Ego appears! "The Super" is a magnificent name for such a one! The patriarchy loves superlatives, but to be a true moralist, Super-Ego has to see both sides and act from love, not from a sense of superiority or a duty to shame. Super-Ego, being the moralist, always looks for perfection in all things. It reminds us of our imperfections and blames us when we do not reach the target set by her. The Super-Ego with a religious bent is horrific! Hell and damnation are forever hovering over one and "it is for your own good" has been the reason it has given as an excuse for the beating of children and judging our actions with critical analysis. Super-Ego is not happy. After all, who would have such a profession? Maybe it is also looking for acceptance through its untiring efforts to keep us good and acceptable to others.

## The Second Force in Psychology

Behaviourists believe that all one has to do is change ones overt behaviour and all would be well. They feel that inner states of consciousness are not reliable and not amenable to testing. Data from internal subjective experiences were not verifiable; so many tests were done on animals. As children learn in different ways, behaviourists show us how to present knowledge in ways that can accommodate them better. There are seemingly two different types of learning: classical conditioning, such as the example of the salivating dog that begins the digestive process of eating the meat by salivating at the sight of it, and operant conditioning, where we reward certain behaviours and punish others. The latter is often used in the treatment of anorexia, whereby if the patient takes food she is rewarded and when she reuses food, she is punished. J.B. Watson and then B.F. Skinner introduced the idea that we do not need to consider inner states when trying to change certain behaviours. Often inmates in prison are subjects for behaviourist intervention, where unsociable behaviour can be changed to acceptable behaviour. They learn that behaviour has consequences and so by changing their unacceptable interactions they no longer have to suffer.

Environment is, of course, important for our overall sense of wellness in body and mind. An environment that does not offer a small child proper stimulation inhibits its growth. Whilst the master of behaviouristic psychology might possibly be J.B. Watson, men like I. Pavlov and E. Thorndike also contributed to its social position, known as the Second Force in Psychology.

Dipping into the earlier work of behaviourists one can see the benefits and also the limits imposed by their theories. We learn how classically conditioned we are in our interactions and we also learn about how this conditioning can be manipulated, so that the human being can be used to promote another's will that is other than their own.

This was certainly true with Nazism during the Second World War. At one time, behaviourist psychology was very innovative but now that our integral evolution is happening, the old bottles can no longer hold a new wine. Changing ones unacceptable behaviour, whether it is an obsessive-compulsive one or an addiction to a substance or attitude, does not necessarily mean that the old behaviour is healed; it means that in the new scenario the behaviour is more socially acceptable and less difficult to live with, both for the client and for society. But what about the reasons, the root causes for the behaviour?

It seems to me, having worked in the field of psychotherapy for 25 years, that if we do not get to the cause of the problem, as dear Freud suggested, we will only experience temporary release. Like the "cover up" stick conceals the blemish on the skin of the young woman, behaviouristic therapy is a way of pretending that the emotional acne does not exist. The behaviour has changed, so all seems well.

I know, of course, in lots of cases it is the only viable solution to be found and it does work for many people. But to say that it is a way of healing an emotional problem from childhood is like saying that prunes are the consistent way of treating constipation.

Now-a-days, cognitive psychology gets good press as it uses our in-built, natural, internal reasoning to help us become more self-regulating in our unhealthy patterns of behaviour. This self-help encourages us to recognize the disturbing patterns so that we can apply a cognitive strategy to release them. The idea put forward by A. Adler, E. Erikson and C.G. Jung et al, that the integration of the unconscious and conscious is imperative, was refreshing. This helped us to recover some of our dislocated, fragmented personalities and gave us cause to believe that maybe our unconscious could one day become conscious and all would be well! In the seventies, when I studied psychology, we were interested to hear of the Third Force, which was more holistic in its concepts and teachings. I recognized it also as a psychology with soul. Later, having realized my Celtic roots, I saw that according to Celtic beliefs, behaviour can be deceptive, it can be about appearances and we must not judge appearances as "we do not know the landscape of the inner story."

## THE THIRD FORCE: HUMANISTIC PSYCHOLOGY

The humanistic tradition can be traced back to the beginning of psychology. William James' definition of psychology as "the science of mental life" indicates the emphasis he placed on consciousness and experience as subject matter. For James, the relevance and significance of knowledge was the primary criteria of its value - a very humanistic approach. Humanistic psychology also has fragments of psychoanalysis as several humanistic psychologists were originally psychoanalysts e.g. R.D. Laing, Fritz Perls and Robert Assagioli.

Human beings, according to Humanistic Psychology, constitute more than a mechanistic make-up that can be manipulated or trained or conditioned to act in a certain way. We are not simply a mass of repressed childhood-based dysfunction, full of darkness and inherently unconscious. Abraham Maslow, Fritz Perls, C. Rogers, Rollo May, Gordon Allport, et al suggested that the creative self, the soul self, was a very real presence within the human psyche and could be accessed through visualization, meditation, symbols etc. Rather than viewing the person as an external observer of her world (for example, an extravert or anal retentive) the focus was on subjective awareness, how one experiences the world from ones own perspective. This was known as the phenomenological approach. These psychologists also believed that we possess the power of choice, leaving us open to changing what does not serve us. Peak experiences, according to A. Maslow, were within the reach of everyone - people just had to let go and allow the pleasure principal, that forbidden fruit of Freud, to show the way. No doubt the great soulful mind of C.G. Jung influenced this new psychology greatly. For his ever-creative psyche everything on the planet seemed to be rich in information, from astrology to esotericism, from ancient wisdom to Buddhist mandalas.

It was wonderful to learn in Humanistic Psychology that the internal structures of human beings were all helpful components contributing to self-actualization and not pathways to hell. The integration of the Id, or shadow self, was considered all-important in order for people to be holy and wholesome human beings. Maslow maintained that "when basic needs are provided for, higher motives towards self-actualization can emerge." These basic needs, or meta needs, if unmet, will create a backlash in adulthood relationships. Whatever part of us we refuse to love will come back at every possible opportunity, asking for admittance. I believe that as long as we forbid the inner, wounded child an entrance to our hearts we will stay cold and isolated. There will always be a part of us wandering the inner streets alone, waiting for that morsel of love, as the song says: "any kind of love will do."

As the wounded child and the Id are synonymous in my thinking, so the free child and the Soul are also synonymous. When we accept that our Id, our inner child, can teach us what we need to know about our sadness, our grief, our guilt and our shame, then we will be able to communicate lovingly with the part of us that was deemed unworthy and unclean. Then the higher consciousness of self-actualization that was central to the Third Force will be ready to sing in us.

## ME AND MY SHADOWS

C.G. Jung certainly was inspired when he looked at symbols and soul markings. As I have said before, the inclusion of Soul widened the whole story of psychology to include mystery, symbolism, paradox, ritual, art, self-authority and shadow work. It is interesting that when Jung introduced the Soul-self, the concept brought with it the imagery of a shadow-self too - the golden and dark shadows. It is all-important that we work on these components of the psyche, call them the Id and Ego, if we are to be fully integrated as human beings. The wonderful dark shadow-self, as Jung explained, is just an accumulation of the parts of me that are not easy to approve of. For that reason we hide them away - in the Id no doubt! However, when they appear within the form of another human being we re-act to them. When we recognize our dark shadows as parts of us that are looking for love that changes the whole scenario. They are not bad or sinful or shameful, they are just survival mechanisms that got hidden because they were certainly not approved of by the tribe or church.

When I began to look at the so-called dark shadow in myself I could not believe it (Id)! I knew for a fact that my partner was very arrogant - it was plain to see! When I studied my own re-actions to him, I realized that what I had condemned in him was exactly what I had not, until that blessed moment, seen in myself! It was so much more pleasant to call him arrogant than to name it in myself. The problem with the dark shadow is that we were taught that it was evil, black and sinful. In actual fact, it had too much Id and Ego in it to be anyway acceptable to the Super-Ego. Later we learned that the shadow-self is rich beyond words in self-information and not a terrible force that is there to condemn us. It is simply that which has not been revealed yet!

Most of us choose to hide our golden shadow, since actually owning it would mean accepting the fact that we are essentially good! That would, of course, not be acceptable to any religion that has stated the opposite and teaches that only God is good and only pride could lead a person to believe she was partly golden. Honouring saints and angels is very easy since they do not have egos. The mantra, "Lord, I am not worthy!" kept us mortals in our place. Thus some of us learnt from a young age to fear dark shadows and to pray against them since they often jumped out at us when least expected in the form of temptation. The devil was always depicted as the dark shadow, the fallen dark angel who also tempted us to think we were worthy. To believe in a golden self was not acceptable. So we just lived life in the not-too-bad but not-very-good lane, the way our parents lived thinking if that was good enough for them, then it was good enough for us. That kept us safe within the tribe and safe in our own internal rationale. It also kept us small, stopped us from risking too much and prevented our reaching inwards or indeed outwards. It kept us walking the path most travelled, as we wanted to remain mostly anonymous.

Believing in our own inner golden selves releases us into the abundance of life, instead of living half lives from birth to death. The language of a New HalleluJA lifts us up where we belong, as the song says, and that means: out of the shadows of the past into the brilliance of our own enlightenment.

When C.G. Jung spoke of the golden shadow, he referred to the divine in us all. According to the Christian church, only Jesus could say, "I and the father are one." And yet, to denounce the truth of the indwelling divine in all of creation is to deny life itself. We were never told we could contribute to the spiritual and psychological evolution on our planet since that, supposidly, was the prerogative of priests, gurus and psychologists.

## THE NEW CONSCIOUSNESS OR FOURTH FORCE

A new consciousness for a new time is calling us now, calling us out of the past and into the present moment. The inner child can heal here and the dark shadows can be revealed as great teachers along the journey to the centre of our self. Our defence mechanisms can be given their honour at the side of compassion and grace from the golden shadow can whisper to us to be still and to know that we are divine beings in earthly form. The new consciousness reveals that our gender is our particular way through which and in which and by which the divine can be expressed without restraint or judgement. The Id, that ancient reptilian self that holds all wisdom from the ancestors, is the witness to all our experiences. And the dear Ego self can be so wonderfully accepted into the depth of the heart and be loved into Soul.

The time is now in which we can release all that we are into the open arms of our golden selves, our divine natures, our healed Egos. It is time for us all, men and women, to ground this divinity in our physical selves. We are all responsible for doing this with joy and integrity, with sharing and with the knowing, the sure knowing that whatever part of us is hurting, whether it is the dear Id, or Ego, one thing is for sure: every painful part needs my love, the love of my Soul self that loves without conditions and serves without seeking a reward. In the end, the Soul self, that container of all life in which we live, move and have our being, can join with Ego self and the two will become one and the one is unity consciousness, is love.

We all have a personal and collective challenge at this time in the integral evolution of the planet: to integrate the old religions and the old theories of psychology and from the ashes, giving great thanks, birth a new age, the age of the Fourth Force, and a new psychology that includes the great consciousness of Soul. Integral healing is here for us all. Quantum healing is happening. We only have to raise our own consciousness to accept it.

Our collective consciousness is spreading for everyone to embrace. All we have learnt from our ancestors and teachers has been stirred in the great Over-Soul. The critical mass has been reached. The Third Reich in Germany and Austria and in Europe is over. The instinctual self has been healed and the dimension of heart is opening wider and wider. The next generations will not have to suffer as the last ones suffered. We are free to speak of and free to remember the past, free to learn from it and to create a new HalleluJA without fear and without judgement.

May we all play our part to serve this consciousness of the Fourth Force in psychology that sees the human being as a divine manifestation of love on earth.

## AN OPEN LETTER TO MY DEAR EARTH MIND OR EGO

Dear Ego self,

It is time I wrote to you as I have much to say to you and much to thank you for and also because I believe it is only fair that you should know why I have not given you much attention in the last years. This is not a goodbye letter, dear one. Instead, it is an explanation as to why our worlds are drifting further and further apart.

You see, we have been friends for a long, long time and you have taken really good care of me. I am grateful for that as I depended on your guidance. You helped me to stay safe and without emotional expression since childhood. When the old memories came back, memories that brought me pain, you kindly erected fences around my heart so that I could not feel anything. This was so thoughtful of you, I know. Many times when I felt the hurt of rejection and abandonment, you just stepped in and reminded me that I did not need anyone, that I was just fine all alone. And this was fine for a long time, until I realized that I also needed others. But I seemed to have driven others away in my pain. You guarded me well from reaching out for help and healing by letting me know that I did not need this. "You do not need to go into the dark again and deal with all the wounds of the past." Those were your very words. Yes, dear Ego mind, you did it all for my own good, I know. And yet I felt that it was not doing me any good.

   This thought kept coming back time and time again, no matter how you tried to help me forget it. And you tried very well, dear. I indulged in too much work and too much shopping and too much chocolate. I remember the time when I thought I might go beyond my fears and say no to my mother. You reminded me that she would be annoyed and it was better to keep the peace in the family. And that I did for many years. I wonder if that was why I got so many sore throats and colds as a child and young person. I wonder why I was always in another world. I guess it was easier to abuse myself than annoy my mother. I had learnt well to disappear as a child so it was easy to become invisible as a young woman. You said it was better to look after the needs of others than my own, as I was ok and I did not have needs really, not like others. You also said that when I cared for others they really approved of me and loved me. That was great for a while. I remember feeling I had worth. You really let me see that everyone else's problems were much bigger than mine and you also let me see that it was better to keep people happy as it made things easier for all.

   When I decided to become an artist you said it was really not so important and, anyway, artists don't earn money. You were always right in those days. I guess that is why I trusted you. I was surprised then when you said I should try teaching as I would be a good teacher and it was a more secure profession. But then you set goals that were totally outside my reach. That was not easy for me as I was not as bright as the others in the group. I seemed to be always preoccupied with the past or future. You said it was better to look to the future and worry about my exams instead of being occupied with the mess my life was. I remember well the goals you set for me. I must do so and so before I am 30 and have achieved so and so by 40, etc. I lived for some years in deep fear of not reaching those goals. But you said everyone else was in the same boat and it was normal to have such stress. You said stress meant that I was getting somewhere. But I also remember thinking I was stuck, really stuck. I had no free time, always doing something, anything to distract myself from the pain that was mounting in my heart. I tried relationships but they were disastrous, as I could not open my heart. You said it was dangerous, as I would get hurt, and advised me to stay distant. You also said that men were not to be trusted. My dear, you were relentless in your advice and I guess you really meant well.

The day I decided to go for therapy was a terrible day for me. You had said only the weak do such things and that I was not weak, I was strong and self-sufficient and did not need such self-indulgence. When I started to work on my childhood you were raging with me. How dare you, you said, how dare you think you are special when you are not. "Everyone had an unhappy childhood. That is just the way it was", you told me. You also said that it was much better to forget it all and live for the future, that the past is over and done and it does no good at all to rake it up. You said that therapy just made me disturbed; more disturbed than before, and why should anyone with any sense pay good money just to feel so bad. "It just does not make any sense," you scolded. Then I really felt stupid and did not go for a while, just to please you. Well, I saw then that you were not right with your assumptions and I went back to therapy again, shaking in my shoes. I am so glad now that I for once defied you, dear, and did what I felt was right. I really had a lot more courage than you gave me credit for.

When I used to cry at night you told me I was now becoming childish and soft. When I was angry and my therapist allowed me to let the anger out, you said it was very dangerous, that I could go mad, and also I could alienate others by my doing therapy. Remember the day you told me I was getting to be a problem with some of my friends? You said they hated me, as I was changing too much. They could no longer rely on me for help at all times and I was starting to become selfish too. That was hard for me to hear and yet something in me kept going, some small voice kept saying, "Go on, the truth will set you free." And it has.

Dear Ego, there is so much more I want to say but I do not really need to say it. I want to be clear with you and our relationship. I want you to see that although I am really grateful for all I have learnt from you, I am beginning to see that if we continued our faded relationship, you would want to take over. It is too late for that now. You see, dear, there is someone else in my life now who guides me and cares for me, one who really knows what is good for me, even though at times I feel like running back to you again. You both know me well. This other being is my soul and we have really got a good thing going. It does not ask me to forget the past, but to honour it and integrate it. It actually loves you too, believe it or not. It does not tell me that I am selfish, but that I am self-loving, which is important if I am to really love others. It reminds me that this present moment is all I have. You will not be happy when I tell you the real truth, dear Ego, and that is that I have surrendered to this relationship fully. We create beauty together, I sing and it loves it, I dance and it encourages my steps, I cry and it does not try to stop me. I am angry and it allows me to feel it without judging me. You see, this other relationship really serves me and others. You, my dear friend, are full of illusions but I do not cast you out because I honour each experience whether painful or full of joy.

So, dear Ego, I will now finish this letter by telling you that there is also a place for you in my heart. You can come here and be warmed at the fire of my love. You are not abandoned at all. In this opened heart of mine there is place for you and all other so-called dark shadowed beings. You are allowed to be who you are in my heart, but you should know that you will never have first place again. This is sad for you and yet maybe you are also glad that your work is nearly over. All you have to do now is to make sure that I live a natural life with my wonderful natural feelings and with enough input from you to ensure that I remain on the earth as long as my contract lasts. You see, dear one, in a short time you will be fully integrated into this soul self and the two of you will be able to dance as one, to sing as one and to enjoy the total freedom of full unity... at last.

With gratitude and love for you, dear old friend,
Phyllida

CHAPTER 9

# Beyond The Fear of The Feminine

## PATRIARCHAL RELIGION AND ITS FEAR OF THE FEMININE

In the Axial age, feminine intelligence was also deemed inferior to that of the male. In her acclaimed book, "Buddhism After the Patriarchy" (State University of N.Y. Press, 1993) Buddhist scholar Rita Gross wrote, "Many of the barriers to women's development and recognition as Dharma teachers remain firmly entrenched." We also read in her paper, "Are We Equal Yet?"(Buddhadarma practitioners quarterly 12 August 2010), "Men dominate at the high ranks while women do most of the teaching at the lower ranks." She asks why Buddha seemingly concurred with the male dominance of his culture and she adds, "but there is little question that he did." It would seem that even today many women have to "sell their souls" i.e. lose something of their creative selves, in order to compete with males, even though they are as advanced intellectually and have the same competence. In the Catholic Church today women are not allowed ordination and they are still considered inferior to men, both intellectually and spiritually.

For centuries the fear of women has been very present in the patriarchy of the institutionalized churches. For example, in the 4th century Saint John Chrysostom decided that "among all savage beasts, none is found as harmful as woman!" Then in the 4th century Augustine met with his bishops to decide if women actually had souls. Tertullian of Carthage, 160-220 AD, the great founder of Western Theology, acclaimed: "Women are the devil's door. Through them Satan creeps into men's minds and hearts and works his wiles for their spiritual destruction." When Pajapati Gautama, the widow aunt of Buddha asked him for admittance to the monastery he adamantly refused even though, as the story goes, she begged him three times to change his mind. The idea of an older wise woman begging for the chance to become enlightened would be horrifying to us today. But in those days women were seen as unworthy and therefore they behaved subserviently. When the Buddha eventually allowed his aunt to enter the monastery he made very strict rules for her, in addition to the ones that applied to the monks.

However, when Buddha saw how well the nuns were keeping the rules and following his words without fail, he actually praised their virtues and decided that they could be seen as equal to monks. He also prophesied that he would not die until he had enough wise monks and nuns, lay women and men followers. Women had to really persevere in order to be included in the ways of enlightenment at that time. Many monks in the first century blamed women for their own sexual lust and this may have been one of the reasons it became an all male club. Buddhism thereafter adopted a patriarchal approach to their teachings.

In the past women and men have accepted Buddhism as a way to enlightenment, often without knowledge of the deeper commitments insinuated. With no wise women to advise them, women adopted a philosophy that, if strictly adhered to, indeed robbed them of their femininity. One such woman confided in me ... "If I had realized how the patriarchy really treats women, I would have left the monastery before now. I had to wait until I got very sick before I became aware of this." The price of so-called enlightenment included selling her soul. In other words, she had to give up her own inner intuitive knowledge as woman for a male orientated philosophy that denied her biology. Perhaps it was because of Buddha's own inner fear of the feminine that he told Ananda to be careful around women and, if possible, not to speak with them ... (Karen Armstrong "*Buddha*", 2002). Buddha left his wife and child on the night his son was born without saying goodbye to them. Perhaps his fear of attachment to his family was the reason. This was a difficult way to learn to detach. Many men upon becoming monks were asked to give up or let go of their family ties so that they could better concentrate on scriptures and be more disciplined. This is also a rule in Christian communities of monks and nuns. Seemingly, family life was and still is not conducive to enlightenment. One wonders what would have happened if women had also decided to go on their own pilgrimages and leave their husbands to care for their families!

Enlightenment according to Buddha was a state of ego-less involvement with the world, freed from all vice (what we in the West call free from sin). To be able to live in harmony with ourselves and all beings is a wonderful goal that we all seek. It is, however, how we go about it that is important for us to ponder. Surely enlightenment must include the possibility of abundance of life and joy, as well as the so-called ordinary familial joys and sorrows. A joyless awakened state is surely not a sacred one. We see many statues of Buddha smiling and laughing but this is a far cry from the Buddhist monks who sit motionless for days, seeking enlightenment. One such person told me that he sat for eight hours a day without any movement until, in the end, his back was so painful he needed help to rise up. When I said I thought this was more like self-abuse that spiritual practise he replied that it was necessary to go beyond the pain and the monkey mind had to be disciplined. Whenever there is so much bodily pain it is not a sacred practise, but it could become an addiction to self-abuse. St. Paul the Apostle, the initiator of Christianity, also talked about living in the world but not being of it and suggested that he, Paul, must decrease so that the Christ could increase. There was, however, a lack of compassion in his words; self-love and self-honouring had no place in Pauline theology.

To teach that the ego must be loved into the openness of the universal heart, where the so-called darkness and fear can be transformed into love, is at the root of feminine Spirituality. As most of Paul's lectures were addressed to men only, the language had to appeal to the male populace; therefore, the language of war and inner struggle was more acceptable. Paul stated that it would be better if women were seen and not heard and they should remain quiet in Church, believing them to be ignorant of a higher consciousness. So in reality Paul's church, which later became the Christian Church, was directed towards the male gender.

## JESUS AND WOMEN

It would seem that Jesus had no fear of women or the feminine. In actual fact, it was women who followed him on his journey to Golgotha, women who stood at the foot of the cross, women who attended him when he was taken off the cross and it was to a woman that he first appeared after his death. When Jesus spoke of enlightenment, as we call it, he referred to caring for one's self and others. He spoke of forgiving one another. Jesus was openly emotional; he grieved loudly and was in fear in the garden of olives. His sweat fell like heavy drops of blood to the ground. He was surely human like us, following the way of the heart and having the courage to love. His teachings on enlightenment seem to be best described as "the way of love." He advised not to be anxious over so many things, and reminded people how deeply they were loved. These are the words not of a strict bishop of the church, but words of a loving, compassionate being, showing us that to be enlightened is to be in love with all beings, including our so-called enemies, as well as the ones who are close to us. This is not an easy path but it is filled with the deepest love - love of self and love of one another. Jesus also reminded us that the darkness we see in another is but a reflection of the darkness in ourselves. In the gospel of Thomas, verse 26, and in Matthew, chapter 7, verse 3 we read of the great moat we see in our brother's eye whilst ignoring the big beam in our own. Learning to love ourselves is the first stage in real healing. It is strange that we do not read very much about love in Buddhist teachings. Again, it may be because of cultural differences. Yet the Christ came from the East and spoke of following the heart. Of course, we need the combination of sound philosophy and the practice of the open heart.

Each man must now open himself to the feminine heart within him and find the pearl of great price, his soul, which the patriarchy has denied him for so long. He has to return to the Anima within and be nourished by her spirit before he can open into the wider dimension of compassion and love for others. I know many wonderful men who are risking the opening of their hearts at this time. They are the men who have been touched by grief and inner conflict and have gone on the pilgrimage to the inner grail. There they have found healing for themselves and their sons. It is the father's job to go into the wilderness of his own inner jungle, engage with his instinctual self and express his rage with the support of his male friends. After that the son can be nourished by his father's wisdom, instead of having to take on the "Sins of the Father".

Now is the age for the male to feel the world from a brand new perspective, the perspective of creativity that is not unintelligent, gentleness that does not negate strength, meekness that is not weakness and grace that cannot be earned or bought.

Perhaps Jesus was the first spiritual teacher who recognized the value of the feminine and who used a language that answered the inner feminine within his own psyche. Perhaps Buddha was the forerunner of the Christ. May they both find true relevance in the lives of people who have a devotion to their ways, and may that serve their souls.

## THE AGE OF AWAKENING

One age must give way to another naturally, and the age of reason and mind is now giving way to the wise heart of compassionate love. The New HalleluJA of male and female balance and harmony is here. We are moving up the spiral of energies within ourselves and in the planet. All is quickening within and without. I tell my students in Germany that we have healed the Third Reich of instinctual re-actional patterns to include the abuse of power and patriarchal control and we are now entering into the domain of the heart: the fourth dimension.

If we stay stuck in past beliefs and past tribal illusions we abandon ourselves and remain in isolation and fear, forever spinning on the wheel of the polarization of shadow and light, forever caught up in the illusion that all is suffering, all is Calvary, without the glorious resurrection of enlightenment. This awakening is happening. Self-actualization is at last not just a dream; we have reached the critical mass and are beginning to feel the urgency of our new birthing into a brand new world - the world that John Lennon spoke of, where there are no more religions, no more hunger, no more possessions, no more war or rumours of war. A time is coming soon when we will all be able to build a Brand New World from the pieces of broken hearts that have dared to open and widen into the world and be helpmates for the ones who are still caught up in the old institutions, still obeying and fearing the abusive God of wrath.

Whatever opens the heart into a deeper experience of love is to be welcomed. No philosophy can open the heart as much as a deep, painful grief experience or a deep, joyful ecstatic experience. Wisdom comes from intimate experiences of our oneness with all beings, while maintaining our own individual experience of love. This interconnection must be authentic and from the heart. If we connect with other beings from the basis of rational thinking only and do not engage the heart we are, as Goethe remarked, "strangers on this dark earth." As human beings who have been given emotions to help us to deal with living on the earth, we would be foolish not to engage them.

Of course, to live only from the emotions is also foolhardy and unwise because emotions are forever in flux and cannot be trusted as the real and true barometers of our inner states. To delve deeper and deeper into our own inner worlds of the divine, we must engage the wise heart, as the contemporary meditation Buddhist teacher Jack Kornfield's book, "A Path with Heart," suggests. I believe that the heart has only the tenderest love for the ego. It is the melting pot where all is accepted in love. It discerns what is true and what is not, what needs to be let go of and what needs to be nourished. The immature heart is the unhealed inner child that has irrational outbursts. Clinging to materialism, family or belief system seems to bring only suffering and pain. The love with which Jesus loved had nothing to do with the personality; it transcended the earth mind. Healing happens when we are not attached or anchored to outcomes.

When we connect to the intention to release pain in another being with inner joy and love, grace flows in and healing happens. To say that one must have no attachment to form at all is also an aspect of ego involvement, a judgement, a rule. It is again polarization. So the idea of "not this, not that" became the language with which Buddha later spoke his truths. This was also the way of Celtic Christianity before the language of judgement and dualistic thinking took over.

May we all benefit from the past and have the courage to combine the philosophy of non- grasping with letting love in, so that we may heal.

## RELIGION, ENLIGHTENMENT AND THE FEMININE

The state of enlightenment, referred to mostly in Buddhist sacred texts as Nirvana, teaches about an awakened place of pure consciousness, unadulterated by the ego. Buddha sought a way of being in form whilst experiencing formlessness - as Christians would say, being in the world yet not belonging to it. Though Buddha himself tried many ways towards this end, he finally realized that the middle way served humanity best. He saw that extreme asceticism was just as ego centric as was self-indulgence. Buddha was not opposed to the idea that the release of the mind could be achieved through joyful experiences, because when one is full of joy, the ego no longer controls the thoughts. Whilst the idea of *no mind* might seem quite radical and for many may be seen as a denial of our physicality, it does, however, appeal to the masculine mind-set with its emphasis on the mind. To a Celtic woman, whose belief it is that the body is the sacred landscape through which and by which we reach our awakened state, this belief would be rather alien. Still, I can easily connect with the core of Buddhist teachings when I somehow transcend language and find a meeting place at the centre of the heart, the only place to meet.

Buddha believed that the way out of suffering in this world was to recognize it as belief in the unreal. When one detached from the world of Mara and Samsara, or greed and clinging, and practised the many exercises he devised, one did not have to suffer.

When read along side one another, the eightfold path of Buddha and the eight blessings of Jesus would seem to support each other. Buddha advised on having a

- *right view (perhaps it also means to have a clear perspective, to see what is not obvious)*
- *right intention (intention is the first step of manifestation)*
- *right speech (our language, when conscious, is prayer)*
- *right action (by their fruits can we know someone, not by words alone)*
- *right livelihood (to love what we do and bring consciousness to what we do)*
- *right effort (when we drive ourselves we are not honouring our bodies and minds, so moderation in all things is important)*
- *right mindfulness (again the word consciousness, letting the mind be focused)*
- *right concentration (concentration can also be self-absorbing when only the ego is involved).*

By practising the above (minus my own interpretations!) Buddha maintained one could escape the wheel of life. The above entries might seem rather primitive, yet they are not easy to live out each day with consciousness. Nor is it easy to follow the blessings of Jesus, which are as follows,

- *"Blessed are the poor in Spirit" (when translated in the heart this might mean, blessed are the ones who live from the heart and not from concepts in the mind).*
- *"Blessed are the gentle" (we need gentleness with ourselves and others).*
- *"Blessed are the mourners" (grief opens the heart and widens us into the world of vulnerability).*
- *"Blessed are those who hunger for justice" (it is a human attribute to want balance and harmony).*

- *"Blessed are the merciful" (to have mercy is to see myself in all beings).*
- *"Blessed are the clean hearts" (those who see clearly from a place of unconditional love).*
- *"Blessed are the peacemakers" (creating peace in our own hearts is the beginning of world peace).*
- *"Blessed are the persecuted ones" (to have integrity and courage in the face of all adversity).*

All these teachings are about becoming more conscious. In their time these teachings of Buddha and Jesus were very radical since the consciousness of the people was not so evolved. "An eye for an eye" was more acceptable than "turn the other cheek". Buddha also recommended that by joining a community of like-minded people and meditating together, one can live a life with less grasping and so remain unattached to the world of form. Jesus was a wonderful example of one who was unattached to the world of form. "He had no place to lay his head" (Matthew 8.20). A lot of his time was spent on the beach or out in the boat with his own Spirit. But the idea of Sangha, or community, was also important to Jesus. His words, "Where two or more are gathered together, my Spirit is also there," suggests that there is a loving, powerful energy in the collective. To be able to be alone and also to be part of a bigger reality is to be able to hold the energy of paradox: I am alone and I am not lonely. I am one of the whole.

Women live very happily in the world of paradox, since they naturally adapt the sense of *I am this* and *I am that* without attachment to either *this* or *that*. Every month, beginning with puberty, women have encountered death and bloodshed in the form of releasing the egg that holds the potential of life. So whilst fully in life women also learn at an early age that birthing the woman within can be a painful experience, can seem like death. It was said of Brigit the Celtic Goddess that she embodied all life and creativity to include the antithesis of life i.e. death and destruction.

A poem I wrote some years ago in honour of Brigit was actually meant for me after I realized I had had a miscarriage. It is about life and death belonging together in life.

> *I am*
> *The water of the seas*
> *That welcomes*
> *Your skin*
> *I am*
> *The same water*
> *That devoured*
> *Your son*
> *Hardly formed in your womb*

Whilst the Eightfold Path and the Eight Blessings are for all people in general, I believe that women walk these paths more easily than men. It is inherent in woman to nurture, to have feelings, to let go, to be peacemakers, to live with fewer concepts than men, to look after the poor and needy. It is interesting that both Buddha and Jesus attracted many men around them, according to the local culture; the men followed the master whilst the women looked after the children. Therefore, one might conclude that the men really needed to hear the messages. Perhaps the women had already internalized them.

Buddha decided that the whole of life represented only suffering: all is "Dukka" and all form leads to suffering. This belief is not a happy state of consciousness. According to his view at that time, all attachment to form led to suffering. I want to emphasize the importance of: "at that time". True, we all have problems with living the fullness of our lives, but I like to think that humanity has evolved dramatically since Buddha's time in all areas of existence. It is true, the problems of being human have not disappeared but the stuff of life surely is to accept what is here and now, without the endless insistence on clearing the mind and that all is suffering. When I looked into the eyes of my day-old grandson my first thought was not that he will have to suffer because he is incarnated but, wow! What an almighty being! I felt such a sense of the beauty and wonder of Soul in form at that moment and how this thought brought me closer to truth and joy and hope and heart. I was filled with awe at the pure passion for life in this tiny powerful form. Those thoughts kept me aware of what was in the present and I had no thoughts of the suffering his life may hold. Can we in truth use age-old methods of transformation while dealing with our evolving organic psyches? No matter how powerful and effective the methods for the release from suffering were 2500 years ago, they cannot fit an on-going, ever-changing evolutionary planet.

Celtic Spirituality translates suffering as our way of deepening into life by means of organic transformations. We can accept the changes and be reborn or resist and stay stuck. Just as nature welcomes each season with a sense that the time for change and renewal has come, so can we learn to do the same by releasing the old with honour and gratitude. Jesus saw suffering as a result of unconscious actions i.e., "Father forgive them for they know not what they do" (St. Luke's gospel, Ch. 23 V. 34). He also taught the universality, the impersonal aspect of love which, when achieved, ends our suffering. Jesus once asked the question: "Who is my mother, who are my brothers?" (Matthew, chapter 12, verses 46-50.) Believing in collective consciousness and the oneness of all beings, here also is the theme of detachment. Celtic consciousness also states that suffering or, to use the Gaelic word *bronach,* comes in the form of judging the appearance of things. When I judge myself or others I am seeing only the personality. Jesus advises us not to judge the outer appearances of things. For instance, he reminded us that many people pray out loud "Lord, Lord" but their hearts are not engaged. (Matthew Ch. 15, Verse 8) In other words, we need to open the heart. This is a true devotional practice. The words "love yourself" seem very simple, on first reflection. But we have to open our hearts to ourselves, otherwise they are just sentimental words.

I believe that in this age we need a new translation of ancient teachings, a more subtle approach to the old truths, translated into a language that the heart can hear and the soul can live. We have to allow for an ever-changing consciousness in an expanded and ever-transforming universe. We have to learn the language of symbols, the language of Soul. This idea of liberation from suffering through an ego-less Nirvana existence must be seen as a philosophy geared mostly to a male oriented philosophy. If we still display the crucifix as a symbol of love and compassion we remain attached to the ideology of suffering. The fully enlightened Jesus was the Christ who died and rose again, just as we all do when we die to the outer form, the appearances of things. We have to let go of the so-called images of love, of life, of God, of ourselves that we have created i.e. the illusions, and conditions created by culture, religion and the institutionalized ego. When we treat the scriptures symbolically and not literally then we go beyond "seeing with the physical eye and hearing with the physical ear," as Jesus advised. But currently the insistence is still on the word, the logos, the intelligence, the literal, the patriarchal approach. The emphasis is still on understanding from the intellect rather than experiencing in the heart.

Celtic consciousness, which appeared on the earth around the same time as Buddhism, has something in common with Buddhist teachings. Sometimes only language separates meaning. Whilst Buddhist language insists on male orientation in argument and style, Celtic Christian language is one of the heart and engages more with soul and soil. Thus it appeals more to women, or the feminine soul in man. For this reason, Celtic Christians saw suffering as the unhappy result of having made decisions from a place of unconsciousness. When we do not have the whole story, we make premature decisions. Words that came to me some years ago when I was having a lot of grief over a relationship speak of this:

> *I will not judge the appearance of this loss*
> *Because I do not know its story*
> *But I will heal no matter what the cost*
> *Surrendering yesterday's glory.*
> *My heart now widens to my soul*
> *And sweet compassion gently holds me.*
>
> (CD "TOUCHED", PHYLLIDA ANAM-AIRE, 2005)

As I said before, according to the Celtic belief, suffering opens the heart and purifies the mind, so it is seen as a catalyst. The problem, though, is that many people view suffering as a way of life. I have often heard Catholics say, "God sent me this suffering as a cross to bear." That is a very violent theology to have to live. It amounts to the same as, "God sent his son to suffer, so if you are loved by God, you will suffer." Perhaps it is time to be released from this old HalleluJA that insists that *all is suffering* and introduce the mantra, *all is grace*. Everything I experience is information for me about my precious sacred life and how I choose to live it today.

Physical pain does not necessarily lead to suffering, according to Celtic belief, as one can ease such discomfort with methods of shape shifting and breath control. The suffering of the mind is a whole different story, as it also interferes with the equilibrium of the physical being, leaving the subtle energies weak. If we continuously make decisions based on past conditioning that, as we know, keeps repeating the same old results, we will suffer both mentally and physically. Consciousness is about coming out of the past and being with what is now in this breath.

According to the Celtic beliefs, Soul experiences herself through the medium of the personality and in all created phenomena. There are no judgements of these experiences; they are not deemed good or bad, just experiences. (You will read this sentence many times in this book!) Naturally, as we evolve as human beings on the earth our consciousness will also change.

Whilst Buddha viewed old age as a time of painful existence, a time of dependence on others for our temporal welfare, Celtic Christians viewed old age as a natural phenomenon, a natural unfolding of life. It held no fear for them. Naturally, the children cared for the old as the old had cared for them earlier. Old age was a result of being in the earth, which was a great grace and privilege. Death itself was honoured and, indeed, welcomed at the end of a well lived life. A prayer to death from my Celtic heart suggests this friendship with death, the one who unites Soul and Spirit at last.

> *Come dancer of life*
> *You who would dance us together*
> *Me and my beloved*
> *Now whisper my name, softly*
> *And I will breathe into you at last.*

This dancer of life, Soul, keeps on dancing, both within and without the physical form. Life as seen by our Celtic foremothers was regarded as independent of form and the formless contained all life. So they bowed low to the might of the sun, the sustainer of life itself, and called on Moon Mother to bring clarity and a sense of belonging. This magnificence called life, or "Beatha" (Gaelic word) was neutral and without an agenda as such. One did not look for so-called solutions to life, as life itself, a continuous flow of ever transforming consciousness, was not a problem. Clearly, societal tribal conditioning brings the problems. Our individual personalities, our tightly held traditions with their prejudices and judgements bring the agendas to life. Like the artist colours the canvas with her own colours, so we also colour our lives with our own individual and collective experiences. When we finally awaken to the love we are, when we live only love, we will live the consciousness Buddha called enlightenment.

As I have already stated, religious systems or ideologies that served us 2.500 years ago cannot do so now, as they were stages in our spiritual development, albeit, very important ones. A workable spirituality for this age has to include our evolution in psychology, technology, science, politics, community, medicine, industry and a deeper appreciation of all things related to Gaia. A more honest appraisal of institutionalized religion and its usefulness in this new age of personal and collective maturity is relevant at this time. Ken Wilber, a contemporary American scientist and psycho-spiritual guide, maintains that we need "Integral Spirituality" if we are to experience enlightenment (see Integral Spirituality 2006, Integral books, Boston).

## INTEGRAL SPIRITUALITY OR FRAGMENTED PATRIARCHAL BELIEFS?

Integral Spirituality must also include the feminine because teachings from patriarchal elitism and hierarchy do not serve the feminine, the soul, in either female or male consciousness. Theories and dogmas can only instruct. As I see it, it is also time for Buddhism to honour women teachers and include the language of the feminine so that the heart can be opened. Pema Chodron, a very wonderful Buddhist nun has written many books on the subject e.g. "Awakening Loving kindness". It has become more and more important for female Buddhist teachers to teach from the heart. Green or white Tara or Quan Yin, whilst very beautiful and effective as Buddhist deities, are still not flesh and blood. Their images will forever hang on a wall or remain as lifeless statues on the altar. Stone images of female catholic saints and martyrs, all of them virgins, cannot touch the hearts of contemporary women who now need a human voice to language for them a way to personal and collective freedom. We need our stories to be embodied in flesh and blood.

My friend Suzanne Dance from Edinburgh Scotland is a theatre actress and a practicing Buddhist. She accepted my invitation to come to Germany and dance for us the aspects of Tara, the Buddhist Goddess. Suzanne brought Tara from the statue of stone into a woman's flesh and bones and warmed her at the passion of her own inner fire. As Suzanne danced, we could feel Tara enter into our own bodies, naming again our female bodies, sacred and powerful. Now Suzanne is preparing to dance Magdalene for us. This is the kind of teaching and pure inspiration that reaches the soul of the feminine in a way that dull doctrines and scriptures cannot. This is soul in action, soul in form. Thank you, Suzanne, for your great courage, beauty and willingness to bring the feminine form of Buddha, of a Christ, alive in and for us.

As I see it, meditation has its limits regarding the healing of our psyches, as integration of the shadow has to be included if one is to reach "self actualization" (as Abraham Maslow called it in the ‚80s). The feminine energy welcomes this integration as a prerequisite to self-actualization or enlightenment and she insists that the integration of one's shadow-self is absolutely necessary, if we are to heal psycho-spiritually. In other words, we need to be able to be at peace in our own darkness if we are to know enlightenment. Women are quite content with the dark side of the moon within themselves and in the world for they know that the insistence on the external-internal dichotomy is the greatest duality. Indeed, women know that they have internalized the patriarchy so much so that they identify with it quite easily. Now we are disengaging from our own re-actions to the outer patriarchy and now we are doing it without judging men. The sacred marriage of male and female energies is imminent and we are all part of the marriage. In her book "Unplugging the Patriarchy" Lucia Rene concluded: "There has never been anything outside of you, nothing at all."

I believe, as my book Celtic Book of Dying suggests, that we are coming away from systems of instruction, such as institutionalized religion, and are creating a more soul-infused way of looking at Spirituality. We are moving away from reading books about freedom and self-acceptance to actually experiencing these realities in our daily lives. The idea now is to live what we have read about since the sixties, integrate it all and with courage step into the brand new world of the awakened. Love consciousness, or universal love, which, according to contemporary female spiritual teachers such as Joanna Macy and Joan Halifax, constitutes a very powerful experiential healing energy on the earth. This energy initiates a sense of interconnectedness with all creation, a sense of unity-consciousness. In other words, we are seeing that pure spirituality, or spiritual essence, the energy that constitutes consciousness is a vast, open, all-enveloping energy and is limitless, timeless and spaceless. It calls us all individually to experience its power and clarity.

At this time that is so filled with grace, we are also delving into the great awareness that consciousness transcends the death of the physical. It is clearly that which keeps all things in motion in all worlds of being. I quote a Christian belief: "In it we live, move and have our being." This "IT" would seem to refer to a mighty life force, a creator of vastness and unbounded creativity in which and by which all creation has its origin.

This widened awareness of the divine opens our enquiry into a more universal experience of what this force is, so we are less likely to claim IT for a particular religion or confine IT to a particular gender, truth or dogma. As our humility deepens, we are disinclined to limit this vast intelligence to our small, yet beautiful mindsets. Perhaps it is time to rename the sacred, to reclaim the divine, to include the feminine and the soul. The great paradox of consciousness is that, whilst IT is limitless and cannot be confined to space and time, IT takes up residence within the tiniest cell of dense matter in a holographic pattern. Thus, to answer the question, "where does God live?" one must reply, "within each particle of form and in the formlessness of the world of Spirit." So we have to believe that form is a symbol of formlessness and should not be discarded as less sacred than its essence, which is pure love.

We see by our more extensive research into various religious doctrines that whilst patriarchal dogmas and theologies did not serve women, they did not serve men either. Its emphasis on control, overpowerment, harsh discipline, the killing off of the ego mind, the non-physical, whether it was in Buddhism or in the insistence of Christianity on suffering now and gaining heaven later, did not help men to progress spiritually. This emotional abuse held them in a place of obedience to the elite administrators of God on earth in the form of popes, abbots etc. The so-called pure male lineage that transmits teachings to the Christian church via the pope is said to come direct from Peter. It is clear from the last decree from the Vatican that Peter did not like women very well!

Psychologically, individuation is an important stage in letting go of childhood and stepping into adulthood. The Christian beliefs concerning the child/father relationship would seem to keep one back from this natural progression. Disobedience and rebelliousness are natural expressions of such individuation where the child can also test the relationship and see if the love of the parents can stand it. The Christian church does not allow for such grown-up spirituality. God, the father up in heaven, provides us with a sense of irresponsibility: I am only a child, I do not know the facts, therefore I do not have inner authority. Though the rules are less stringent these days, in the past and up until the sixties in monasteries and convents the total adherence to the letters of the dogmas and encyclicals, no matter how stringent and how harsh, had to be maintained. There was no space allowed for self-expression, intuition or self-love.

Enlightenment for monks and nuns in many traditions meant a life of self-sacrifice to a God, or a philosophy that demanded total and radical surrender of the will to the Father Superior or Mother Superior. I am saddened to know that such superlatives still exist in convents today. I imagine if there is a Mother Superior then there must be inferior nuns! If there exists a head nun surely there must also be a heart nun!! This idea of hierarchy has been the cause of much terrorization in Christianity since the inquisition and even before. It is strange that no one questioned the results of the demonizing of the ego in all patriarchal religions and ideologies. This practice paralyzed the heart, suppressed and subdued the living waters of imagination and creativity in women and men alike. How different this is to our Celtic beliefs that:

- *The human being is the beauty of the divine on earth.*
- *Humanity is the answer to creation's longing to experience herself in fullness and joy.*
- *The creative force in the world is an expression of loving compassion.*
- *The soul, the feminine expression of the Great Spirit, loves us into union when we leave the earth.*
- *The earth herself is holy and is an expression of the sacred, an example of how we can live and die according to the rhythms of nature.*
- *We are not sinners and never have been, but we are a continuous source of blessing to one another.*

These beliefs were not future dreams, but reality in Celtic Christianity. When we lost sight of the feminine energy, the counterpart to the Great Spirit, we lost sight of love, of compassion, of the rich inner wilderness landscape, of the abundance of our precious living that includes the dark and chaotic, whose depths and richness are containers for clarity and creativity.

Soul is the very antithesis of patriarchy. It moves us in a way that overpowerment and dominance never could. It moves us in the direction of inner self-authority and intuition. These amazing graces then move us in the direction of healing the past and help us to rely more on our own inner wisdom than on any authoritative voice from without. In this place of self-knowing, we as women begin to awaken to the inner voice of love. Love alone can lead us to the state of nonjudgement of ourselves. That love is then projected to all beings, excluding none -not even the so-called enemy, for there is and shall be none. We now see the patriarchy for what it was a stage in the growth of individuation that was necessary in order to understand the states of polarization in which we have lived for so long, but which only brought us duality and suffering. The feminine archetype is teaching the men and women of our time about balance and equilibrium, about heartfelt involvement in the world. Now we realize that nature is our true mentor in timing and transformations.

For us women, the dark and all its richness hold no fear; rather it is a place of amazing growth and evolution. The language of the inner patriarchy is also very different to the language of the heart, as we have already seen. Men are discovering the language of feelings rather than merely expressing their thoughts. I feel, therefore, that I am the new adage. During his talk while visiting America in 2008, the Dalai Lama said that it would be western women who will bring enlightenment to the West. And we are all ready with a New HalleluJA.

Enlightenment, as woman has always known, is about befriending the dark so that we can see more clearly, with more light and more knowledge. It is about returning to innocence, to carrying out an unconditional appraisal of our place in the family of things, as men and women of great faith in the healing of ourselves and our planet earth. Now we can really see through the veils of illusion. Although we cannot return to the Garden of Eden, we can welcome a brand new dawn in which all beings can raise their own divine voices and sing an ode to love, pure and unconditional.

Enlightenment is, then, about birthing a truer consciousness, more awareness, more balance and greater harmony. As woman is the natural birther, she is also the container. So in this Age of Aquarius the water carrier encourages self baptism so that the masculine and feminine energies can unite in creating unity consciousness. Woman and man must cooperate as mother earth is depending on our togetherness to co-create with her. Woman is saying to her male counterpart:

*Come with me; be baptized by your own Anima.*
*Open into the creativity in yourself.*
*Open into compassion in yourself.*
*Come, we know the way.*

*Our tears of longing have long since watered the earth.*
*We women have hewed and scraped and planted seeds of regeneration.*
*We have waited long enough, we have longed for your inclusion with us.*

*Our power is gentle yet strong.*
*We will not overpower nor will we want to control.*
*Neither will we use defences.*
*We are not in competition with you or with ourselves.*
*We have inner authority now.*

*We show a way of inclusion.*
*We introduce you to an age where guns will be obsolete,*
*Where the language of war will be replaced by a language of the heart.*

*Come and lead with us together.*
*Stay no longer shut out of your own heart.*
*Come now, or stay in bondage to the old age.*
*No need for confrontation; there is no war raging.*
*Come, we know the timing of things.*
*The choice is yours, dear man friend.*

## WOMEN'S WORK AND WORTH

In matriarchal times, ca. five thousand years ago, things of the hearth, family, sharing with one another, networking, helping one another, caring for children and the aged was a way of life. Although hierarchies were also part of the culture there was a sense of integration and respect for the ancestors. People knew their own places in the order of love. Stories and sagas of old were told and feelings expressed. Songs and dances were enjoyed as part of ceremony and ritual. Food and fruits were eaten as Holy Communion and fasting to the death as a form of self-punishment was not adhered to. Animals were also part of the family of things and man honoured the animal kingdom as a source of food, companionship and clothing. It was also the woman's role to teach the young about life and how to gather and create from the earth's abundance. Healing remedies from trees, herbs, grasses and plants were prepared by the women while children learnt by watching and experiencing.

Men honoured the ways of the women and their hearts were open to their female power and grace. Women were the keepers of the hearth and were also the ones who sat in a circle when a punishment had to be dealt to a member of the community. Thus was the power of women.

Something terrible happened to human beings and to nature when we exchanged living with and on the land for so-called "progressive" institutionalized living. Something green in us withered when we exchanged the riches of the brown earth for the so-called wealth of industry. Success and achievement became the goals and inner states of honour and respect for all living things were neglected. Soul was neglected, to our downfall as spiritual beings. When woman's roles were disrespected by the patriarchy, something also happened to the collective soul. Men left the heart opening business to the women and women gave their power roles over to the men. In the end, women were forced to emulate male dominance in order to find what was seen as success and power. In doing so, women forgot, as did men, that female power had nothing to do with male power. Hers is a subtler and more imaginative creative force that is all about inner authority and not about physical toughness or mental achievement. Woman-power includes intuiting the world around us, creating communities, gleaning inner wisdom from healed experiences, keeping the old creative traditions, such as weaving, story telling, and the making of all things beautiful alive.

Sadly, women exchanged their internal knowing about the timing of things, the birthing and dying of things, for ready-made, instant solutions with an emphasis on production. Financial reward, instead of internal peace and soulful connection with all beings, increasingly became the goal set for her by a so-called progressive world that did not acknowledge her worth or her wisdom.

When woman sold her creative soul for a wage packet, she displaced herself. Now many women are still trying to regain their places in their own stories, in their *"herstories."* Woman's story is an internal one, one that keeps writing itself over and over. Every woman holds a part, a chapter of the collective *Herstory* and one day when we awaken fully, our own sacred scriptures will be heard and sung throughout the planet. In 1960, feminist Betty Friedan wrote the following:

> "When every woman learns to listen without fear to the voice inside her instead of smothering it, it may lead perhaps even more surely than rockets into space to the next step in human evolution."

I am a woman who had to read silently her own internal scriptures, because of fear of ridicule from the outer patriarchy and from other women, still attached to the internal patriarchal messages. I look forward to the time when women all over the world can stand up and be heard to sing a New HalleluJA, one that honours her glory and her message of inclusivity instead of hierarchy, in all walks of life. Then the voice of the soul will sound her healing throughout the planet. Then we as women will be strong enough to really obey the inner voice and not smother it by rushing to the call of a so-called progressive society that uses men and women as machinery for the advancement of technology and multi-national corporations.

We forgot that woman's timing is not like that of the man. Her inner clock obeys the moon, which has her own particular stages and vibrations. When woman neglects her own inner rhythms, her own inner voice she dishonours her gender and exchanges her own natural timing for the clock on the wall of the office. Enlightenment for women in earlier days was seen as the so-called freedom to be an economic unit, to work outside the confines of housekeeping and children and to be allowed to plan a family by using contraception. She happily worked to pay a good child minder. Now she was at last respected in the community and known as a "good hard working woman."

This new status for women contributed greatly to the continuation of patriarchal values since usually the jobs allotted to them were greatly inferior to those of men. This is still the norm in most parts of the world. When woman can no longer create something very naturally alive she becomes depressed and like in the story of Persephone, she goes underground. Although she is physically present to her friends and family, she is invisible to herself. She loses her own sense of who she is. Slowly she chooses ill health as an alternative to numbness.

## FROM HISTORY TO OUR STORY

The patriarchal archetype i.e. a left brain, conditional, male dominated reality is the starting ground, so to speak, of our journey from the base instinctual energies of our psyches to the fully awakened state of consciousness of pure love. So I see it as a journey from an internalized archetypal patriarchy to pure love.

If the patriarchy represents the first three chakras in our energetic field of evolution, i.e. survival by using defensive mechanisms and the over-use of power and control, then love consciousness is the state of the fully awakened abiding in the 10$^{th}$ chakra. As we evolve from warring and the inappropriate use of power i.e. fear, we begin to walk the earth with more open-hearted energy for all beings and so are less inclined towards the polarization of mind. It is these polarized thought processes that bind and attach us to the past, therefore reinforcing our habit of re-creating history. As we evolve spiritually we have less need to recycle the old stories and we delight in building up a New Gospel, chapter for chapter, one that includes all our stories, so that, in the end, we are woven into mystery. We women are beginning to believe that all our needs are being met, moment-by-moment. Our story is not just about survival; it is also about abundance. And with this abundance we naturally live more truth and less illusion.

The issues around money, science, politics, religion and terrorism take up a lot of our nervous energy at the moment. People are so engrossed in these issues of the first three instinctual energetic centres in our psyches that they have no energy left for joy and laughter and things of the heart. Blaming the patriarchy, the external male generated world, does not help. Yet we have to be allowed in the beginning of our awakening to vent our natural anger against such institutions. Being able to find safe places to do so is essential to our psychological and spiritual health. Soon we will recognize that blame is a form of irresponsibility. The age of blaming and pointing the finger is also past, as it belonged to the old order. When we blame we also have an inner need for punishing someone. This creates terrorism in the psyche and the next seven generations will have to carry this bitterness if we do not release it and find a return to innocence, yours and mine.

We know the history and now we will create our own story by taking responsibility for our own actions and re-actions. When we move out of our internalized patriarchal dominance as men and women, we move into soul.

In this place of self-knowing and self-consciousness, we as women begin to awaken to the inner voice of love. Love alone can lead us to a state of non-judgement of ourselves. When we listen to the compassionate voice of love within us, we move gently into the belief that we are one with all and so, as we have compassion for ourselves, that compassion, that love without limit is then projected to all created phenomena.

## WOMAN SOUL AND SEXUALITY

In the Christian church, the soul was not referred to as a feminine aspect of God or life, but that which kept us in order and reminded us of our unGodliness. It was the antithesis of ego and kept check on our sinful state as human beings. Somehow Spirit took the place of real honour and the soul, that aspect which had earth connection took second place. It may be seen as the one who reported us to the head man! It demanded the bending of the spiritual knee, the beating of the spiritual breast, the chanter of "Mea culpa, mea culpa, mea maxima culpa." The inquisition was a clear example of religious brutality "in the name of the father". The soul it seems, was forever trying to purify and cleanse humans from sinfulness of the flesh, that thorn which Saint Paul spoke about, that gnawing ever present shadow self that needed so much purging and thrashing in order to subdue it. Teresa of Avila spoke of her soul as the purger of her Ego (see "The Interior Castle" by Teresa of Avila). This emphasis on violence to the persona was seemingly a pastime of middle age religion. Whosoever could mortify the physical to the extent of near death was seen as the holiest amongst them. Monks and nuns of different religious persuasions were advised to subject their sinful bodies to terrible tortures "for the love of God" or as a means of controlling the mind. One can hardly imagine the absurdity of a father God delighting in the sufferings of his children.

Such acts were possibly sexual by nature, but the nuns at least insisted that they were holy purifying encounters with the suffering Christ. Saint Margaret Mary Alacoque, (1647-1690) founder of the visitation order of nuns, allegedly practised whipping her body in front of a bloody picture of the crucifixion. Seemingly when the other sisters found her, she was in a great spiritual ecstasy. I prefer to name it an orgasm. Repression of sexuality of course is one of the greatest abuses in the Christian faith.

Whilst voluntary celibacy can be used as a source of grace and self development, when it is forced becomes a great dysfunction within the psyche of men and women. The result of such repression can be seen today in the overwhelming accounts of continuous sexual abuse of priests with young boys and girls. There is a very close connection between repression and perversion which to its chagrin the Catholic Church is now realizing. Perhaps it should have taken Freud's advice about this. The financial drain on the Vatican purse because of moneys being awarded to the victims of clerical sexual abuse might be an incentive to revert the laws of celibacy. Thus, allowing men their natural right to express their sexuality in a loving relationship.

The addiction to brutality and outbursts of rage afflicted on innocent students who attended colleges and convents in the past in my own country Ireland bears witness to the curse of repressed rage and sexuality. The film about the Magdalene Laundries is one of truth saying and is an example of how young women were treated by nuns, women who had dedicated their lives to the God of love. The order I had joined the Irish sisters of charity was also involved in the scandal. Now, we are able to name what is no longer acceptable, and let go of what no longer serves us, as beautiful manifestations of divine love. We have come a long way and we are still moving on further and further as we name the sacred for and in ourselves as women. And some men are supporting us to do this. According to the hierarchical status of women in the Christian church in the past centuries and indeed up until the 70s, nuns were the purest species; as they lived holy "non" sexual lives and were known as the brides of Christ. I was one such bride in the 60s. I had dedicated my young life to prayer, penance, service of all, poverty and fasting into anorexia. Self love and honouring of our bodies were not part of religious practices. Motherhood whilst seemingly respected in the Christian religion, still demanded that women go through the purification ceremony after the birth. Only after this so called purification ritual was she admitted into the Catholic so called "Mother church" again. Saint Marie Goretti, the young Italian girl 1890-1902 a virgin martyr, was venerated as holy because she refused sexual pleasure with a young man. Virginity in men and women was blessed and encouraged, and sexuality outside the institution of marriage was a sin. It was doubly so if the poor girl/woman got pregnant , as it was always her fault, the fallen woman , the whore , the wanton woman who would always lead men astray with her wiles.

The gospel stories written by men ,do not refer to the holiness or joy of sexuality, or to the sacredness of giving birth, but refer to the sinfulness of the woman taken in adultery and to the inferred loose living of the Magdalene. The very thought of self pleasuring was a mortal sin when I was a young woman in the early sixties. Ignorance about ones own body led many young men and women to believe that if they indulged in such disgusting habits they would go to hell.

The fathers of the church had a great fear of all things connected to the physical body, even though it was known in theory as the "Temple of God". The inclusion of body as sacred was also not accepted in Buddhism. How delightful then, my own Celtic tradition in comparison, whereby the body is seen as the means to liberation and great freedom. We believe that through the body one becomes enlightened. What a relief for many to know that their sexual energy is sacred and when appropriate to the couple, may be expressed as a spiritual practice. This amazingly powerful energy is deeply spiritual in essence and may be a means of reaching great union with Spirit. Such a belief honours our incarnations.

It seems that the Great War between piety and pleasure arose out of one woman's courage, to disobey the father and say yes to life. Even at the risk of being disowned. This is the story of our first mother Eve. What an example for her daughters to follow. She is saying,

*Be fully in your life as woman.*
*Your garden of paradise cannot be dictated*
*By male programming*
*To disobey the father*
*Is a natural progression of individuation.*
*His punishment of you is sadly,*
*The betrayal of his own soul.*

*Find your inner authority.*
*Source out the sacred in everything*
*Shake off all guilt.*
*Welcome the symbol of the serpent,*
*The powerful energy of transformation.*
*Go forwards in truth and joy.*
*Have no fear, I am with you.*

*Honour your sexuality as a facet of divine beauty.*
*Do not betray who you are in the face of great trials*
*For who you are is a reflection of the greatest love.*
*Know that, so that your daughters will know it for all time.*

## THE CAULDRON, THE GRAIL AND THE SOUL - THE TRINITY REVISITED

In my old Seabheannach mythical Gaelic language, the Cauldron is called Caildran, that which holds all without judgement; that which cradles paradoxical energies equally. It was known as the great balancer, the harmonizer of all life, coming and going. The shape of life is said to be that of the womb, rounded and swollen like the cauldron itself. And like the womb, it carries life within it with the ease of transformation. As the womb awaits the birthing of a new life, so also it was said, that the cauldron continuously, in ever growing spirals births new life, until that life is no longer attached to a body. Until such maturing, the cauldron expresses the life within it and loves to feel the abundance of that life.

In Celtic lore it is also known as the mysterious one, the secret one, because the Great Matair Mor, Grandmother Earth stirs all the stories of her creation to include the stories of animate and so called inanimate beings. Thus we are all connected; we are all part of one another.

Cerridwen, the Welsh Goddess was said to have been given the cauldron of plenty by her father. The father had no fear of the powerful feminine energy, embodied by his daughter, and symbolized by the great cauldron. He presented it to her, with the knowledge that she would experience the overflow of life, the abundant dance of all life and so, she could penetrate the deeper mysteries of creation. The father's responsibility was to allow the daughter to experience life, with the protective container of his love to support her.

When we say that the cauldron holds mystery, we also mean that life contains the stories of every incarnation of all created phenomena.

At death; or the passing over of the soul to Spirit, each story is presented to Spirit in the shape of a cauldron, the shape of soul. So, our stories, our *mysteries*, our actions and re-actions are all held in the great cauldron of life. Eventually, after many journeys to earth plane and other dimensions, after aeons of experience all gets stirred back into love, into divine life.

This great cauldron of life holds all our experiences without judgement. This is difficult for us to imagine as we have been conditioned to believe that judgement is important, even necessary in order to live good and holy lives. The Christian Church whilst teaching us that judgement is reserved for God, she pours her judgement on her children if they disobey her spiritual standards. In the confessional, the priest decides who will be absolved from sin and who not, thus giving him the power to judge. We have of course safe societal rules and laws from which if one digresses one is also punished. Deciding who will live and who will die is also the prerogative of some societies. Parents also judge or at least make decisions which are based on judgements, when they reward or punish their offspring for certain behaviours. So, in reality, the idea of judgement is an old one, and is part of our familial, social and religious conditioning. No wonder then we find it unimaginable, that we could live without the unnecessary burdens of inappropriate guilt we carry, because of our so called sinfulness. We have been taught that God loves the sinner but hates the sin. This is impossible as God does not have a personality, without which he is incapable of emotion therefore incapable of loving or hating. Then we have to conclude that God whom-so-ever or what-so-ever this magnificence is, is incapable of judging.

Again I reiterate emotions belong only to a personality, an earth mind, with human qualities. We reduce God or life to our restrictive conditioning, and cannot believe there is anything outside our small imaginings. We have been taught that God sees all our actions and is judging them, ready to pronounce hell fire or heavenly reward! We have also learnt to judge ourselves without mercy, and so continue the same with others. In the old shamanistic languages there is no proper word for sin or sinner. We have made, and do make mistakes, which means, we ache in the midst of not seeing clearly. We do not have the whole story so we judge the part of the story we see.

As a child growing up in the catholic religion in Ireland in the late 40s and 50s, the emphasis was on the love and fear of God. If you loved God you also had to fear him. This was so confusing for a child. Later on we were instructed that perfect love casts out fear, but as we were incapable of perfection, we were left with only confusion and feeling stupid as we could not fully grasp the meaning. How easy it is to shame the innocent, to lay on their small shoulders a sense of guilt and self abasement. I believe that a religion that emotionally abuses the innocent is neither holy nor good.

Again I say the time has come when the laity has to determine within themselves what is sacred and what is profane. We have to rename the sacred to include the whole human experience, from birth to death. This journey has to include our feelings and emotions and our right to define what the sacred means in our own lives. Perhaps it is also time to be more transparent in all our interactions, so that we can all work together towards a Spirituality that serves us as human beings with divine natures. So, perhaps, the cauldron, the container of life, that unconditionally accepts all our stories, "*mystories*" is the true pot of gold at the end of the rainbow, for which we all at some time search in order to find healing balm. Perhaps the cauldron is also the Grail, from which the golden elixir of life flows to all who would search for the answers to their soul's quest. Perhaps the cauldron IS the great rejuvenator.

## THE GRAIL

The story of the grail is an old one, known to most cultures. It is said that the Grail king Amfortas, who was wounded by a spear in the groin (seen symbolically as a sexual male wounding), needed healing. This healing could only happen with the assistance of a Fatherless youth, who was to find the Holy Grail out of which would flow the elixir that would heal the king. His nephew Percival (one who is pierced to the heart) was chosen to go on the grail quest. But the youth, being insecure, was not sure of his quest, or how to maintain the secret of the grail. He did not have enough experience in the ways of mystery and like most youths, he was impatient. The second time he went on his search however, he was successful. He knew the right questions to ask, with the help of many women including Genevieve, the wife of Amfortas and his own mother Herzteloyde, meaning "heart-rending". He also implored Sophia the Goddess of wisdom for help. So, equipped with this feminine wisdom he had access to the healing elixir from the grail. And so, the wound was healed and the King was free.

It is interesting that the king could only be helped by a youth, willing to journey and find the healing balm. It is said that if the father does not finish his journeys the son will have to complete them, and so the father receives healing from the son. His lack of a good male role model, left Percival quite helpless, but the feminine, the anima led him to the grail. The masculine, animus, the patriarchy alone could not take him to the place of healing.

The personal wound that Percival carried was that of the absent father. This wound could only be healed when the king was healed. The old male must find inner congruence, his sense of his own gender, his own power as a man, before the youth can be free to experience his masculine nature.

The feminine also brought Percival into experiencing his own Anima, his own sense of opening to the feelings of piercing. This was done by the opening of his heart, by being willing to be vulnerable to his own sensitive nature, by being willing to experience his sense of failure also in the beginning, and the realization that he needed help with the great task of helping the king. Then with the right questions, with that sense of humility, and a willingness to learn from his own anima, he was given access to the regenerative power of the Grail.

The king also known as Fisher king, belonged to the Age of Pisces, was also affected by the patriarchy at the time; his strength left him and he was both physically and mentally impotent. The fact that a youth alone could save him was humbling. The fact also that he had to wait whilst the youth made a second attempt to find the Grail, also taught the old king about the feminine attribute of patience. He had to wait for his needs to be met … and not judge the youth. The youth in him needed honouring also. Percival had the wisdom to ask how he could serve the Grail, not how it could serve him. This is important as service is synonymous with the feminine, the nurturing of another before the needs of one's own ego mind.

So we see that the Holy Grail can be interpreted also as a symbol for the feminine, the Anima, the Cauldron in disguise. Since the story of Arthur and the Knights of the Round Table, men have been searching for the Grail and their quest takes them deeper into the world searching for that which though illusive is yet important. Although we are not told the secret of the vital questions Percival asked in order to have access to the grail, we can only surmise that they were deep questions regarding the mystery of life. Perhaps Percival realized that one must integrate the Grail within oneself. Perhaps the grail is actually the container of our stories, or mystories … that which holds our experiences of life without judgement.

When the male honours and accepts the wise counsel of the feminine, his own gender is also honoured, and he becomes whole in himself, being led by the heart and soul rather than by his intellect alone. The intellect by itself cannot ask the deeper questions about life, it does not have the creative inspiration of intuition to do so.

## THE SOUL

What is the soul? Theologians have been debating this question for centuries and because of theological terminology it has been difficult to really grasp the true meaning of soul in our everyday lives. Certainly one can say that soul is that which animates form, whether that form is human, animal or plant. It imbues all form with being ness i.e. with aliveness, with consciousness albeit manifesting itself variously in different forms. The energy of soul is that spaciousness wherein we live move and have our being. It may be seen as the messenger or the agent of Spirit. When Spirit inspires one, it is through the soul that such imagery flows and we say, we are inspired, literally "in Spirit".

The Celts believed that the soul is that which experiences the divine in form. Soul finds soil in order to ground Spirit, to expand it into the worlds of created phenomena. No doubt soul has other worlds and galaxies in which she grounds Spirit, as she activates all creation since the beginning of time. It would seem that the only time we actually hear about soul connection is when someone is dying. We are told by religious instruction, that at the time of death, the soul leaves the body and goes to Spirit. We are not instructed as to when soul enters the body whether it is at birth or before birth, whilst the foetus is still in the womb.

Like the Cauldron and the Grail, soul is recognized by many esoteric groups as symbolizing the feminine because she is a container for life and birth. In Celtic Spirituality she is also the container for death. At the moment of death she is breathed back into Spirit, into pure consciousness.

Celtic consciousness speaks of the wildness of soul, her willingness to be always in life, whether life in form or out of form. She is the instinctual being of the animal self, and it is soul that creates imagination and brings out the wilderness beauty in humans. Her gifts are so great that she pours her abundance on nature with sheer abandonment. Nature reflects her extravagance in the seasons. From the wild storms and devastation of harsh winters, to the delightful warm colourful growths of summers, everything is done with abundance.

Soul in us asks us to widen our experiences as human divinities. She supports us in all our experiences, and never judges, or scorns us.

I often imagine her to be the antidote for the guilt and shame imposed on us by our conditioned earth minds or egos.

Like Perivale's search for the Grail, we have to also go in search of the soul. When we suffer a great trauma, we are bereft of soulfulness and so we are said to become numb, numb of feelings and responses. In order to find our soul, we must do as Percival did and that is to go on a quest.

And this quest is not an outer one; it is an inner journey, right to the centre of our own selves. We have to be in touch with our own inner voice, our inner reality, our creative Spirit. We have to ask questions, and we have to have patience, as Percival had, and wait. This is not always easy for us and we often want answers overnight. When answers to our painful questions are not immediately available, we look to other agents like alcohol, sex, drugs, other addictions, in order to push the pain away. We get temporary relief, and then are thrown into the depths of depression as these other agencies do not help us to retrieve the soul. Percival asked important questions and we must do likewise. But the content of the questions is not as easy as it may seem. The questions are not about finding easy solutions for the trials of our lives, they are more challenging.

The answers will be found as they were for Percival within ourselves, within this cauldron of creation. The elixir of soul is within me, as it was within the cauldron of Cerridwen. This non judgemental balm can heal the wounds of guilt and blame and fill me with the abundance of life. I may be healed by allowing the Percival, the innocence in me to ask the questions, which will lead me to the Holy Grail, the soul. When I have reached the goal, i.e. live from soul, I will have found the eternal Anima, and I can experience my precious life fully without judgement.

Then I will have found the grail and the cauldron of healing, for myself and for the collective.

CHAPTER 10

# Letting Go In My Time

**A CHILD LEARNS ABOUT GRIEF**

When you were a small child and you did something wrong, what happened? What was the immediate response or re-action of the parent? *"Don't do that again!"* So what do you do instead of that? Supposing the child hits another child because she has taken something from her. The hitting of the child was the natural response to grief. It is anger: "That's mine! Give it back to me! I had it first!" It is the same in regard to adult grief when we declare: "That was my husband or wife or friend, or that was my breast that's been taken away, or that is my child that has died." What the young child did by slapping the one who took her toy was the result of natural anger. The other was seen as the perpetrator, the one who comes and takes away. When the child is not allowed to scream, to shout out: "That is mine, give it back" and she represses the feelings and sounds in order to be good, this will become a learnt response to grief and so she will continue this pattern of non-expression until she can have the chance, maybe years later, to express the pain. The body also needs to expresses its grief, as it is also feeling the loss.

*What is not natural,* but what we call normal, is all about socialized conditioning. When the parent says in her own annoyance (because now she has two children crying), "Don't you smack your sister! Don't hit the wall! Don't bang that on the floor! Now tell your sister you are sorry and give her the toy!" - can you hear what's going on here?

Not only is the child not allowed to express her grief and feelings of loss, but she has to give the love object to the one who took it away, thus denying that it was hers. And then the child has to say: "I'm sorry", as well. Can you see the seed that is being planted in the psyche of the young child? She has to say "I'm sorry" to the one who took her toy away. This is very confusing in the heart of the child. Is it any wonder that adults get very frustrated when they feel grief and do not know how to express it naturally? When everyone is saying: "Everything is God's will", it is difficult to grieve. The situation with an adult grieving is very like the story of the child. For example, the grieving one may say, "God took my dear husband away, and I am not allowed to be angry with God or to shout at God or even with the doctors. But I am supposed to thank the doctors and thank God that I had my husband for 30 years." Or they may say, "I am supposed to thank God because my husband was taken quickly and didn't have to die in agony" or, "I have to thank God that he was 58 and not at 40!" or, "I have to be grateful because I can have another baby. But I want this one that died." It is strange how uncomfortable we are with people in grief. We would like them to heal quickly in our time, not theirs.

These are some of the ways people cope with grief in the community. We are still not allowed the natural expression of loss, neither are we supposed to be too full of joy! It is embarrassing to others that we should express our feelings. At the funeral of Princess Diana a newscaster reported that the two boys, her sons, were valiant and did not cry at the grave. I can imagine what it took to keep the tears from falling.

If you can allow a child the natural anger of grief, even when in her agony she throws something at the wall, if you can sit back for a moment and just breathe and not re-act this will help a lot. If you can just be with your child and not give attention to the wall that has been dirtied or the thing that has been thrown, you will help your child to deal with the pain. If you can take the emphasis off what has been outwardly disturbed in your room and be with your child in her inner disturbance, she will have learnt to honour her feelings and know that she is still loved through them. Later, when she is older you can explain that when she gets angry it might be a good idea to punch a ball or throw stones in the pool etc.

We say to a young girl whose boyfriend has broken up with her, "You are young, and there are plenty of better boys around!" But first she has to grieve the loss of this boy, just as the young child had to grieve losing her toy.

Grief is about here and now. It does not have a future that is bright and clear yet. Grief will teach you about presence, and we all can learn from it. We try to hurry grief in the young and the not so young, and yet it demands time, space and its own unfolding. And it unfolds differently in each person. When we can express our pain in grieving we do not have to try and accept the death or the loss. Acceptance comes as a natural stage after we have allowed grief its say.

## LETTING GO IN THEIR TIME

When an older person in full capacity of their mind is dying and they specifically say they do not want life support machinery, this wish should be granted. What they are saying is: "I do not want to stay alive, supported by machines. Please let me go and do not keep me longer on the earth." Now, what happens when this request is not heard and the hospital rules are that they have to be artificially supported, even though that person cannot maintain life on their own?

I have seen old people being wakened out of their daytime sleep and given injections. Once when I asked what the medicine was, I was told that it was antibiotic for a mild chest infection. When I asked if the patient had any signs that the infection was troubling him the answer was, "No, but it could get worse if they do not get it." The injection was given every four hours for eight days. The arm of that dear old man was blue and black due to the painful intrusion on his crinkled old skin. It is so difficult for nursing staff to do what they themselves feel is right, as the nurse told me: "I don't want to bother the old fellow as the injections are a bother to him, but these are the rules."

In many hospitals the rules of the medical staff are still more important than the wishes of the dying person. Many people who are very near death are being fed intravenously, when food is the last thing they need. Often, on the other hand, when they need water they press the button in vain, as the nurse is too busy with other patients. This is not the nurse's fault and no one is to blame; it is the way things are when the institution is ruled by the patriarchy, the old way of "rules rule OK."

The administration of water, even in the form of swab sticks is all-important for the person dying. When they reach the stage when the water element is drying up, the mouth and tongue dry up too and it is very discomforting for them. When a dying person asks not to be resuscitated in any way and the medical staff refuses this wish and keep on bringing them back into the body time after time, this is not acceptable. This is abusive medical practice, in my eyes. Whilst I am not advocating actively helping people to die, as in euthanasia, I do believe, having been with many older people who were dying, that compassion for their needs is the only important issue. When the soul needs to let go of the body and be united with Spirit and the physical is being strengthened by various medications, this is confining for the soul.

Maybe we need to look at our denial issues around death and our unwillingness to see death as the great adventure that begins with the letting go of the earth element (see "Celtic Book of Dying", Phyllida Anam-Aire, 2005). When the dying old man is ready and willing to surrender to Spirit and can no longer sustain his vitality without machinery and added drugs then, one might ask, is this life that is being maintained, or is it an unnatural practice maintained by the medical field in its own unconscious fear of death?

### CONSIDER THE STATE OF THE SOUL

In many hospitals the spiritual life of the dying person would seem not to be considered. Life is seen as functional and mechanical, whereby the heart beats, the breath flows and the internal organs work, etc. The sacredness of the physical is not taught in medical school and the spiritual life of the patient is not their concern. The concern of the medical staff is to keep the physical machinery operating with added appliances of machinery. The Hippocratic Oath is, of course, a very honourable statement of altruism and many doctors are true to it. The problem lies in how we view and define life and death. When we react to death with denial and see it as a failure, something that really should not happen if one is a good doctor, then problems arise. When the patient is young and has a strong life force and can recover quickly what modern medicines can do to aid their recovery is to be applauded. Many lives have been brought back to good health because of such machinery and modern medical technology. We are speaking only for the older patient who does not want resuscitation and has specifically asked and documented that this wish be granted.

The soul of the older person hovers between the worlds of living and dying. The body cannot release it when artificial programming is applied, as the electric magnetic field of machinery is a different energy frequency to that of the soul. The soul is expanding its energy to include the electric machinery around it and this affects the soul's ability to leave in peace and with ease. At death the body can no longer hold the soul's expanded energy field and the earth, fire, water and air elements naturally need to leave the restrictions of this very constricted and limited space. One must understand that when one is dying one's own energy field is quickened up, as the life force leaves the form. When too many unnatural mechanical forces are around the bed, the charge is too great for the release of the soul and so it has to stay close to the body, thus keeping the dying person still grounded.

The soul needs to be gently facilitated to get on with its own closure and although the soul cannot suffer, it is still limited in its journey to full consciousness by a force field very alien to its own. If an old person has requested that they have no resuscitation or supportive machinery when dying, why is this wish not granted by the medical staff?

Imagine if I were 84 years old and I were dying. I have made good choices, or not, throughout my long life. Now I want to make my own choices about dying. Imagine I have inner authority and have been able to lead a good full life. Supposing I had arranged with my family that I did not want to be resuscitated or given any artificial help when I was dying and I had made this decision with a very sound mind, witnessed by family and friends. Imagine, however, that when the time came and I was dying, the doctors decided to sustain my life with supportive machinery to feed me intravenously. How would I feel? I think I would feel dishonoured, disrespected and not heard. Many old people have told me that this is how they felt a lot of the time regarding hospitalization.

It is natural that once an old person has gone into unconsciousness they should be allowed to remain so, without any assistance from machinery.

As I have already said, it is the presence of foreign bodies, such as electrical machinery that curtails the soul's agenda for leaving. Indeed, all electrical appliances ought to be shut down in the room of a dying person. When we understand more about subtle energies, we will understand about the exchanges of energies that take place whilst we are living and dying and indeed after death.

Many times one hears how the family goes against the wishes of a dying relative. There is a deeper psychological story here. The family does not have the right to resuscitate a family member if they have requested the contrary. It is selfish on behalf of the family to bring back an ageing relative to so-called life after they have requested be allowed to die naturally in their bed. Perhaps the person "stays" for another 2 weeks. Does that help the dying one or the relatives?

In the state of unconsciousness the patient can, because of the appliances, energetically attach themselves to the people around the bed. If the family are crying loudly and saying words like, "Don't go mother!" or "Keep fighting!" or "We need you!" this is not respectful to the dying person who is longing for relief.

We need to learn more about the inner journey of the soul and not always put the emphasis on maintaining the life of the body at any cost, that is a sign of our ignorance regarding the value of life, or perhaps our own unwillingness to let go. Perhaps it is our own insistence that life at any cost is worth it, even though that life is struggling under machinery and that soul is ready to depart. Many people say: "I am glad we saw her again. She looked much better and I think she smiled." If she smiles without the help of machinery, that is fine, but whilst there is machinery any movement from the body at this stage is usually a muscle reflex and must not be seen to be voluntarily initiated. Many people say the same about babies…e.g., "He smiled at me" or "He moved his hand towards my face." This is usually the result of muscle reflex actions and involuntary in the young child. It is not conscious action. Of course one must always make space for miracles, but please check first if it is a physical reaction or ones own projected spiritual need for connection.

I was sure my father smiled at me when he was dying and this is the image my heart accepts with gratitude although the medical staff assured me it was a muscle reflex. Our thoughts are very powerful, especially when we are vulnerable and needy.

- *Imagine you are trying to let go and machines are keeping you back.*
- *What do you imagine happens internally with soul awareness?*

We need to be more aware of how to help each other to look at the meaning of life and the adventure of dying. We can support our older dying relatives by asking them what they want to happen when they are dying and get it written into a living will so that the hospital staff, if need be, can have access to the legal form. We have to speak on behalf of the dying; we have to let the doctors know the wishes of the dying person. Have the faith and the strength to say your words clearly for the dying when you feel they are not being adhered to. A friend of mine did this some time ago and although he found it difficult to insist that his mother's wishes be adhered to, at last the doctors gave in and granted his mother a natural death without the previously applied machinery.

The medical people are doing what they learnt - maintain life, save life. This is great, this is wonderful, but also they have to hear the wishes of those who have enjoyed a good long life of decision-making. Now, when they really want some control over the way they depart their lives, some of the medical staff does not listen because they want to be in control. Older people know the timing of things, especially if they were reared on farms. Many have a natural fear of hospitals and do not want to be kept any longer than their own natural timing when dying. An older woman who had lived on a farm all her life went to hospital for a hip replacement. During her time there she developed pneumonia and was dying. She had told me the year before in the presence of her son that if she had to go to hospital she hoped she would be allowed to die without "all that stuff around me", meaning life machinery etc. "I don't want machines to help me stay alive, Phyllida", she told me. "I want help to die well." Her family came with me to see the doctor in charge, who decided she should be fed intravenously every day. When the doctor heard our story on behalf of the old woman, she said that she was sorry but she could not help us as the rule of the hospital was that all patients had to be helped to stay alive. This was her sacred trust. I actually felt pain for this woman as she was just keeping the rules and she was not allowed to change them. The old woman had an "accident" that very night. She fell out of the bed whilst trying to get to the switch to switch off the machinery and was found on the floor, dead. Maybe this is why I want to speak on behalf of the dying.

> *May we all live fully and die the way we wish, in peace, and in complete union with the wishes of our souls.*
>
> *(May I add that whilst I am in agreement that old people should be allowed to die in dignity without machinery if that is their will, I also believe that medicine does a lot to help others to maintain life. Through the help of machinery and wonderful advanced medicines we have seen virtual miracles happen, for which I am deeply grateful.)*

### WE ARE NOT ALONE

Some years ago I composed a song that I had forgotten until lately. The words are as follows:

> *I am energy moving freely*
> *I am living, cosmic energy*
> *All creation is within me*
> *Moving freely moving freely*
> *I am body, I am intellect*
> *I am floating creativity*
> *I am no thing, I am everything*
> *Celebrating my humanity*

We are a part of a whole, making a deeper consciousness than that of the individual self. This is a powerful concept and a very responsible one. I am not an island and although I may feel very independent, I am none-the-less part of a collective consciousness that operates in a holistic and integral way to achieve harmony and balance for all beings in the Universe. It has always been so throughout the centuries of our individual and collective evolution. As one aspect of creation evolves, so do all others with it. As new stars and galaxies are named, so we are also being named and renamed. As new beings are coming to the earth and others are leaving, we are also being reborn.

At this critical time of the mysteries of humanity, we are also being called out of our past identity into a whole new awareness of who we really are. We are realizing that our contribution is vital if we are going to rise up from our individual and collective past conditioning and realize our potential as powerful human/divine beings who are here to fulfil an old prophesy, which was foretold by Brigit of Ireland, daughter of the High Druid:

> *A time will come when fear will creep*
> *Deep into your sleepless eyes,*
> *When nature's bones will break*
> *The boundaries of her waters.*
>
> *Soon then, those eyes more bright*
> *Will open wider to her fire*
> *And a new voice will sing*
> *The song of her desire on the land.*
>
> (FOR PHYLLIDA ANAM-AIRE, A GIFT FROM BRIGIT, 2004)

Maybe our eyes have now opened, maybe we can again begin to listen to the wisdom of nature and allow her teachings to guide us to our new place in the family of things. Your contribution is essential, my contribution is essential and our inclusion is fixed; there is no escaping our involvement. In joining the song of love's desire, a New HalleluJA on the land, I need to be awake with you.

> **There cannot be collective evolution without individual progress. Neither can there be collective evolution without individual involvement.**

As one cell of an organism expands in evolution, all other cells are consequently affected. Earth is a field of great moving transforming energy and, like human beings; it is a living, breathing, vibrating organism. We affect one another, whether we are aware of it or not. Now we are becoming aware and that makes a great difference.

> *Could I have a loving thought?*
> *Hidden in my own*
> *Imagination*
> *Without a star*
> *Blinking its approval?*

More and more we believe that thought affects matter. The creative forces of my thoughts through the medium of my heart take on form, and so my world is created. Does it also follow that my thoughts can affect my neighbour, or that my thoughts today can have far-reaching effects on my future? Again, tests done by various scientists (e.g. Vladimir Vla 1993) have shown this to be so. As there is no time scale regarding consciousness or soul, time and space are irrelevant. We know that throughout the world collective prayer is used for healing. If we believe that there is greater power in collective than in individual thought, because it produces more electromagnetic energies (which is really an accumulation of spiritual energy) then when we can visualize, indeed, we will actually see the future we can create.

We are, from the moment of incarnation, vibrating at a frequency suitable to our own inner stages of evolution. This is clearly shown in Kirlian photography. This type of photography shows the aura in various stages of consciousness. I was surprised to see the difference in my photograph before and after I sang a song. The colours were very different. When four of us sang the same song, the light and the colours were much more illuminated.

As consciousness uses our brain mechanisms in order to transmit its life and movements to us, it is completely independent of it. It is life power itself. People who have had near death experiences have shown this clearly. Naturally our E.M.F. (electro magnetic field) is affected by the frequencies emitted by our consciousness and as we evolve in consciousness so do our electromagnetic fields. The electric element is that of the masculine energy and the magnetic element is that of the feminine. When both fields are vibrating at the same frequency, then we are well in our body-minds. That, in turn, affects others and the entire planet. When there is disharmony in the relationship between the electro and magnetic fields, then dis-ease can occur. It first begins in the thoughts and in the emotional tension held in the frequencies. From there attitudes are formed and emotions gather to support the attitudes. Attitudes become embedded in the cellular, endocrine, lymphatic, and glandular systems and manifest at last in a mass of incongruence in the physical being.

When we change our thought patterns to harmonize with the E.M.F. of our souls or consciousness, we are again in perfect balance with the pulsating energy of the cosmos. But we often wait until the dis-harmony, the unease or dis-ease has inhabited the cells and shows itself in various disturbing ways in the body-mind. The inner landscape needs to be tilled and hoed, cleansed, watered, replenished and loved, as it is a living being.

At death, the body deteriorates; the brain no longer connects with the world as we know it, and we are decathexing (disengaging from life) from a world in which we participated. In our decomposing state we are also affecting the world of matter all around us. Our soul is leaving form and although we are not aware of it, others can, and do notice the change in the vibrations in a room where someone is dying. It is as though that which kept the person in the here and now, the very life force, the animation, has left the space. This naturally will affect the E.M.F. all around the room. Kirlian photography, again, has actually shown how and when death occurs by revealing how colours leave the body.

Life is a spiralling continuum, consisting of various magnificent electromagnetic fields of vibrations that, although individual, are interdependent, because they all affect one another. Advancement in one field of consciousness affects all other fields. Decay in one field also affects all others. The more we give ourselves to thoughts of bitterness and interreligious hatred, the more we are responsible for bringing about disharmony and unrest not only in ourselves, but in the Universe. Although the earth can adjust to all unrest and change of frequencies, we, as human beings, are not always so adaptive. One thought of hatred leads to another and fear takes over when two or more agree; then the hatred is multiplied until we have wars. Until we get back to a place of balance the energetic messages we send out will be unhealthy and the opposite of love, thus creating spiritual pollution.

The earth has existed without us human beings and other animals for centuries and will continue to do so. But we, as more fragile organisms, cannot exist without the earth and other planetary systems. So let us remember that although we are wonderful as individual, unique forms of created consciousness, we are still dependant on the earth and the planets for our existence. Without air, fire, water and earth we cannot exist, so let us take care of the elements that serve us so well.

Let us take care of one another and our planet, for we are the outpouring of our own making. And let us take care of our thoughts, which are the carriers of our creative forms that affect ourselves and all other beings.

**A BLESSING TO ALL**

*What would your life be like if you were truly healed?* If you were truly healed you would no longer have re-actions to anything or anyone in your environment. You would walk the earth with grace and be a blessing to all creation, to the animal kingdom, to the plant kingdom and all creation would rejoice because you would bless them with your breath. There would be no part of you living in the painful past. Your love would be purified in the waters of divine grace and would be unconditionally available for all humanity. There would be no self-judgement of any of your actions or those of others, even though their actions might be unloving. You would be able to look past their ego fear and see the divine spark behind their pained minds. Your compassion would be great and non-personal, therefore spiritually imbued. You would live free from all conditioned fear. It is hard for us, at the moment, to understand this because our lives contain re-active emotions. Sometimes our emotions are wonderful and we can express them through the open heart. Even our righteous anger can be expressed thus.

Happiness is a feeling dependant on something outside our selves e.g. somebody that we love makes us happy, makes us smile, so we are full of happiness. But when the object of our good humour is removed - what then? It seems to me that there is a vital difference between happiness and joy. Happiness is brought about by external influence. It has to do with conditions from the past; it is from the ego, so to speak. For example, we say something or someone "makes" me happy. Joy, however, is indwelling compassion and indwelling light. Joy is love within our selves, our indwelling divinity and cannot be taken from us. It fills us up with grace because grace and joy are the same being, the same energy. To be filled with joy is to be filled with inspiration and creativity. This state is always available as it is independent of external stimuli. To be creative is all-important for us if we want to be healthy in our bodies and minds. This place of creativity is our joy and others feel it also, as it draws on the soul for its essence. Our joy, when expressed, becomes contagious and can affect plants and the animal and mineral worlds. Inanimate beings also respond to our joy. Because it is non-conditional, it shines on all alike, just as the sun in the sky shines on all without conditions. Because we are all essentially energetic beings, everything is energy, moving freely in us and in all.

Imagine you see your picture on a computer. Now enlarge this picture as much as you can. What do you see? You see a system of dots and symbols. You do not see an outline of your face anymore. Imagine you enlarge your image until you come to a place where there are just particles of energy flowing around. Those electromagnetic fields of energy come together to give you form. Basically and intrinsically you are light energy and you are creating from that energy all the time. You are creating vital health or ill health. As the nuclei in the cells in our bodies constitute light, we are, in truth light, beings full of light. When we feel low in our vital energies, the light is not so bright and we say we are feeling a bit "off" - literally, the light is rather dim. We have learnt ways whereby we can "lighten up" our thoughts again.

What are you thinking at this moment as you read this page? You are bringing many thoughts together, forming ideas and creating something from them. Maybe you will stop reading and remember something you read some time ago, similar to this, and you will begin to create other ideas from them. As thought builds on thought you will reach a conclusion. The mind loves reaching conclusions about ideas, loves the stories around ideas. And on and on it goes, adding information to information. We are also stories around the great intelligent idea of the creator!

When we think only of the past and the mistakes of the past, we begin to live these thoughts in our daily lives. If thoughts from the past bring delight to your heart, that is wonderful and light enhancing. Do not create dead messages. Create vital, living impulses here and now, that you may become enlightened in this lifetime. Enlightenment does not mean that you are no longer a human being. It means your humanity is healed into unconditional love for your ego and also for other beings, animals, plants, flowers, herbs, grasses, mountains, seas, galaxies, stars, the sun and the moon. Unconditional love, because it is unlimited and without boundaries, can extend to all beings in all worlds of creation. Just because someone is no longer on the earth does not mean they cannot be touched by your pure, loving thoughts, for unconditional love is the strongest force in the universe that transcends matter. You were always one with all, with earth, fire, water and air. In the end, when you return these elements to the earth plane i.e. when you die, they will appear as loving energetic beings that you have left behind to help all human kind.

*Thought cannot*
*Go astray*
*I pray*
*One day we'll see*
*That thought creates*
*Eternity*

(WRITTEN IN THE CONVENT WHILST
I WAS A NUN, 20 YEARS OLD)

## *Gathered*

*Love gathers life*
*Into death*
*Ah! Life!*
*Ah! Death!*
*Gathered in*

*The gathering*
*Of me*
*The gathering*
*Of you*
*Gathered*

*Not just you*
*And me*
*Not you along*
*With me*
*But all of us as one*

*Fully shaped to the Eagle*
*And the tree*
*Oceans breathe us*
*Safely in*
*No other saviour.*

(PHYLLIDA ANAM-AIRE, 2010, WRITTEN ON THE TRAIN)

## NO OTHER SAVIOUR

It is now time to gather in all our prodigal parts safe into heart. In this way peace will sing to us and all beings will rejoice. The internal patriarchy will meet the soul and the sacred marriage of soul and spirit will take place. Horus and Isis, Animus and Anima will reign again in love. Buddha and the Christ can find a new belonging of the heart in the language of soul. The symbolic lion will have lain down with the lamb and the patriarchy will have been loved into the universal heart itself.

Perhaps then Magdalene, followed by Buddha and the Christ (intellect and heart), will break open the alabaster box of blessing and bless us all with a new song of songs, and the sacred will be renamed in a new HALLELUJA.

# Books I have referred to

**Karen Armstrong**, *"Buddha"*, Phoenix, 2002
**Louise B. Young**, *"The Unfinished Universe"*, Oxford University press, 1986
**Malcolm Hollick**, *"The Science of Oneness"*, O books, 2006
**Pim van Lommel**, *"Consciousness Beyond Life"*, HarperOne, June 2010
**Lucia Rene**, *"Unplugging The Patriarchy"*, Crown Chakra publishing, Dec. 2009
**Rita Gross**, *"Buddha After The Patriarchy"*, State University of N.Y.Press, 1993
**Jack Kornfield**, *"A Path With Heart"*, Bantam Books, 1993
**J.W. von Goethe**, Poem *"The Holy Longing"* Translated by Robert Bly
**Dorothy MacLean**, *"An Ordinary Human Mystic"*, 2010, Findhorn Press
**Alan Featherstone B.S.**, *"Trees For life"*, Findhorn Press
**J. Kenneth Arnette PhD.**, *"The Mind Body Problem"*
**Amit Goswami PhD.**, 1995 *"Self Aware Universe"*, Publ. Tarcher, March 1995
**Neville Goddard**, *"Power of Awareness"*, 1952, Reprint by De Vorss Publ. 2009
**Phyllida Anam-Áire**, *"Celtic Book of Dying"*, 2005, Findhorn Press/ Ennsthalers Verlag
**Christopher Hitchens**, *"God Is Not Great"*, Atlantic books, 2007.
**Caroline Myss**, the American spiritual teacher, talks about *"Mystics without Monasteries"*
**Mark Fox**, singer, CDs from info@markfox.de
**Ken Wilber**, *"Integral Spirituality"*, 2006, Integral books, Boston.
**Pema Chodron**, *"Awakening Loving Kindness"*, Shambhala pocket classics

**Roger Woolger**, *"Other Lives, Other Selves"*, Doubleday, 1987
**Alice Miller**, *"For Your Own Good"*, Noonday Pr. 1990
**Mary Oliver**, Poem "Wild Geese" from *"Dream Work"*, Atlantic Monthly Pr. 1986
**T.S.Eliot**, Poem "Burnt Norton" from *"Four Quartets"*, Faber & Faber, 1998

## Also available

Phyllida Anam-Áire
CAULDRON OF SONG

*Audio-CD, 79 min., with Booklet.*
**ISBN 978-3-85068-790-4**

Phyllida Anam-Áire
LET LOVE IN

*Audio-CD, 51 min., with Booklet.*
**ISBN 978-3-85068-791-1**